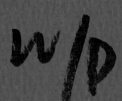

NANCY LINDHEIM is Associate Professor of English at the University of Toronto.

The argument of this study is that the *Arcadia*, like the High Renaissance painting analysed by Heinrich Wölfflin, is characterized by what may be called 'multiple unity.' The complexity of its organization, whether examined rhetorically in terms of language and thought or tonally through its sequence of events, or narratively through the relation of episode to main plot, is an expression of Sidney's need to control and arrange experience for aesthetic and moral purposes without giving up his perception of its chaos or unmanageability. The nature of Sidney's complex vision, in spite of the apparently pastoral title of *Arcadia*, is not pastoral but epic. Like much important Renaissance writing, the work is a *paedeia*, an education of princes, in which the narrative seeks what Sidney considered the paramount object of learning: 'the knowledge of a man's self, in the ethic and politic consideration.'

Professor Lindheim finds that the key to the greater stylistic and narrative complexity of the revised *Arcadia* lies in the larger and deeper reading of experience that it offers. The *New Arcadia* is not merely the *Old Arcadia* heavily ornamented and reassembled in quaint ways, but a radically reconceived work, a re-vision as well as a revision of the earlier version. The radical (root, upwards from the very foundation) coherence of the work is here explored by tracing its rhetoric to an inherent rhetoricism and by analysing its style stylistically. The *Arcadia* is a masterpiece of Elizabethan literature because of this integrity: because Sidney's technique, whether stylistic, rhetorical, or narrative, has a direct bearing on his humanist understanding of experience.

THE STRUCTURES

OF

SIDNEY'S

Arcadia

NANCY

LINDHEIM

UNIVERSITY OF TORONTO PRESS
Toronto Buffalo London

© University of Toronto Press 1982
Toronto Buffalo London
Printed in Canada

ISBN 0-8020-2374-6

Canadian Cataloguing in Publication Data

Lindheim, Nancy, 1936-
    The structures of Sidney's *Arcadia*
    Includes index.
    ISBN 0-8020-2374-6
    1. Sidney, Philip, Sir, 1554-1586. New Arcadia.
    I. Title.
    PR2342.A63L56   821'.3   C81-095005-7

This book has been published with the help of grants from the Canadian Federation for
the Humanities, using funds provided by the Social Sciences and Humanities Research
Council of Canada, and from the Publications Fund of the University of Toronto Press.

Once and for all

Dad and Miriam, Ralph, Sara and Rachel

and in memory of my mother

CONTENTS

THE STRUCTURES OF
SIDNEY'S *Arcadia*

INTRODUCTION

E.M.W. Tillyard, lecturing at Johns Hopkins on the question of whether there was such a phenomenon as the English Renaissance, found it possible to decide the issue affirmatively, on the basis largely of the existence of Sidney's three major works.[1] If the English Renaissance can thus be said to find quintessential expression in Sidney, the work that quintessentially expresses Sidney's genius is his *Arcadia*. While interest in this work has grown significantly from the virtual neglect of only thirty years ago, the *Arcadia* probably remains the least read masterpiece of our literature. The excitement of discovery still lies ahead for most readers. It is heady enough stuff to have generated the extraordinary estimate from the Shakespearean critic John F. Danby that Sidney and Shakespeare are 'twin miracles,' 'the two giants of the Elizabethan scene.'[2] I like to think that this book presents a Sidney who might, in the excitement of discovery, be considered in such a light.

My examination of the *Arcadia* focuses on the structures of the prose narrative. Two points need clarification: why 'structures,' in the plural, and which version of the *Arcadia* will be studied?

To begin with the easier question, the matter of texts. Three distinguishable *Arcadias* have survived from the sixteenth century. The *Old Arcadia*, apparently begun in 1577 but composed mostly in 1580,[3] is a neatly structured work in five 'Bookes or Actes.' Printed for the first time in 1926 as Volume IV of Albert Feuillerat's edition of Sidney's *Works*,[4] it is now available in a blessedly more accurate and readable state in Jean Robertson's Oxford edition. The *New Arcadia*, probably written between 1582 and 1584,[5] revises and expands the first two books of the earlier draft and adds a totally new Third Book, which, despite its considerable length, is incomplete, breaking off in the middle of a sentence. It was printed in quarto by William Ponsonby in 1590 under the editorship of Fulke Greville, Matthew Gwinne, and perhaps John Florio.[6] The third version is that of the 1593 folio (and all subsequent editions until the twentieth century), published under the direction of the Countess of Pembroke. It is a composite text, formed by adding the *Old Arcadia*'s Books III-V to all the revised material of the *New Arcadia*; its major independent contribution is four passages in the later books which Sidney apparently had rewritten to conform with his new plan.[7] The text is still divided into five books, since the old and new Third are joined as one, though without any attempt to fill the narrative gap.[8]

The structures I examine are mainly those of the 1590 text, but it is necessary to go beyond these 500-odd pages to determine how the revised material fits into what we can determine of Sidney's plan for the work. The existence of three texts, though universally recognized since 1907 when Dobell published his discovery of the *Old Arcadia*,[9] has oddly enough failed to make its full impact in critical studies of the *Arcadia* not concerned mainly with textual comparisons. Two valuable analyses of the work[10] ignore the fact and the implications of Sidney's revisions and use the 1593 text as though it were a unity. Others have chosen either to deal exclusively with one of the versions or to treat the two versions separately, as different works.[11] This book is concerned with the purpose and tendency of Sidney's revisions. These become especially important in the chapters on narrative structure where the relation between the two versions is examined, but throughout the discussion I have given alterations and additions special weight because they help to define the total vision that the *Arcadia* was meant to express. And that vision, I shall be arguing, amounts to a re-vision of the original text.

The second point requiring clarification is the plurality of structures in the *Arcadia*. It can perhaps be said of any work that it has more than a single structure or ordering principle. For example, dramas and narratives are 'put together' on the basis of both action and theme; lyrics are structured by their thought as well as by patterns of repetition (formal repetition in grammatical and rhetorical figures, rhyme and meter, thematic repetition in the words and ideas themselves). To some extent the plurality of structures discussed here is the result of a multiple approach to the work of art; most analyses, in contrast, are content to establish the existence of the one pattern which most fully accounts for a given work. Yet if it were only a matter of approach, identifying several kinds of structure that operate simultaneously in the *Arcadia* would say something about critical methodology, but not much about Sidney's ideas of composition. Validation for a multiple approach to the *Arcadia* may be found, however, in studies of Sidney's poetry which suggest that conscious structural complexity is indeed the hallmark of Sidney's writing.

These studies have recognized in Sidney's poetry an overriding concern with what may be termed 'multiple unity,'[12] the drive for a complex though still coherent structural pattern. The concern is significantly manifested in all levels of composition, from sound and word schemes to placement of completed units within larger wholes:

[Sidney's] special contribution was the use, not of one or two figures in isolation, but of a wide variety of figures in intricate combination ...

His own central preoccupation was with structure, and in his search for form he not only produced single excellently fashioned poems, but also sought to relate them to one another to produce larger and more complex unities.[13]

It is logical to suspect that this need for pattern and coherence is an ingrained habit of mind, a standard of personal aesthetic satisfaction that will show itself in all Sidney's work. Reading the *Arcadia* with this in mind, one discovers that several kinds of structure do operate simultaneously, and that subordinate units are organized within themselves as well as being structurally functional in the work as a whole.

The fascination with complexity, with both cross-patterns and analogous repetitions on smaller and larger scales, is as much the result of a world view as it is a personal compulsion. A multiple approach to the *Arcadia* is not a purely arbitrary methodological decision, nor are the multiple structures an accidental result of Sidneian composition. Multiplicity is inherent in both the way Sidney saw his world and the way in which he organized it for literary purposes.

Three types of structure are dealt with: rhetorical, tonal, and narrative. I have defined each term in ways that depart from its normal usage. By rhetorical structure I mean local organization of language and ideas undoubtedly derived from the practice of rhetoric, but without sharing the traditional aim of rhetoric, which is to persuade. These organizing principles are found in terms such as partition and division, especially by means of antithesis. Tonal structure expands the notion of tone from its usual concern with local textural devices that indicate attitude and judgment to explore grosser elements of composition, notably the arrangement of sequences of events, that likewise convey attitudes and judgment. The third kind of structure, narrative structure, is rather more conventional, treating such formal elements as episode and plot, but without emphasizing linear or causal movement. A frequent concern of this book – the way in which the episodes of the *New Arcadia* fully articulate and sometimes modify the assumptions of the basic fable – is here extensively examined. This aspect of the *New Arcadia*'s construction also seems to me to have been neglected. It will offer more evidence as to the nature of the re-vision that lies behind the alterations Sidney made to his text.

To a certain extent, these categories overlap – for example, arrangements for tonal manipulation have some relation to other means of narrative progression – but I think clarity is promoted by keeping them isolated for separate study.

It may help to think of the classification as offering perspectives, selections from among several possible ways of viewing a single phenomenon. I emphasize the arbitrariness of the selection here: I have discussed thematic or amplificatory material more extensively than plot; I have omitted consideration of the *Arcadia's* poetry and its structural functions within the whole work in favour of concentrating on the prose narrative. Mere multiplicity of approach will not result in comprehensiveness; neither this nor any other classification can exhaust the meanings of a great literary work.

One result of this multiple exploration of how the *Arcadia* is put together is the discovery of a unifying core to its deliberate complexity. Many structures turn out to be related to a tension between Sidney's analytical habit of mind and his temperamental need for synthesis, which becomes matter for literary study through his use of antithesis or other sharply disparate or contrasting elements. In rhetorical structure the units are antithesis itself (or codified antitheses which I call antithetical topoi, such as doing-suffering, matter-spirit) and certain figures such as *antimetabole* and *correctio* that are means of simultaneously establishing and superseding antitheses. In tonal structure (Chapter 4) the manipulation is done by arranging the sequence of action and theme into an evaluative pattern that is first positive, then negative, then parodic or humorous. The particular narrative structure discussed in Chapter 5 exhibits two alternative accounts of virtue that are reconciled by being related hierarchically, and this kind of pattern is perceptible in the other two chapters on narrative structure as well, which see the second element in oppositions such as those between chivalry and pastoral, public and private, active and contemplative as being not finally antithetical but subordinate to the first, finding its fruition and fulfilment in the perfection of the dominant term. I have not, however, reduced the explorations of this book to make them demonstrate the validity of this stylistic observation. My emphasis is as much on the actual variety of the *Arcadia's* structures as on the temperamental unity discoverable within them. Moreover, the *Arcadia* is an important work for the English Renaissance precisely because it raises many large problems and asks for wide-ranging comparisons. This is not a book for people who see Sidney as a fellow of Lodge, Greene, and Gascoigne in the writing of Elizabethan fiction.

To the first of these larger issues I want to turn now. Before exploring what I have termed rhetorical structure in Chapter 2, there is a matter that might be called, only a little facetiously, rhetorical substructure. The subject, rhetoricism, is crucial to our understanding of the kind of work Sidney was writing.

More than thirty years have passed since literary criticism began to study rhetoric in earnest, but just as critics have always talked about 'style' yet rarely pursued the implications of their discoveries to what we today call 'stylistics,' so in this time we have extensively explored the use of rhetoric without seeking the meaning inherent in 'rhetoricism.' Sidney's *Arcadia* is a case in point. It is, by common consent, a fundamentally rhetorical work: the style is rhetorical because it is florid and dependent upon a wide range of figures and tropes; its fictional shape is rhetorical because significant junctures of the action are marked off by formal oratory; the poetic theory underlying the work is rhetorical because it aims at moving the will to virtuous action.[14] I take all these statements to be valid – and others like them, some to be offered in these very pages – yet they do not do justice to the work's innate rhetoricism, its essentially rhetorical perception of experience. What then does a rhetorical consciousness imply?

A recent brilliant study of Florentine humanism, Nancy S. Struever's *The Language of History in the Renaissance*,[15] has supplied the groundwork for answering such a question. Professor Struever's account begins with the quarrel between Plato and the Sophists over the validity of philosophy and rhetoric as educational disciplines, in which she is concerned to defend the Sophists' much-maligned position. The decision of Protagoras and Gorgias 'to deal with the impure: to shun the ideal sphere where pure reason and perfect justice reside for the shifting and uncertain field of action and discourse' is not, as Plato would have it, cynical opportunism, but is based upon a contrary epistemological insight, namely, that 'reality' is either unknowable, or if known, not communicable. 'Only a world of flux and impurity exists, and ... a mental operation cannot be divorced from this disorderly matrix. The desire for purity of thought and communication is a delusion, and even the force of logic is a force of violence ($\beta \iota \alpha$) mediated through the passions.'[16] According to Mario Untersteiner, whom Professor Struever follows in these matters, this epistemological belief in turn shapes the Sophists' understanding of art, ethics, education, political action, and language theory.[17] The result of this epistemology is a sense, differing strongly from both Aristotle's and Plato's, of what can be known about things and about right and wrong and also of what one in fact does in composing a work such as an oration or a formal history. Although one may reasonably question the evidence Untersteiner offers for the total coherence of Sophistic thought,[18] the description of the historical practice of Thucydides, Polybius, Sallust, and the Florentine humanists that Professor Struever arrives at on the basis of this interpretation of rhetoricism seem valid to me, and suggestive for reading English Renaissance literature as well.

The relevance of rhetoricism to Elizabethan narrative (and drama), for example, can be seen in the following account of the salient characteristics of rhetorical history. It is a history which emphasizes human will and choice, insisting on the way action is conditioned by circumstances and capable of ambiguous and conflicting interpretations. In structure it often employs antilogy – full presentation of opposing arguments – to give pluralistic illuminations to 'truths' and motivation, in style it makes use of antithesis to highlight contradiction and of irony to achieve detachment and awareness of discrepancies between the intention and effect of action. Having no commitment to transcendence, it deals intensively with 'appearances' (with this-worldly cause and effect, with human psychology), and it uses whatever rhetorical tools are available to create the strongly affective form of verisimilitude called *enargeia*.[19]

One may well protest that such rhetoricism ought not to be relevant to Elizabethan literary practice because its unknowable and contradictory reality is as much opposed to the Christian universe of absolute truths and hierarchies as it is to Plato's idealism. But it is not the epistemology as such that is significant for the Renaissance, which after all receives the rhetorical tradition through Aristotle and especially Cicero, neither of whom share the Sophists' view of reality. What is important is that embodied in the origins of rhetoric is a bias that is this-worldly rather than transcendent, emphasizing on the one hand the speaker's manipulation of words (and therefore his mediation of reality) and on the other, the contingent, imperfect nature of the reality in which we must operate. A fundamental rather than a superficial commitment to rhetoric will inevitably transmit repercussions of this bias.

Thus Aristotle's *Rhetoric*, although conceived to fit into a system bearing quite another epistemology, of necessity still reflects some Sophistic insights. Aristotle seeks to make rhetoric more philosophical, to see it as an 'art' capable of generalized statements and applications rather than Gorgias' collection of ad hoc pronouncements tied to specific subjects and circumstances,[20] but the root of his rhetoric remains appearance, contingencies, and the uncertainties of civic life. If human discourse has a need for rhetoric and not merely dialectic (Plato himself conceded this in the *Phaedrus*), then the Sophists' exploration and mastery of this territory – 'political reality' if not reality itself – had to be taken into account.

As for Cicero, the eclecticism of his approach to important questions means that one finds in his writings both the rhetorical (Sophistic) and the philosophical (Platonic) traditions discussed above, and further, that his works on rhetoric express both the serious and the debased or mechanical strands of rhetorical practice.[21] It is important that the full range of questions is available in Cicero's work because he is the decisive figure in transmitting classical ideas of rhetoric to the Italian humanists and thereby to the Renaissance period in general.[22] Cicero's own epistemological position, being Stoic, defuses the original Sophistic insights sufficiently to make them acceptable to the later Christian period. In contrast to the Sophists, who present a reality which is either unknowable or capable of generating contradictory statements about itself, the Stoics believe in a rational and knowable universe and assert the 'congruence of the structure of the cosmos, of the mind, and of language.'[23] Cicero's Stoic rationality seems to reflect Plato's philosophical stance, but his work is actually quite different in emphasis. As

Nancy Struever notes, where Plato suggests 'fitting rhetoric into a philosophical framework, Cicero inserts philosophy into a larger context of eloquence.' For all its reminiscences of the *Phaedrus*, a crucial dialogue like *De oratore* transmits ideas about language and the function of the Orator in society that are alien to Plato.[24]

Cicero derives his understanding of invention and the topical tradition and perhaps even his starting point for what constitutes the Orator's field of knowledge from those parts of Aristotle's *Rhetoric* that are related to Sophistic.[25] His subordinating of philosophy to eloquence reminds one of the way Aristotle subsumes ethics and politics into his rhetoric by considering them the background knowledge necessary for generating arguments. But Cicero's exalted view of the province of the Orator is light years away from Aristotle's concrete sense of ethics and politics anchored in psychology, human motives, and notions of the good.[26] Cicero sees the Orator's significance as well as his area of competence in inflated terms. That which differentiates man from the beasts is λόγος, a Greek word translatable either as speech (*oratio*) or as reason or thinking (*ratio*). For Cicero as for Isocrates, λόγος as speech rather than as thought is man's distinguishing characteristic: the Orator does best what is man's single advantage over brute creation.[27]

Cicero's ideal Orator proved congenial to the Renaissance mind, which thought in a similar way about the symbolic significance of special figures, notably the King, who embodies and represents all mankind because of his position at the head of the social (and therefore human) hierarchy. This formal connection between the Orator and the King is of special interest for Sidney's *Arcadia*, which uses oratory conspicuously to demonstrate educational, political, and heroic values. The *Arcadia* is concerned with the education of the Orator almost as much as Cicero and Quintilian, because the knowledge garnered and displayed during this education is for Sidney chief among the requisites of the King.

Yet for all the *Arcadia*'s kinship with Cicero's conception of the ideal Orator, Sidney's sense of rhetoric in the work is closer to Aristotle's. The lessons that the princes learn are concrete and lie mainly in the areas of ethics, psychology, and politics. Even those philosophical issues that are germane – the conflict between the active and contemplative life, the immortality of the soul, and in the *New Arcadia* Pamela's proof of the existence of God – may be said to resemble Aristotle's treatment in the *Rhetoric* of common topics such as what men think is the highest good rather than to display Cicero's requirement of 'universal culture.' In this light John Hoskins' statement that Sidney once translated the first two books of Aristotle's *Rhetoric* becomes significant.[28]

Sidney's rhetorical bias therefore implies something about the content as well as the style of the *Arcadia*.[29] The original quarrel between philosophy and rhetoric may be reworked to provide illumination of an issue broached in Sidney criticism by the studies of John Danby and Walter Davis, namely, to what extent the *Arcadia* can be described as primarily seeking to embody Christian or Neoplatonic doctrine. (I lump the two together because of their other-worldly orientation, although both are not equally relevant to the work. The *Arcadia* is unquestionably Christian in its assumptions, though this does not, I think, form part of the crucial thematic interest of the work. But Neoplatonism, I am convinced, is largely a red herring.) Much recent criticism has moved away from this question, but not, it seems to me, because it has been answered. One purpose of this book is to anchor the *Arcadia* firmly enough in *this* world – from its rhetoricist substructure to its preference for Aristotle over Plato and its decision for action rather than contemplation – that the issue can be laid to rest satisfactorily.[30]

The problem of Christianity can perhaps be treated as a permutation of the original conflict between philosophy and rhetoric that we have been tracing. Reconciliation between these two, always necessary because people immediately perceived the weakness of either in isolation, was traditionally effected by subordinating one to the other: for example, as noted earlier, Plato's *Phaedrus* fits rhetoric into a dominantly philosophical framework, whereas in the *De oratore* Cicero merely accepts philosophy as a necessary component of true eloquence. So too with the conflict between Christianity and rhetoric (or the this-worldly orientation implied by rhetoric). For Augustine, to cite an obvious example of someone who felt the conflict and decided that Christianity was dominant, rhetoric had to be purified before it could be allowed to fill religious needs;[31] in the *Arcadia*, on the other hand, the dominant concern is the life of the heroic Orator-King,[32] and certain Christian attitudes and beliefs are merely shown to be consonant with it. Were the existence of two schemes of values – the Christian and the heroic – the conscious thematic concern of the *Arcadia*, one is tempted to think that Sidney's mind would have been at least as intellectually alive to the possibility of conflict as Spenser's is in Book I of *The Faerie Queene*. But the this-worldly concerns of Sidney's rhetoricism in the *Arcadia* finally preclude his giving primary attention to a transcendent doctrine like Christianity or Neoplatonism. When in the last chapter of this book I examine the handling of an absolute value such as Justice, the trouble it causes will be apparent.[33] The pull of rhetoric is towards καιρός or the particular matching of time and circumstance, that is, towards people and their associations, not towards the discovery of abstract 'truth.'

Sidney's relation to the ideas traced here is largely conjectural, but we may interpret the evidence of his writing. He obviously grew up with the 'abuse' of the rhetorical tradition even as Shakespeare did; it was enshrined in their education (the emphasis on *elocutio*, on codified 'decorum' and lists of appropriate topoi). But just as the Florentine historians rediscover the essential implications of rhetoric, so Sidney (again like Shakespeare) with the intelligence and honesty native to fine writers who explore the tools they work with, seems intuitively to rediscover the roots of the rhetoricism he employs and then to live with this insight as part of the total fabric of his work.

The similarity between the *Arcadia* and certain aspects of classical and Renaissance history is of course not accidental. Sidney's age did not in practice distinguish among poetry, rhetoric, and history as we do today. The Renaissance notoriously held a theory of poetry that was contaminated by rhetoric, and their new classicizing unearthed a body of history that was largely rhetorical as well. It is this rhetorical bent to history as they discovered it in Sallust, Tacitus, Polybius, and others that may have made it seem to literary theorizers that epic was a form of versified history. Indeed, one of the excellences of poetry for Sidney's *Defence* is that its content may come from history: 'whatsoever action, or faction, whatsoever counsel, policy or war stratagem the historian is bound to recite, that may the poet (if he list) with his imitation make his own, beautifying it both for further teaching, and more delighting ...'[34]

The revolution in historical writing of the Tudor period, which saw the change from medieval chronicle to something more oriented towards secondary causes and political activity,[35] demonstrates how important it was for the historian as well as the poet that the main result of humanist rhetorical activity was the 'defence of poetry,' that is, a defence of the *creative* role of the rhetor (poet, historian) in selecting and moulding his material.[36] Some of the passages Nancy Struever quotes from Salutati concerning the historian might have come from Sidney's own treatise on poetry. In fact, although the *Defence* seems clear enough on the relative merits of history, an important letter to his brother Robert reinforces one's feeling that Sidney has distorted the treatise's argument concerning poetry's superiority for the sake of persuasion. On the basis of the letter it seems that history might have urged a stronger claim to the palm for teaching: 'So lastlie not professing any arts, as his [the historian's] matter leads him he deales with all arts which because it carrieth the life of the lively example, it is wonderful what light it gives to the arts themselves ...'[37] Here in the letter, history is not reduced to a 'bare was' (though philosophy is still pure dialectic); instead, it makes its effect through 'lively example' (ie, *enargeia*), the effectiveness Sidney assigns only to poetry in the *Defence*.[38]

Sidney's understanding of poetry, at least of the sort the *Arcadia* is, thus seems intertwined with his understanding of rhetoric and history. Together they indicate the intellectual and emotional preferences that are built into that work. The bias is active, historical, and this-worldly rather than contemplative, philosophical, and other-worldly, though the pull of the latter set of alternatives is not altogether absent. Nor could it be for a sixteenth-century Christian. But the

Greek setting of the *Arcadia* is as deliberate, I think, as More's decision to locate his 'Utopia' outside the Christian world.[40] In a way it parallels the attempt of Dante to work with 'natural virtues' for the first two books of the *Commedia*.

By way of introduction I have suggested some implications of Sidney's particular kind of rhetoricism. The remarks are meant to stand as a background or resonator for the ensuing discussion, which begins with an attempt to set out more limited and specific kinds of rhetorical influences that operate in the *Arcadia*. Periodically, however, I shall either explore further some of these opening remarks or support their assertions through insights gained from closer reading of the text. The overall view of the work that I shall offer has already been adumbrated: it is not primarily concerned with transcendant doctrines like Christianity or Neoplatonism, nor is it (and this follows from its active bias) primarily pastoral, although pastoral is clearly crucial to its conception and design. More positively, I see the *Arcadia* as an heroic poem in prose, fully engaged in the problems of history, philosophy, politics, and ethics (and love) that the Renaissance assigned to the domain of epic. But we must now turn from substructure to structure, from rhetoricism to rhetorical organization.

RHETORICAL STRUCTURE:
THE TOPICAL TRADITION

The *Arcadia* expresses the pervasiveness of rhetoric in Sidney's thought not only through its 'rhetoricism,' but also through its *informal* rhetorical structure, by which I mean methods of arranging material that are stated and implied in rhetorical manuals when discussion does not concern the formal divisions of an oration. It is thus organizations of language and thought which derive from the practice of rhetoric without necessarily in themselves contributing to the rhetorical aim of persuasion. The term can be applied to many kinds of organization, from simple problems of arrangement and sequence to patterns of balance and repetition, from sentence structure to the structure of episodes and books. The meaning of the term 'rhetorical' here is much more limited and rather more technical than in my introduction, yet it does not represent the usage of either scholarly or popular discourse. In spite of the multiplication of meanings, the term seems particularly useful for conveying the idea that Sidney's solutions to problems of organizing his fictional narrative often parallel the treatment of language and thought in rhetorical handbooks.

Since the basis of the Elizabethan education was classical rhetoric, the habits of mind it instilled were largely those necessary for oral discussion and argumentation.[1] Oral communication implies emphasis on organization itself; one must always be sure that the audience can follow the thread of the argument, that it knows at all times the relation of the parts to the whole. Though of course desirable in all forms of discourse, clarity is particularly urgent for the orator, and it leaves its stamp on the writings of a rhetorically trained culture, usually as an explicitly articulated structure or outline of thought. Conversely, this kind of skeletal clarity is generally absent from our own age, which thinks of formal communication as being written and of form as arising 'organically' from the subject instead of being mentally imposed upon it.

THEME AND ACTION: ANTITHETICAL TOPOI

Sir Fulke Greville's analysis of the *Arcadia* in his biography of Sidney offers a fair example of Elizabethan rhetorical training in practice. Commentators generally dwell on the content of his statement, since it represents an important contemporary view of the work; I should like here instead to draw attention to its structure:

> in all these creatures of his making, his intent, and scope was, to turn the barren Philosophy precepts into pregnant Images of life; and in them, first on the Monarch's part, lively to represent the growth, state, and declination of Princes, change of Government, and lawes: vicissitudes of sedition, faction, succession, confederacies, plantations, with all other errors, or alterations in publique affairs. Then again in the subjects case; the state of favor, prosperitie, adversity, emulation, quarrell, undertaking, retiring, hospitality, travail, and all other moodes of private fortunes, or misfortunes. In which traverses (I know) his purpose was to limn out such exact pictures, of every posture of the minde, that any man being forced, in the straines of this life, to pass through any straights, or latitudes of good, or ill fortune, might (as in a glasse) see how to set a good countenance upon all the discountenances of adversitie, and a stay upon the exorbitant smilings of chance.[2]

One immediately notices the verbal devices that today we consider 'rhetorical' – the antithesis, word play, metaphorical language – but just as obtrusive is the skeleton of the thought itself: the central idea is stated (turning barren philosophy into pregnant images of life), divided into two component parts (monarch-subject or public-private), and then each of the parts is amplified at will.[3] The unity of the passage is ensured because there is a single idea from which all the parts have been derived; the contrasts and antitheses, far from intruding upon the unity, become the pattern through which it is effected.

The main device of the passage, division or partition of thought, is important enough to appear in some form in the subject matter of every section of a rhetorical manual, as well as to constitute much of the manual's own method of presentation, since the procedure is obviously well suited to pedagogy. The standard manual generally had three parts: *inventio* (finding of arguments), *dispositio* (arrangement of the material once found), and *elocutio* (language, ornamentation, and whatever the author has to say about memory and delivery). For most theorists, *partitio* is one of the formal parts of an oration [*dispositio*];[4] Quintilian, on the other hand, feels that because division is relevant to every aspect of a speech it should not be treated as a separate element.[5] Various forms of division are catalogued among the figures of thought [*elocutio*]: *Rhetorica ad Herennium* includes *divisio* and *distributio*; Puttenham adds the dilemma (*dialisis*, or the Dismemberer).[6] Division is also treated as a topos or commonplace (ie, a form or line of argument) by Aristotle, Cicero, and the later theorists, whose lists of topics [*inventio*] invariably include some consideration of parts and wholes.[7] Division may of course result in any number of component parts, but a preference for antithetical contrasts, if accidental, is still readily understandable. While the *Ad Herennium* warns the orator that a useful partition contains no more than three members, a common pedagogical dictum was that 'every good division ought to be two-membered.'[8] Father Walter J. Ong asserts that Ramus' famous dichotomies merely exaggerate a tendency clearly discernible in scholastic and Renaissance thought, and that, ignoring questions of influence, both phenomena reflect 'a bi-polarity in being, which echoes everywhere through philosophical history: form and matter, act and potency, Yang and Yin, thesis and antithesis, the one and the many, and so on through an indefinite number of epiphanies.'[9]

One certainly need not wait for Ramistic discussions of method to find division by dichotomy at work. For example, here is the treatment of the deliberative speech in the *Rhetorica ad Herennium*, conveniently tabulated by the Loeb editor:

A Deliberative speech concerns a choice among two or more courses of action; the question may be examined either on its own account or on account of a motive extraneous to the question itself. The aim in a deliberative speech is Advantage, to be studied in accordance with the following topics:

Advantage

1 Security		2 Honour	
Might	Craft (strategy)	The Right	The Praiseworthy, in the opinion of
a Armies	a Money	a Wisdom	a The proper authorities
b Fleets	b Promises	b Justice	b Our allies
c Arms	c Dissimulation	c Courage	c All our fellow-citizens
d Engines of war	d Accelerated speed	d Temperance	d Our descendants[10]
e Manpower	e Deception		

One can readily use this model to construct a similar table from Greville's analysis of the *Arcadia* quoted above: philosophy has two aspects, public (politics) and private (perhaps ethics); politics can in turn be broken down into acts of peaceful evolution and of violent change, ethics into a paired series of contrasted activities which are misleadingly said to fall under the headings of good or ill fortune. There is a major difference between the two analyses – the topics of the *Ad Herennium* pretend to exhaust the possibilities, while Greville's suggest almost unlimited expansibility or amplification[11] – but either type of analysis adheres to traditional interpretations of the term topos.

Since the topical tradition is central to the analysis of the *Arcadia* in this chapter, let me clarify the notion of the topos. There is much confusion surrounding the subject,[12] but for our period one may follow Sister J.M. Lechner's division of topoi into two categories, the analytic and the subject topic:

[The Renaissance 'analytic' topic is] usually thought of as a concept which could be used in asking oneself questions about a subject which would generate ideas concerning the subject: for example, such 'places' as definition, division, etymology and relation, when applied to a specific subject, would 'spin out' the full meaning of that subject. The 'subject' topic or heading, on the other hand, represented a heading more usable for organizing material gathered in a commonplace book, where one 'located' an argument named according to the subject matter of its contents, such as virtue, physics, peace, or ethics.[13]

The two separate traditions are also recognized in Francis Bacon's distinction between Commonplaces and Topics as the two main categories of aids to rhetorical invention. The idea of differentiating the terms seems to be Bacon's own; the words were apparently synonymous before him. He defines topics as 'directions or guides for undertaking ... investigation and for retrieving ideas previously discovered.'[14] The topic is therefore a place for storing arguments, while the commonplace is for storing dilations and expansions of a theme:[15] 'one is led to believe that 'common-place' may be a class name applicable to any idea which either recurs often, or is likely to recur often, during a speaker's career, and whose repetition, accordingly, justifies cataloguing it together with related ideas, for future reference.'[16] The subject topic, what Bacon terms the 'commonplace,' is the one more interesting for our purposes.

It is thus possible to view the content of Greville's statement, the particular topoi or contrasts he chooses, as well as the mode of thinking that encourages him to write antithetically, as aspects of rhetorical training. One can see this operating clearly in a passage where there is no possibility that the subject matter itself imposed the scheme for its interpretation, as might have been true for the description of the *Arcadia*. Greville talks about Sidney's life in the same way he speaks of his work: 'But the truth is: his end was not writing, even while he wrote; nor his knowledge moulded for tables, or schooles; but both his wit, and understanding bent upon his heart, to make himself and others, not in words or opinion, but in life, and action, good and great.'[17] Greville saw the *Arcadia* in terms of public and private activity and of behaviour in prosperity and adversity; the central contrast in Sidney's life is between knowledge and action. I have analysed these passages of Greville because the issues are particularly clear in his prose, but neither the mode of thinking nor the particular sets of contrasts are peculiar to him. They represent the basic formulations of moral and literary thought inherited from antiquity and the Middle Ages, common formulations with the important virtue of being able to serve as headings under which to assemble a coherent interpretation of experience.[18] These traditional sets of conflicting values, such as are found in debates between body and soul, will for convenience be called 'antithetical topoi.' The name indicates their relation to Curtius' work on the topos, though the topoi I discuss do not resemble most of the formulae, images, and motifs he treats under this term.[19]

Greville might have included the 'life' version of the active versus the contemplative virtues in his discussion of Sidney's work, or with equal justice to the *Arcadia*, he might have opposed reason to passion, doing to suffering, or matter to spirit, or he might have chosen the equally familiar conflict between art and nature. They are all present in the *Arcadia*, at various times and to varying degrees providing the subject matter, themes, and narrative sequence of the work. Sidney, in sharing Greville's education, also shares his habits of thinking and organizing experience. Earlier I rejected the possibility that Sidney's plan in the *Arcadia* had been solely responsible for the form of Greville's commentary. Neither is the opposite true: Greville's analysis does not impose a foreign schema on Sidney's thought. In fact, both the form and content of his remarks find strict parallels in Sidney's own *Defence of Poesie*, for example, in the famous statement that 'the highest end of the mistress-knowledge ... stands (as I think) in the knowledge of a man's self, in the ethic and politic consideration, with the end of well-doing and not of well-knowing only' (82-3).[20]

I wish to turn now from Greville's commentary on the *Arcadia* to the *Arcadia* itself, from the use of the topical tradition in composing analytical or expository prose to the use of one example of that tradition, the antithetical topos, in solving problems in the invention and disposition of narrative materials.[21] I shall discuss two of the major antithetical topoi present in the text – matter-spirit and doing-suffering – in order to make two points. The number and significance of the examples will demonstrate the pervasiveness of these topoi in the *Arcadia*, the way they supply thematic content and help determine certain features of the action. The second point, more important than mere pervasiveness, is the apparent perseverance of the topoi's original function in generating argument. The evaluative bias seemingly built into them, the need for ranking and decision, is something that Sidney explores and subtly manipulates. I shall begin, as the *Arcadia* begins, with the figure of Urania.

The conflict between matter and spirit, the antithetical topos clearly announced in the Urania prologue, is related both to the medieval debate between body and soul and to the familiar conflict between appearance and reality. Though Sidney's handling of his topos treads a neutral ground between the religious and philosophical biases of these other two formulations, he still often employs it in assessing moral value. The result of his particular shading of the antinomy is to permit a more complex or equitable weighing of the contending possibilities, a complexity necessary to his total design. For example, although the reader's expectations of moral evaluation are apparently satisfied by the opening passage of the revised *Arcadia*, it is crucial to the work's final assessment of other antinomies *related* to the original matter-spirit antithesis (public-private, active-contemplative, doing-suffering) where the issues can be more evenly balanced, that Sidney complicate our automatic moral response. He sees to it that we are simultaneously satisfied by the value placed on spiritual good and yet kept responsive to the claims of physical pleasure.

The very warp and woof of this opening scene of the *New Arcadia*, the lament of the shepherds Strephon and Claius for the departed Urania, is provided by the conflict between matter and spirit: all that remains to them is a memory of her physical presence; other shepherds delight in material gain and physical exercise but they improve themselves through contemplation; her physical beauty is overmatched by her spiritual qualities. Yet Sidney is not willing to allow his Urania to be simply the Heavenly Venus of the Neoplatonists.[22] Though he goes as far as he can with this vague Neoplatonic love theory in the initial pages of the *Arcadia*, he also undercuts the simplicity of the vision with Kalander's playful suggestion that their improvement has not been caused by love at all (I, 27).

Even the elaborate description of Urania reminiscent of the Song of Songs cannot be considered an unqualified assertion of spirituality. Instead, one is faced with a considerable discrepancy between explicit statement and the total effect of the passage. The 'argument' is that Urania is 'a maide, who is such, that as the greatest thing the world can shewe, is her beautie, so the least thing that may be praysed in her, is her beautie':

Certainely as her eyelids are more pleasant to behold, then two white kiddes climing up a faire tree, and browsing on his tendrest braunches, and yet are nothing, compared to the day-shining starres contayned in them; and as her breath is more sweete then a gentle Southwest wind, which comes creeping over flowrie fieldes and shaddowed waters in extreme heate of summer, and yet is nothing, compared to the hony flowing speach that breath doth carrie: no more all that our eyes can see of her (though when they have seene her, what else they shall ever see is but drie stuble after clovers grasse) is to bee matched with the flocke of unspeakeable vertues laid up delightfully in that best builded folde. (I, 7)

The idea is developed in three parts: a comparison between her eyelids and the eyes contained in them, between her breath and the speech it carries, between whatever the eye can see and her inner virtues. The passage is richly evocative and pictorial, yet the descriptions given to the spiritual qualities it purports to praise are comparatively flat: 'day-shining starres' for eyes,[23] 'hony flowing' speech, and a 'flock of unspeakeable' virtues. Physical things, on the other hand, have lavished upon them all the striking detail of the white kids, tender branches, creeping wind, flowery fields, shadowed waters, dry stubble, and clovers grass. (The result of Sidney's working in the style of the Canticles, incidentally, is to 'chasten' the physical import, since the images convey no sensuality.) Moreover, to speak of final impressions, there can be no doubt which of the two elements of the last set is climactic. The 'unspeakeable' virtues may be made subtly concrete by the association with kids and sheep perceptible in the word 'flock,' but the force of even that comparison is not realized for us until they are 'laid up delightfully in that best-builded folde.' We have not given up physical for spiritual pleasures nearly so much as Neoplatonists, Strephon and Claius included, would have us believe.

In spite of these tensions and qualifications, it is still accurate to say that the revised opening of the *Arcadia* employs the antithesis between matter and spirit as a balance for weighing moral value, with spirit bearing the heavier weight. Whatever equivocation exists is submerged in the formal and ceremonial quality of the passage. As the *Arcadia* unravels, the special atmosphere of the prologue disappears, but the contrast between matter and spirit, along with the allied antithetical topoi suggested above, continues as a dominant thematic element. The most important examples of the matter-spirit topos in Book I occur in the disguise or transformation sequences, which include both the trial of Argalus and Parthenia for constancy and the effect of love on the two princes.

The story of Argalus and Parthenia again works with the moral implications of the topos: Argalus' continued love for Parthenia after her beauty has been disfigured by a rejected suitor is explicitly called a 'rare ensample' of 'trueth of love' and 'vertuous constancie' (I, 35). Faithful to the amplificatory tradition of the topoi, the contrast between body and mind offers 'a fayre field to use eloquence in' (I, 35). Argalus' plea runs thus:

that her face, when it was fayrest, had been but as a marshall, to lodge the love of her in his minde; which now was so well placed, as it needed no further help of any outward harbinger: beseeching her, even with teares, to know, that his love was not so superficial, as to go no further then the skin; which yet now to him was moste faire, since it was hers ... (I, 35)

His rejection of Parthenia's 'double' after her supposed death strongly restates the same position; its moral correctness is underlined by the revelation that Parthenia has devised the story of her death 'to make this triall, whether he could quickly forget his true Parthenia, or no':

Excellent Ladie, know, that if my hart were mine to give, you before al other, should have it; but Parthenias it is, though dead: there I began, there I end all matter of affection: I hope I shall not long tarry after her, with whose beautie if I had onely been in love, I should be so with you, who have the same beautie: but it was Parthenias selfe I loved, and love; which no likenes can make one, no commaundement dissolve, no foulnes defile, nor no death finish. (I, 50)

Parthenia's being disfigured, which the 1590 Quarto interestingly calls 'disguysed,'[24] is therefore just an outward or exterior alteration. Her 'true self' remaining intact, the exterior blight creates an absolute divorce between her physical and spiritual being. More positively, the external disfigurement, being a kind of adversity, strengthens the inner beauty that the lovers' constancy represents and makes it visible. Thus the radical disproportion between body and mind here is not in itself a moral tension, though like all the effects of Fortune, good or bad, it tests morality. The disfigurement becomes a means of discovery for both Parthenia and Argalus, an outward, incontrovertible assurance of their virtue.

The metamorphoses of the two princes into Amazon and shepherd play a variation on this exploration of inner being and outer appearance. One would expect Sidney to focus on the discrepancy between princely reality and disguised appearance, and though this forms as it were the continuo to their lament, the melody is concerned not with the divorce but the parity between the real and the apparent self. 'Transformd in shew, but more transformd in minde' (I, 76), Pyrocles dressed as Zelmane assures us, and Musidorus (now turned Dorus) echoes the lament: 'Come shepheards weedes, become your masters minde: / Yeld outward shew, what inward chance he tryes' (I, 113). The revised *Arcadia* makes their transformations more clearly psychological and ethical, the result not of impersonal Fortune but of Love. In the *Old Arcadia*, both princes 'would yield out suchlike lamentations':

Alas! What further evil hath fortune reserved for us, or what shall be the end of this our tragical pilgrimage? Shipwracks, daily dangers, absence from our country, have at length brought forth this captiving of us within ourselves which hath transformed the one in sex, and the other in state, as much as the uttermost work of changeable fortune can be extended unto. (*OA* 43)

In the *New Arcadia*:

O heaven and earth (said Musidorus) to what a passe are our mindes brought, that from the right line of vertue, are wryed to these crooked shifts: But o Love, it is thou that doost it: thou changest name upon name; thou disguisest our bodies, and disfigurest our mindes. But in deed thou hast reason, for though the wayes be foule, the journeys end is most faire and honourable. (I, 117)

Though the revision forgoes the interesting metaphor 'captiving us within our-selves,' it gains precision for the idea of similarity in inward and outward effects, while at the same time enhancing the ethical implications of their actions through the contrast between foul means and honourable ends.[25] The function of the antithetical topos in this passage is to use opposition for suggesting 'range':[26] it casts a simple statement into antithetical form by saying that something is true not only for A but for Z also, that the transformation is total, entailing the mind as well as the body. Perhaps the marvel of the total effectiveness of Love's transform-ing power over one antithesis is meant to hint that the further, redeeming, trans-formation from foul means to fair ends is possible too.

The final example of the matter-spirit topos to be discussed here illustrates one of the more complex structural functions that antithetical topoi may take on. In the splendid Triumph that precedes Phalantus' tourney (I, 101-4), the sequence of the conquered women is determined largely by a movement within the bounda-ries of a contrast between physical appearance and spiritual value. The design of the eleven descriptions breaks into two parts: the first six or seven seem to develop in pairs; the second group achieves what may be called a pictorial bal-ance, weighing a single, elaborate contrast against the three briefer contrasts of the first part. The opening six portraits probably represent a linear progression through beauty as judged by some absolute standard; taken in pairs, however, they each contrast physical attributes with 'spiritual' qualities.

The first two portraits in Artesia's Triumph present women who are not beau-tiful. Andromana is described purely in physical terms; she has 'exceeding red haire with small eyes' (I, 101). The next picture 'taught the beholders no other point of beauty' than that someone, in spite of her plainness, thought she was beautiful enough to appear as her champion. Thus we have in both the same physical fact, once merely stated and once mitigated by a 'non-sensory' judgment.

The second pair, Artaxia and Erona, repeats on a more theoretical level the interplay between fact and judgment of the first. The question seems to be whether beauty consists in physical proportion or inner grace.[27] The point is quite clear in the description of Artaxia: 'a Lady upon whom Nature bestowed, and wel placed her <most> delightful colours; and withal, had proportioned her without any fault, quickly to be discovered by the senses, yet altogether seemed not to make up that harmony, that Cupid delights in ...'[28] Erona's features are finely assessed as if to show that physical beauty with its chief criteria of symmetry and colour has been fully considered before the decision is given to inner grace:

> Of a farre contrary consideration was the representation of her that next followed, which was Erona Queene of Licia, who though of so browne a haire, as no man should have injuried it to have called it blacke, and that in the mixture of her cheeks the white did so much overcome the redde (though what was, was very pure) that it came neare to palenes, and that her face was a thought longer than exacte Symmetrians perhaps would allow; yet love plaid his part so well, in everie part, that it caught holde of the judgement, before it could judge, making it first love, and after acknowledge it faire ...

The next two portraits, of Baccha and Leucippe, are explicitly introduced as a pair. The order of presentation is the same as in the first two pairs, the less attractive member preceding, but the basis for contrast is now clearly moral. As the culmination of this sequence of three, it asserts most strongly the underlying physical-spiritual duality. Unlike the first set, both these women are beautiful. Baccha's description emphasizes her physical attributes and evaluates them with words that carry a highly negative charge. Her 'fatnes' allures, her breasts are 'over-familiarly laide open,' she languishes with idleness, invites and finally over-runs desire. Leucippe's 'portrait,' on the other hand, is not physical at all; her features convey only qualities of character, and the many abstract words, though gentle, are morally positive. She shows 'fine daintines,' 'sober simplicitie,' cheerfulness and 'prety demurenes.' The contrast between them is complete, down to the beholder's reactions. We hear of his desire on the one hand and of his 'pitie' for a 'poore soule' on the other.

The seventh portrait stands alone. It belongs to the first group in its concern with fact and judgment in assessing physical beauty, but it is obviously meant as a joke on the nature of *relevant* fact: 'she was a Queene, and therefore beautyfull' (I, 103). As such, however, it offers the maximum contrast both in tone and substance to the portrait of Helen that follows immediately. Helen's description is by far the most sumptuous of the Triumph; one is overwhelmed by the jacinth hair, the ropes of pearl, the small face that is a spark of beauty able to inflame a world of love. The richness is not confined to the objects described, but finds expression in the ornamental style and in the multiplication of motifs as well. Prominent among the new motifs is the nature-art topos:

It was the excellently-faire Queene Helen, whose Jacinth haire [was] curled by nature and intercurled by arte ... In whose face so much beauty and favour expressed, as if Helen had not bene knowen; some would rather have judged it the painters exercise, to shew what he could do, then <the> counterfaiting of any living patterne ... (I, 103)

Previous descriptions did not extend to the clothing each woman wore, but 'as for her [Helen's] attire, it was costly and curious ...' These new motifs are central to the second set of portraits, but among the older motifs continued in them is Sidney's interest in the beholder's reactions. For Helen, the account is extraordinary not only for the emphasis placed on it (it is patterned from three allied sets of antitheses) but for Sidney's refusal to use his loaded terms for moral judgment:

For every thing was full of a choyce finenes, that if it wanted any thing in majestie, it supplied it with increase <in> pleasure; and if at first it strake not admiration, it ravished with delight. And no indifferent soul there was, which if it could resist from subjecting it self it make it his princesse, that would not long to have such a playfellow. (I, 103)

As one would expect, Parthenia, Helen's complementary figure, offers a strong contrast to the concentration on external beauty and ornament. Her physical description is limited to three items: her great grey eyes, her large and exceedingly fair forehead, and the clean simplicity of her attire. As Sidney says, she is of a beauty 'farre differing' from Helen's, though he is quick to add that it is 'esteemed equall' (I, 103). The description proceeds with the kind of abstractions that we have met before in Leucippe, though here they are majestic while Leucippe's were hesitant and personal. In Parthenia 'every thing was goodly, and stately' (note that in Helen 'every thing was full of a choyce finenes'), her 'great-mindedness was but the auncient-bearer to humblenes,' and her eyes and forehead 'with all the rest of her face and body, [were] cast in the mould of Noblenes' (I, 103). She had no need of 'exquisite decking, having no adorning but cleanlines; and so farre from all arte, that it was full of carelesnesse ...' (I, 104). In spite of Basilius' characterization of Parthenia as 'the perfect picture of womanly vertue, and wively faithfulness' (I, 104), the contrast between her and Helen is not primarily moral. If one wished to generalize the implications of the progression from Helen to Parthenia and then to Urania, one could *perhaps* see it as asserting the greater good of the more spiritual factors (here translated into terms of asceticism, simplicity, naturalness, abstraction) while simultaneously suggesting an inability to renounce the lesser good of the sensuously delightful physical universe, which at its best can be accused of no more heinous sin than opulence.[29]

The maximum case for 'spirit' is not found in the description of Parthenia, however, but is worked out with an absoluteness that no royal or noble figure could permit, in the final description of the Triumph, that of the shepherdess Urania.[30] Just as the complex sensuousness of Helen's portrait is reflected in the increased ornateness of the style, the simplicity of the ideal embodied by Urania – and the power it has over men – finds expression in the diction and syntax:

It [the picture] was of a young mayd, which sate pulling out a thorne out of a Lambs foote, with her looke so attentive uppon it, as if that little foote coulde have bene the circle of her thoughts; her apparel so poore, as it had nothing but the inside to adorne it; a shephooke lying by her with a bottle upon it. But with al that povertie, beauty plaid the prince, and commanded as many harts as the greatest Queene there did.[31]

'Apparel so poore, as it had nothing but the inside to adorne it' – an absolute version of the matter-spirit conflict, but translated into pastoral terms. For the princes and princesses who are the key figures in the story it cannot therefore represent a viable choice. For them the significant emblematic figures must be Helen and Parthenia. The refusal to treat *that* choice morally is especially significant, considering the moral potential of the relevant topos.

In this discussion of Sidney's use of antithetical topoi, interest has thus far been primarily thematic. As thematic motifs, the topoi of course also perform the usual function of unifying the total work through recurrence, but with the matter-spirit conflict my focus has rather been on the individual sequences themselves.[32] The next antithetical topos to be considered, the contrast between doing and suffering, controls larger blocks of material; since it is concerned intrinsically with the idea of action, it readily projects itself as narrative events. I have chosen the terminology 'doing-suffering' because it is Sidney's own in the *Arcadia*, but the topos has had varying forms in its long classical and Christian history.[33] It is similar to what John Danby, using the *Defence*, has called the antithesis between patience and magnanimity. Danby connects 'the outer world of public events' with magnanimity and the 'inner world of private affections' with patience, suggesting at one point that the princes' pre-Arcadian exploits of Book II portray their magnanimity while the Book III captivity displays the princesses' patience[34] – which gives some idea of how the topos may be converted into a structural concept.

Walter R. Davis, following Danby's lead, traces a precise pattern in the scenes comprising the captivity episode in Book III: 'The siege is part of a pattern by which scenes within Cecropia's castle alternate with events outside it: Cecropia's first set of arguments, a skirmish between the two armies; her second set of arguments, the series of single fights; and Cecropia's set of tortures (proceeding to the conclusion of the episode as it stands).'[35] He finds that the episode illustrates

Danby's scheme 'quite neatly, the actions outside the castle representing the public world, those inside, the private.' This is on the whole justifiable, yet something can be gained by a shift in terminology that would allow us to consider the pattern a projection of the doing-suffering topos. The often explicit relation between episode and main plot in the *Arcadia*, discussed further in Chapter 7, makes it probable that Sidney is elaborating a motif introduced earlier into the revision with the story of Argalus and Parthenia:

> But it was hard to judge, whether he in doing, or she in suffering, shewed greater constancie of affection: for, as to Argalus the world sooner wanted occasions, then he valour to goe thorow them; so to Parthenia, malice sooner ceased, then her unchanged patience. (I, 33-4)

The point of this statement, and also, I think, of the captivity pattern, is the equality of the two ordeals: 'it was hard to judge, whether he in doing, or she in suffering, shewed greater constancie of affection.' This may well represent an important clarification in Sidney's thinking. In Book IV of the *Old Arcadia*, Pyrocles justifies his plan to commit suicide by comparing the two conditions: 'For to do requires a whole heart, to suffer falls easiliest in the broken minds' (*OA* 296-7). The *New Arcadia* seems deliberately to demonstrate the error in Pyrocles' judgment, not, however, by making patience pre-eminent,[36] but by insisting on equality between the two spheres of virtue.

CHARACTER: TOPICS OF PRAISE AND BLAME

Sidney thus employs antithetical topoi as the themes and to a lesser extent as guides for the action of his *Arcadia*; his methods of characterization are similarly dependent upon another variety of rhetorical topos, the topics for praise and blame.[37] For example, the young male characters in the *Arcadia* all share virtually the same attributes: noble birth, princely education, virtue, valour that overcomes all difficulties, courage, courtesy, modesty, liberality, and wit or learning. The list is also likely to include eloquence, constancy, and a tendency towards melancholy. Moreover, we are made aware of the sameness of their conception through repetition; Sidney regularly provides such formal descriptions of his characters, as if to do so were an accepted convention of the genre he pursued, though it may well be his own innovation.

Once we perceive the basic pattern of these descriptions – they are moulded also by the decorum governing the 'hero' – it is possible to see shades of emphasis which lend, if not what we would today call 'characterization,' at least what we can recognize as differentiation, subtle discriminations among excellences that are actually predispositions for one sort of behaviour or experience rather than some other.[38] Argalus and Amphialus are cases in point. Argalus is introduced to us by Kalander's steward, apparently to illustrate valorous 'doing,' the action-oriented 'public' virtue of our earlier antithesis. But closer inspection shows that the emphasis in his description is on internal qualities: his learning, modesty, friendliness, courtesy, gentleness, melancholy, moral goodness, and so on. Although these excellences of character, combined with an exceptional degree of martial prowess and endurance, should make up an altogether superlative figure, Argalus is only a secondary hero in the *Arcadia*. This ranking is perhaps conveyed by having his qualities defined in terms of an excess which they do not in fact demonstrate:

being a Gentleman in deede most rarely accomplished, excellentlie learned, but without all vayne glory: friendly, without factiousnes: valiaunt, so as for my part I thinke the earth hath no man that hath done more heroicall actes then hee [except perhaps Pyrocles, Musidorus and Amphialus] ... but I say for my part, I thinke no man for valour of minde, and habilitie of bodie to be preferred, if equalled to Argalus; and yet so valiant as he never durst doo any bodie injurie: in behaviour some will say ever sadde, surely sober, and some-what given to musing, but never uncourteous; his worde ever ledde by his thought, and followed by his deed ... (I, 31)[39]

Notwithstanding Sidney's apparent association of Argalus with Hercules – Parthenia's mother employs him 'in as many dangerous enterprises, as ever the evill stepmother Juno recommended to the famous Hercules' (I, 33) – our chief impression is of fineness and control rather than what we have come to know as the 'Herculean hero.'[40] Even Sidney's handling of the doing-suffering topos in Argalus' story has been geared towards an ethical end, since its purpose is to illuminate the nature of constancy, that is, his 'doing' has been subordinated to an 'internal' quality all along. Though we believe in Argalus' valour and prowess, he is not in our mind primarily a fighter. We are prepared for his defeat in single combat against Amphialus, his counterpart as a secondary hero in the *Arcadia*.

For Amphialus has been described with quite the opposite emphasis. Helen begins with his martial fame. His 'deeds and monuments,' valour and heroism are mostly what we hear about him, although he too is courteous, liberal, virtuous, intelligent, and bears a presence 'full of beauty, sweetnes, and noble conversation' (I, 69). Later, much attention is given to his perfect masculinity, he is 'such a right manlike man, as Nature often erring, yet shewes she would fair make' (I, 222-3).[41] Important among the standard topics for praise is the argument from one's ancestors and parents,[42] and there is clearly some question as to whether Amphialus' character can escape contamination from the wickedness of his mother (though Helen's and very likely the Narrator's opinion is that it has). At any rate, Amphialus is seen as developing against something malevolent, which differentiates him from the other heroes of the *Arcadia*. We can perhaps convert the disproportionate emphasis given to his great deeds into a basis for evaluating Amphialus' behaviour in Book III (as well as in the story Helen tells), where his military intelligence and valour far exceed his ability to understand the princesses, his mother, or for that matter, himself. Is he meant to be an object lesson in 'pure' magnanimity or doing? (Note his connection with Anaxius, who is a caricature or comic version of a man whose sole excellence is fighting.)

If we turn to the two major male characters of the *Arcadia*, Pyrocles and Musidorus, we can see how the existence of a single set of standards for the ideal hero risks yielding soil not fertile enough for developing significant distinctions. In Sidney's original conception of the princes, the primary area for their differentiation seems to have been physical and called for by the plot. Sidney apparently took quite seriously the need for a hero who could be accepted as a beautiful woman, though the *Old Arcadia* makes little attempt to work with the paradox implicit in a 'feminized' hero. The occasions in this version for formal descriptions of any sort are rare, and the few that exist tend not to deal with excellence of character. Pyrocles is said in the Book II eclogues to be 'pure white and red' as against Musidorus' 'sweet brownness' and 'younger and more delicate' than his 'elder and stronger' cousin (*OA* 155). Then in Book V there is a full and gorgeous description of them at the trial, concentrating on their physical appearance and clothing, and not even in summary going far beyond:

Musidorus was in stature so much higher than Pyrocles as commonly is gotten by one year's growth; his face, now beginning to have some tokens of a beard, was composed to a kind of manlike beauty; his colour was of a well pleasing brownness; and the features of it such as they carried both delight and majesty; his countenance severe, and promising a mind much given to thinking; Pyrocles of a pure complexion, and of such a cheerful favour as might seem either a woman's face on a boy or an excellent boy's face on a woman; his look gentle and bashful, which bred the more admiration having showed such notable proofs of courage. Lastly, though both had both, if there were any odds, Musidorus was the more goodly and Pyrocles the more lovely. (*OA* 377)

Much of what seems characterization here is not borne out in the narrative itself. Very little of Pyrocles' 'bashfulness' is discernible and his eloquence in staying a riot outside the lodge and in arguing about immortality gives substance to claims for his intellect pointedly absent in the description. Musidorus' character seems to be shaped for us in the long debate between the princes when Pyrocles first falls in love. Musidorus of course takes the part of Reason and the active life, but considering the sententiousness of both princes throughout, he says nothing there that Pyrocles would not have said were their positions reversed. And the situation rapidly does change towards equality when Musidorus himself falls in love. The original Musidorus is also more playful than he will become in the *New Arcadia*, and this too tends to equalize the two characters. In short, the final words of the formal portraits above are something of an admission of defeat: 'Lastly, though both had both ...'

In the *New Arcadia* Sidney tries harder to differentiate the two princes, but his task is made more difficult by the implicit insistence of the topics for praise that the hero be both a 'doer of deeds and a speaker of words.'[43] He increases the intellectual element in the one formal description of Musidorus that we have – '[Kalander's] having found in him (besides his bodily giftes beyond the degree of Admiration) ... a mind of most excellent composition (a pearcing witte quite voide of ostentation, high erected thoughts seated in a harte of courtesie, an eloquence as sweete in the uttering, as slowe to come to the uttering, a behaviour so noble, as gave a majestie to adversitie; and all in a man whose age could not be above one and twenty yeares) ...' (I, 16) – but he is certainly also pre-eminent in combat. Pyrocles is a shade better at fighting than Musidorus,[44] but it is excellence of character – Pyrocles' political sagacity and ability to lead men – that is more important for the Helot rebellion which forms our first sustained impression of him in the book. The description of Pyrocles which follows the rebellion is a hyperbolic elaboration of the *Old Arcadia*'s description at the trial, but one that explores the ethical meaning of physical facts:

For being now well viewed to have no haire of his face, to witnes him a man, who had done acts beyond the degree of a man, and to looke with a certaine almost bashefull kinde of modestie, as if hee feared the eyes of men, who was unmooved with sight of the most horrible countenaunces of death; and as if nature had mistaken her woorke to have a Marses heart in a Cupides bodye: All that beheld him ... made their eyes quicke messengers to their minds, that there they had seene the uttermost that in mankind might be seene. (I, 48)[45]

Lest we think that we have discovered grounds for ranking and differentiating the princes, Sidney continues: 'The like wonder Palladius [Musidorus] had before stirred, but that Daiphantus [Pyrocles] as younger and newer come, had gotten the advantage in the moyst and fickle impression of eye-sight.'

Within the confines of 'both had both' Sidney does contrive to make the Musidorus of the *New Arcadia* the somewhat more mature, austere, ethically-oriented of the princes, while Pyrocles is rather more emotional and introspective. Though the reader feels the differentiation, I think, it is hardly a major triumph in the art of characterization. The case is quite different for Sidney's women. In

C.S. Lewis' estimation, '[Pamela and Philoclea] can be praised without reservation. English literature had seen no women to compare with them since Chaucer's Crisseid; and, apart from Shakespeare, was to wait centuries for their equals.'[46]

Part of the explanation for Sidney's greater success with his heroines may be that ideal womanhood had never been rigidly defined. It can be argued that the ideal man, being largely a public conception, had necessarily to excel in every aspect of life because the well-being of the state depended upon his prowess. But for women, interest in public affairs was an accident either of birth or of choice, so that at least two kinds of ideals had to be envisioned, each complete in itself and not obviously complementary like the usual wisdom-fortitude dichotomy for male virtues. Aside from the indispensable virtue of chastity, which guaranteed a stable society,[47] women (at least in literature) were free to pursue perfection in ways that ranged from emphasizing those qualities they shared with men to emphasizing those that inhered in their special function as woman and mother. The Aristotelian tradition of condescension towards the female as less perfect than the male, which implied that certain weaknesses, frailties, and passions were natural and therefore excusable in women, allowed the heroine to develop more humanly, thus providing an author with greater possibilities for individuation than the hero.

Whatever the reason for Sidney's greater flexibility in creating ideal women, he exercises it in a manner already familiar from his handling of narrative and thematic material. That is, as in the short formal descriptions comprising Artesia's Triumph (notably those of Baccha and Leucippe, Helen and Parthenia), he often presents character by means of antithesis. Interestingly, as a method of characterization this is largely a New Arcadian innovation. The most important example is of course the sustained comparison between Pamela and Philoclea. It is difficult to imagine them in terms other than the majesty and humility of the New Arcadia, yet the contrast is barely suggested in the original version, and might not even be picked up there if the reader did not bring with him the New Arcadia's more vivid realization of the princesses' characters and its insistence on distinguishing between them. The Old Arcadia actually presents a Pamela who cannot help responding with tears and sighs to Dorus' tale of a shepherd-prince (OA 107); in her place the New Arcadia offers one who 'without shew either of favour or disdaine, either of heeding or neglecting what I had said, turned her speech to Mopsa ... with such a voice and action, as might shewe she spake of a matter which little did concerne her ...(I,164). In the original version, the jewel she wears is not a diamond set in black horn bearing the inscription 'yet still my selfe' (I, 90), but 'a perfect white lamb tied at a stake with a great number of chaynes, as it had bene feared lest the silly creature should do some great harm;

neither had she added any word unto it, but even took silence as the word of the poor lamb, showing such humbleness as not to use her own voice for complaint of her misery.' (OA 37)

In the *Old Arcadia*, Pamela shows 'a countenance more princely than she was wont' (OA 319) when Musidorus is taken from her and imprisoned after their thwarted escape; in fact, almost all suggestions of Pamela's majesty in the first version result from this adventure, whether in response to stress or in recognition of her role as heir to the throne. The latter factor is emphasized in the only explicit contrast of the two princesses provided in the original *Arcadia*, occurring just before the trial in Book V. The seeds of the New Arcadian characters are present here, but they obviously were to undergo still further development in Sidney's mind:

the tender Philoclea who, as she was in years younger and had never lifted up her mind to any opinion of sovereignty, so was she apter to yield to her misfortune, having no stronger debates in her mind than a man may say a most witty childhood is wont to nourish ... But Pamela, although endued with a virtuous mildness, yet the knowledge of herself, and what was due unto her, made her heart full of a stronger disdain against her adversity ... (OA 369-70)[48]

The absence of strong contrast in the *Old Arcadia* can perhaps be explained by considerations of its generic antecedents. As William A. Ringler astutely notes, Sidney moulded his romance material into dramatic form:

The *Old Arcadia* is a tragi-comedy in five acts, with a serious double plot (the two pairs of noble lovers with Basilius, Gynecia, and Euarchus) combined with a comic underplot (Dametas and his wife and daughter) ... The renaissance Terentian five-act structure is followed with its movement of protasis, epitasis, and catastrophe. The various strands of action are cleverly intertwined; there is a climax in the third act, a counter-movement in the fourth, and a denouement in the fifth with a totally unexpected anagnorisis and peripeteia.[49]

The idea of the double plot most concerns us here. Pamela and Musidorus are in many ways a second or subsidiary set of lovers, such as Guarini discusses for Terence's *Andria*.[50] The *Old Arcadia* unequivocally ranks them a little lower than Pyrocles and Philoclea: Pyrocles is 'the younger, but chiefer' (OA 9; he is also a prince while his cousin is only a duke), Philoclea is 'the beauty of the world' (OA 9) and 'to [her] memory principally all this long matter is intended' (OA 108).[51] There is ranking, but little significant differentiation. This conforms to the Terentian double plot, where the contrast offered by the subsidiary lovers need not be insisted upon because it exists more to provide variety within duplication or parallelism than to focus attention on itself.

But contrast *is* part of the purpose and principle of Sidney's revision of his *Arcadia*, and contrast in turn calls for some kind of equality between opposing members. Thus, one may say with greater accuracy for the *New* than for the *Old Arcadia* that it has two heroes and two heroines, though Pyrocles and Philoclea retain the edge.[52] Our first glimpse of the princesses heralds the change; nothing in the *Old Arcadia*'s handling of character remotely approaches Kalander's appraisal of them:

The elder is named Pamela; by many men not deemed inferiour to her sister: for my part, when I marked them both, me thought there was (if at least such perfections may receyve the worde of more) more sweetnesse in Philoclea, but more majestie in Pamela: me thought love plaide in Philocleas eyes, and threatned in Pamelas: me thought Philocleas beautie onely perswaded, but so perswaded as all harts must yeelde: Pamelas beautie used violence, and such violence as no hart could resist: and it seemes that such proportion is betweene their mindes; Philoclea so bashfull as though her excellencies had stolne into her before shee was aware: so humble, that she will put all pride out of countenance: in summe, such proceeding as will stirre hope but teach hope good manners. Pamela of high thoughts, who avoides not pride with not knowing her excellencies, but by making that one of her excellencies to be voide of pride; her mothers wisdome, greatnesse, nobilitie, but (if I can ghesse aright) knit with a more constant temper. (I, 20)

Having thus firmly distinguished their temperaments, Sidney proceeds to make the distinction govern details ranging from the general tone of their courtships to their appearance and demeanour in captivity. In the latter episode especially, he insists upon the contrast. He devotes striking descriptions to the pattern of shadow and sunlight on Philoclea's brooding face (where 'there was nothing to be read but Sorrow: for Kindnesse was blotted out, and Anger was never there' [I, 367-8]), or to 'the dressing of her haire and apparell ... left to a neglected chaunce, which yet coulde no more unperfect her perfections, then a Die anie way cast, could loose his squarenesse' (I, 376) – and these are clearly meant to be weighed against the picture of Pamela calmly embroidering a purse:

it was not without marvaile to see, howe a minde which could cast a carelesse semblant uppon the greatest conflictes of Fortune, coulde commaunde it selfe to take care for so small matters. Neither had she neglected the daintie dressing of her selfe: but as it had ben her mariage time to Affliction, she rather semed to remember her owne worthinesse, then the unworthinesse of her husband. For well one might perceive she had not rejected the counsaile of a glasse, and that her handes had pleased themselves, in paying the tribute of undeceyving skill, to so high perfections of Nature. (I, 402-3)[53]

The contrast shows obvious structural relevance by requiring balanced repetition of Cecropia's assaults. In the first round of verbal persuasion, she virtually becomes Comus tempting the Lady with the fecund blessings of marriage. Philoclea ultimately fends off the attack with a politely evasive manoeuver, saying

> that whilest she was so captived, she could not conceive of any such persuasion (though never so reasonable) any otherwise, then as constraints: and as constraints must needs even in nature abhor them, which at her libertie, in their owne force of reason, might more prevaile with her: and so faine would have returned the strength of Cecropia perswasions, to have procured freedome. (I, 380-1)

Cecropia meets a more direct and sound defeat in the corresponding verbal appeal to Pamela, which calls forth the well-known refutation of atheism.[54] The contrast between majestic virtue and silent humbleness is repeated for the second round, the scourging of the two princesses. Philoclea refuses to alter her resolve not to marry Amphialus, but in tears she pleads with her aunt for death rather than continued torture (I, 471). Pamela's response literally embodies the ideal of conscious self-mastery:

> But if ever the beames of perfection shined through the clowdes of affliction, if ever Vertue tooke a bodie to shewe his (els unconceaveable) beautie, it was in Pamela. For when Reason taught her there was no resistance (for to just resistance first her harte was enclined) then with so heavenly a quietnes, and so gracefull a calmenes, did she suffer the divers kindes of torments they used to her, that while they vexed her faire bodie, it seemed, that she rather directed, then obeyed the vexation. And when Cecropia ended, and asked whether her harte woulde yeelde: she a little smiled, but such a smiling as shewed no love, and yet coulde not but be lovelie. And then, Beastly woman (saide she) followe on, doo what thou wilt, and canst upon me: for I know thy power is not unlimited. Thou maist well wracke this sillie bodie, but me thou canst never overthrowe. For my part, I will not doo thee the pleasure to desire death of thee: but assure thy self, both my life and death, shall triumph with honour, laying shame upon thy detestable tyranny. (I, 472-3)

Sidney's treatment of the sisters during their captivity therefore shows the same partition of a subject into opposing halves that I have attributed to the Elizabethan's rhetorical habit of mind: all experience can be divided into things done and things suffered; the latter can be undergone with impatience or with patience; patience in turn may be the result either of a naturally humble disposition or of a consciously willed indifference to Fortune. The contrasts are thus by no means moral: one must not be misled into considering Pamela's care for her appearance vanity or Philoclea's humility weakness. Sidney is quite clear that in spite of sharp distinctions, the sisters are equally virtuous and equally able to triumph over evil, 'for what majestie of vertue did in the one, that did silent humblenesse in the other' (I, 411).[55]

John Danby's fine analysis of Sidney's conception of the sisters (based on Kalander's description, quoted above) can be applied with equal relevance to the working out of their characters in the Book III captivity. I quote his discussion at length because it suggests some issues to be treated in the following section, where Sidney's use of antithesis becomes the basis for stylistic analysis:

Part of our difficulty here might be that Sidney's discriminations are finer than we have been in the habit of making for three hundred years. The two princesses are put side by side and differentiated. Yet Sidney deprecates any subordination of one to the other. The method of presentation seems comparative, yet comparison is not entirely Sidney's aim: the sisters do not occupy positions on a scale that makes comparison possible. Nor is contrast part of the intention, though the pair are so unlike as to seem poles apart. Each princess is herself a perfection. Nothing could add to either. They are not complementary to one another, for that would argue their mutual incompleteness. And yet when we have said all this there is still the overruling impression of one's being weighed against the other, the sense of scrupulous and fine assessment that saves the passage from becoming merely hyperbole. The main distinction between them is, it would seem, that Pamela's is a conscious and deliberately maintained virtue, Philoclea's a perfection of nature in which instinctive rightness of constitution effects the same as a properly directed will. Pamela would not depart from virtue, Philoclea could not. The desire *not* to compare or contrast, or to consider the sisters as complementary, comes from Sidney's unwillingness to make a doctrinaire decision – a choice which would in a case like this be an impoverishment ...[56]

STYLISTIC ANALYSIS

In Danby's vague awareness of vanishing distinctions lies the key to Sidney's use of antithesis throughout the *Arcadia*: one receives the impression that extreme contrasts are being presented, but under careful examination the oppositions disappear. The differences, though real enough from one point of view, must be called only apparent from another, since no matter how contradictory the causes, the results are identical:

Philoclea so bashfull as though her excellencies had stolne into her before shee was aware: so humble, that she will put all pride out of countenance ... Pamela of high thoughts, who avoides not pride with not knowing her excellencies, but by making that one of her excellencies to be voide of pride. (I, 20)

We have seen the princesses' behaviour in captivity described with the same paradoxical implication ('for what majestie of vertue did in the one, that did silent humblenesse in the other'), and have noted that Sidney's handling of the doing-suffering topos, both for Argalus and Parthenia ('it was hard to judge, whether he in doing, or she in suffering, shewed greater constancie of affection') and for the overall contrast between patience and magnanimity emphasizes what might be called an equality of ordeal under antithetical guises. The same peculiar use of antithesis could have been cited in the earlier discussion of Helen and Parthenia. There, after arranging the two women in an antithetical contrast between art and nature, Sidney undermines the opposition first by stating that their beauty, though different, is equal, and then by turning the antithesis into a paradox, making the studied insistence upon unadorned Nature for Parthenia disappear the instant it receives its most cogent formulation: Her attire was 'so farre from all arte, that it was full of carelesnesse: unlesse that carelesnesse it selfe (in spite of it selfe) grew artificiall' (I, 104).[57]

Sidney's manipulation of antithesis becomes significant partly through mere frequency and partly through employment in passages deliberately intended to weigh opposing values. The description of Kalander's house works the contrast between beauty and utility through a series of paces unusual even for Sidney's habit of scrupulous assessment:

The house it selfe was built of faire and strong stone, not affecting so much any extra-ordinarie kinde of finenes, as an honorable representing of a firme statelines. The lightes, doores and staires, rather directed to the use of the guest, then to the eye of the Artificer: and yet as the one cheefly heeded, so the other not neglected; each place handsome without curiositie, and homely without lothsomnes: not so daintie as not to be trode on, nor yet slubberd up with good felowshippe: all more lasting then beautifull, but that the considera-tion of the exceeding lastingnesse made the eye beleeve it was exceeding beautifull. (I, 15)[58]

Sidney is not satisfied merely to give each aspect its due weight, as is implied by the judicious 'yet as the one cheefly heeded, so the other not neglected' and by the attempt in the succeeding clauses to establish the mean that represents beauty and utility;[59] the final phase subverts distinction altogether by suggesting that at their extremes the two opposing values are actually identical.[60] The same vanish-ing distinction noted in Parthenia's portrait thus appears in the description of Kalander's house, though demanding explanation with greater urgency because the laboured movement of the latter through contradiction and negative compari-son has apparently been directed towards precision in defining outlines. Why then suddenly blur these careful delineations?

The stylistic analysis of the *Arcadia* has therefore begun with an observation about Sidney's peculiar habit of simultaneously constructing and superseding antithetical relationships. In Leo Spitzer's terms, one hopes this will lead into 'the lifeblood of the poetic creation [which] is everywhere the same, whether we tap the organism at "language" or "ideas," at "plot" or at "composition."'[61] The rest of the chapter is an attempt to see if the observation is viable for several other details of the work, in this way to approach what is in the same metaphor the 'inward life-center' that animates the whole.[62]

The examples offered thus far have presented antithesis largely as a conceptual scheme, separated as much as possible from verbal formulation. The two are of course linked together. For Sidney to interpret experience in the manner suggested requires that he use those rhetorical figures which permit him to establish and then overturn distinctions. Two traditional figures, *antimetabole* and *correctio*, are particularly relevant, yet because the important factor is not these figures as such, but the essential connection between them and other loosely related patterns, I refer to them all generically as a rhetoric of reciprocity or reversible balance.

Strictly speaking, *antimetabole* (*commutatio* in Latin) is a special form of antithesis requiring reciprocal exchange of syntactical function, but not necessarily designed to convey the idea of reciprocity. Two definitions and some illustrations should make this clear. According to Heinrich Lausberg's comparison of all major classical rhetorics,

Die *commutatio* besteht in der Gegenüberstellung eines Gedankens und seiner Umkehrung durch Wiederholung zweier Wortstämme bei wechselseitigem Austausch der syntaktischen Funktion der beiden Wortstämme in der Wiederholung.[63]

Commutatio consists in the contrast between a thought and its inversion through the repetition of two words in which their syntactical function is reciprocally exchanged. (my translation)

The author of *Ad Herennium* emphasizes the logical aspect of the figure:

Commutatio est cum duae sententiae inter se discrepantes ex transiectione ita efferuntur ut a priore posterior contraria priori proficiscatur, hoc modo: 'Esse oportet ut vivas, non vivere ut edas.'[64]

Reciprocal Change occurs when two discrepant thoughts are so expressed by transposition that the latter follows from the former although contradictory to it, as follows: 'You must eat to live, not live to eat.'

In this most common example of the figure, or in Sidney's comparison of Arcadia and Laconia, 'the one wanting no store, th'other having no store but want' (I, 14), the exchange is between two independent ideas, without any further sense of mutual experience or fluidity of boundary. This is less true of another well-known example, 'poema loquens pictura, pictura tacitum poema debet esse,' where the distinction between poetry and painting becomes blurred to some extent.

Looser definitions of *antimetabole* forgo the element of antithesis, but as in Quintilian's case, retain the syntactical interchange, or as in Hoskins', retain an element akin to the 'chiasmus' of modern terminology.[65] Hoskins defines *antimetabole* as 'a sentence inversed or turned back'; his list of examples from the *Arcadia* includes several that blur distinctions or point to a fluid boundary between cause and effect:

Either not striving because he was contented, or contented because he would not strive.

As this place served us to thinke of those thinges, so those thinges serve as places to call to memorie more excellent matters.

But with that Dorus blushed, and Pamela smiled: and Dorus the more blushed at her smiling, and she the more smiled at his blushing.[66]

The examples could be multiplied at will; as Hoskins says, 'our learned knight skipped often into this figure.'[67] In one case, Sidney even doubles the effect:

matters being so turned in her, that where at first, liking her manners did breed good-wil, now good-wil became the chiefe cause of liking her manners: so that within a while Zelmane was not prized for her demeanure, but the demeanure was prized because it was Zelmanes; (I, 169)

in another, as in the description of Kalander's house, he sets up and overturns a distinction:

Amphialus seemed to excell in strength, the forsaken Knight in nimblenes; and yet did the ones strength excel in nimblenes, and the others nimblenes excell in strength. (I, 460)

The following examples convey the idea of reciprocity without using the formal device:

... it seemed as he borrowed the horses body, so he lent the horse his mind. (I, 179)

... a rope of faire pearles, which now hiding, now hidden by the haire, did as it were play at fast <and> loose, each with the other, mutually giving and receiving rich<n>es. (I, 103)

... they were suddainely stept into a delicate greene, of each side of the greene a thicket<, and> behind the thickets againe newe beddes of flowers, which being under the trees, the trees were to them a Pavilion, and they to the trees a mosaical floore ... (I, 17)

... there a yong shepherdesse knitting, and withall singing, and it seemed that her voice comforted her hands to work, and her hands kept time to her voices musick. (I, 13)

Sidney often uses the second of these traditional figures, *correctio*, to overturn distinctions initially set up as an either-or choice, for example, 'either with cunning or with force, or rather with a cunning force' (I, 64), or similarly, 'and growen bolder, or madder, or bould with madnes' (I, 69). This use of *correctio* is, as far as I can discover, unusual.[68] Indeed, it would be difficult to conceive of an ordinary rhetorical situation which would set up and overturn distinctions as a strategy of argument. But the strategy is well suited to Arcadian description, and one should not be surprised to discover that the area at the rear of Kalander's house, where the trees and flowers are reciprocally pavilion and mosaic floor, 'was neyther field, garden nor orchard; or rather it was both fielde, garden and orcharde' (I, 17). The psychological movement at the base of such formulations can be compared with that analysed for the description of Kalander's house: in both there is an awareness of distinctions, a refusal to select from among them, and an attempt to find some way to encompass all alternatives.

Though the discussion has been limited to a few figures, these few contain or imply much of what is peculiar to the Arcadian style, its particular handling of antithesis, repetition, and paradox. But this is still description and not stylistic analysis. For the latter, we should note that both reversible balance and the vanishing distinction are manifestations of a still more central attitude towards experience. Frequently, Sidney's use of reciprocal figures occurs in passages describing some sort of perfection. It is this connection that should prove significant, for it tallies with the strategy of the *Defence*, which consistently argues the merits of poetry on the basis of its embodiment of one ideal or another, whether it be of a golden world, a just empire, or a moral man. Because ideality or perfection is philosophically central to Sidney's didactic conceptions of literature, his view of perfection is likely to be reflected in the moral structure of his *Arcadia*. And so it is. An important doctrinal centre of the work, Pamela's refutation of her aunt's attack on religion, proves the existence of a God who imposes 'perfect order, perfect beautie, perfect constancie' on the warring elements of the cosmos: 'for their natures beying absolutely contrarie, in nature [they] rather woulde have sought each others ruine, then have served as well consorted partes to such an unexpressable harmonie. For that contrary things should meete to make up a perfection without a force and Wisedome above their powers, is absolutely impossible ...' (I, 408) Ultimately, all perfections find their reflection if not their origin in this view of the universe. The obvious may still be emphasized: the perfection envisioned here is not the expression of a simple unity, but what has been called, in aesthetic terms, a 'multiple unity.'[69] The man-produced harmony of the

Renaissance lay in 'the complete agreement of the different parts of the art object with each other and with the whole,'[70] and its God-produced harmony resided in the same characteristics: 'Beauty is a certain grace, which is born, above all, of the harmony of divers things.'[71] Thus, the devices Sidney employs in order to bring contraries into harmonious relation, no less than his need to create this particular kind of ideal, can be seen as simultaneously reflecting the philosophical, rhetorical, and aesthetic assumptions of the work.[72]

Sidney views perfection as a reciprocal relation – expressed as mutual dependence, harmonious interchange, reversible cause and effect – regardless of the phenomenon he is describing; it may be cosmological as in Pamela's speech just above, physical as in the earlier description of Helen's hair, or political, psychological, or topographical. The connection between cosmological and political perfection is of course enforced by metaphors of governorship and order. The connection between political and topographical ideals seems to lie rather in analogies based on the idea of dependence.

The ideal embodied in the descriptions of the Arcadian countryside is the poet's golden world spoken of in the *Defence*: 'Nature never set forth the earth in so rich tapestry as divers poets have done; neither with pleasant rivers, fruitful trees, sweet-smelling flowers, nor whatsoever else may make the too much loved earth more lovely. Her world is brazen, the poets only deliver a golden' (p 78). The poet, in 'disdaining' subjection to Nature, frees his own imagination. Especially in the use of *ekphrasis* or formal description, one finds Sidney's idea of perfection in its purest form, that is, depictions of 'what should be' undiluted by shrewd observations of 'what is.' The description of Arcadia is eloquent proof of C.S. Lewis' statement that Sidney's ideal 'is not a reverie but a structure':[73]

There were hilles which garnished their proud heights with stately trees: humble valleis, whose base estate semed comforted with refreshing of silver rivers: medows, enameld with al sorts of ey-pleasing floures: thickets, which being lined with most pleasant shade, were witnessed so to by the chereful deposition of many wel-tuned birds: each pasture stored with sheep feeding with sober security, while the prety lambs with bleting oratory craved the dams comfort: here a shepheards boy piping, as though he should never be old: there a yong shepherdesse knitting, and withall singing, and it seemed that her voice comforted her hands to work, and her hands kept time to her voices musick. As for the houses of the country (for many houses came under their eye) they were all scattered, no two being one by th'other, and yet not so far off as that it barred mutual succour: a shew, as it were, of an accompanable solitarines, and of a civil wildnes. (I, 13-14)

None of the objects stands completely alone, perhaps because the view of nature here is mildly teleological. The degree of dependence is modulated throughout, thematically unifying the passage. The first group of objects representing non-sentient nature shows the two lowest degrees of existence, Being and Life, with the idea of one performing a service for the other constant in each pair (the hills and trees, valleys and rivers, meadows and flowers);[74] this is followed by a slightly more dependent relation between things which have Life and creatures having Sense (thickets giving shade to birds), increasing again in the sheep's dependence on the pasture for their sober security, and culminating in the completely dependent animal relationship of the lambs to their mothers. The link with the world of man (creatures of Reason) through the implied relationship between sheep and shepherd yields a set of harmonious independencies (the shepherd boy here, the shepherdess there, both engaged at their own tasks but still somehow a unit, just as her hands and voice are said to be); and finally there is a similar picture of the social aggregates in which man lives: the individual households balanced between independence and 'mutual succour' are epitomized in the oxymoron of 'civil wildnes.' The suggestion of political organization, perhaps of the small community, is no accident, of course, but the crystallization of the metaphor diffused in the entire description. The next paragraph follows with a discussion of what becomes the culminating entity of this progression, the state, for 'it is evident that the state is a creation of nature, and that man is by nature a political animal.'[75]

Curiously, despite the strong political emphasis of the *Arcadia*, there is no description of an ideal commonwealth. The natural condition of the political state resembles the cosmos in this: without the superior wisdom of the ruler the contrary parts would seek one another's ruin. Whatever 'perfection' the state can achieve occurs when opposites are held in precarious balance, but chaos always threatens. Book IV of the *Old Arcadia* contains a 'notable example how great dissipations monarchal governments are subject unto' (OA 320), occasioned by Basilius' apparent death; Book II of the *New Arcadia* depicts the natural anarchy of democracy, occasioned when the rebels are asked for a list of grievances:

At length they fel to direct contrarieties. For the Artisans, they would have corne and wine set at a lower price, and bound to be kept so stil: the plowmen, vine-laborers, and farmers would none of that. The countrimen demaunded that every man might be free in the chief townes: that could not the Burgesses like of. The peasants would have <al> the Gentlemen destroied, the Citizens (especially such as Cookes, Barbers, and those other that lived most on Gentlemen) would but have them refourmed. And of ech side were like divisions, one neighbourhood beginning to find fault with another. But no confusion was greater then of particular mens likings and dislikings: one dispraising such a one, whom another praised, and demanding such a one to be punished, whom the other would have exalted. (I, 315)[76]

The absence of perfect societies, except perhaps by implication, can thus be accounted for in terms of Pamela's cosmological argument: since elements by nature war with one another, harmony is proof of a wise and beneficent governor – as with God, so with the king. The *Arcadia*, having as one of its main motifs the education of the good governor, is thereby necessarily oriented towards a political philosophy that maximizes the ruler's power to effect good and evil, and this means making the balance among opposing forces in the state both precarious and totally dependent upon his agency. Political perfection, then, lies in the perfect ruler rather than in a perfect state.[77]

Though these political and cosmological implications form as it were a sounding board giving greater resonance to the rhetoric of reciprocity, not all its occurrences are so elaborate or so philosophically explicit. Topographical perfection may be expressed in the verbal formulations noted above for the descriptions of Kalander's house and garden, or like this for the river of Ladon: 'It ranne upon so fine and delicate a ground, as one could not easely judge, whether the River did more wash the gravell, or the gravel did purifie the River.' (I, 216) It is this aspect of harmonious interchange and fluid boundaries that dissolve distinctions which has most relevance for Sidney's view of psychological perfection, that is, the experience of reciprocated love. The subject of course commonly calls forth ideas of mutuality; there is nothing unique in Sidney's defining love as 'that right harmony of affection which doth interchangeably deliver each to other the secret workings of their souls' (*OA* 197).[78] The statement could have occurred apart from Sidney's stylistic predilections, but the effect is richer because its reverberations echo throughout the Arcadian universe.

The most striking expression of perfect love in the work, a description of Argalus and Parthenia, displays such verbal pyrotechnics that one initially questions whether Sidney has not sacrificed content to virtuosity. The dramatic context within which the description appears, however, is in itself assurance that the handling is serious. The point of the episode is that the messenger who summons Argalus to his death arrives at a moment of supreme happiness for the lovers. It is a tribute to Sidney's sureness in discriminating between easy and profound irony that this is not a transient moment of ecstasy, but a moment which expresses the continuing pattern of their everyday lives:

The messenger made speede, and found Argalus at a castle of his owne, sitting in a parler with the faire Parthenia, he reading in a booke the stories of Hercules, she by him, as to heare him reade; but while his eyes looked on the booke, she looked on his eies, and sometimes staying him with some pretty question, not so much to be resolved of the doubte; as to give him occasion to looke upon her. A happy couple, he joying in her, she joying in her selfe, but in her selfe, because she enjoyed him: both encreasing their riches by giving to each other; each making one life double, because they made a double life; one, where desire never wanted satisfaction, nor satisfaction <ever> bred sacietie; he ruling, because she would obey: or rather because she would obey, she therein ruling. (I, 420)

In addition to the virtuosity, one senses a genuine attempt to define the essence of this perfection: here the reversibility of cause and effect and the extinction of boundaries are the necessary if paradoxical goal towards which the analytical search for perfection must tend. The presence of reversibly-balanced rhetoric provides a kind of verbal tension, but a feeling of synthesis and resolution is also present because Sidney makes us accept the wonder of their achievement.

Danby rightly asserts that Sidney's style includes both analysis and synthesis: 'Sidney saw the world in terms of division, balance and resolution. His style is a reflection of his vision.'[79] Neither element can be dispensed with, though one may perhaps reformulate their relation and speak of the tension between Sidney's analytic mode of thought (which sees the world in terms of antithetical alternatives) and the harmonious, synthetic nature of his vision of the ideal.

The tension, lying as it does at the 'inward life-center' of the *Arcadia*, finds expression in various ways, notably in the contrast between the ideal and experienced reality which I argue is at the heart of the princes' 'paideia' in Book II and of the trial scene in the original Book V. It is also possible to discuss the tension in terms touched upon earlier in the introduction, that of rhetoricism and the Renaissance belief in ideals and absolutes. We have had occasion to view two totally different depictions of ideality – the simple rendering of Urania in Artesia's Triumph (p 24) and the virtuoso description of Argalus and Parthenia (p 40). One is struck by what may be called the 'Gorgian' element in the latter, the manipulation of language by the rhetor, the artificial quality which asserts that this is a man-made (and therefore precarious?) achievement, created by a language that cannot be thought to reflect reality but in its self-consciousness must be seen as mediating it. In the description of Urania, on the other hand, the rhetor is absent, and the language seems to try to render directly the reality she embodies. Neither the content nor the style of Urania's description is characteristic of the *Arcadia*. The aristocratic realities of Sidney's and his heroes' experience is expressed in the precarious brilliance of the other description. Nevertheless, both passages share the yearning, perceptible throughout the work, for some kind of ideal.

RHETORICAL
EXPLORATIONS:
TWO TOPOI

Before turning to means of structuring the *Arcadia* other than those derived from rhetorical handbooks, I should like to explore some of the ideas already suggested. This chapter is, in effect, two excursuses: the first section applies the insight gained from stylistic analysis to one main theme of the *Arcadia*, the antithetical topos Reason versus Passion or Love; the second considers the relation between Knowledge and Virtue (which Sidney occasionally treats as though it were antithetical) as an opportunity for organizing contrasts among characters into what may be called a thematic structure.

REASON AND LOVE

One generally thinks of style as peculiar to a writer or an age; in its broadest sense, style is a means of distinguishing one from among many. Stylistic analysis relies upon this assumption, since it begins with the discovery of idiosyncrasy and only at a later stage does it try to set the personal vision within a larger cultural context. For Sidney, the attitude that governs verbal choices such as the use of *antimetabole* also governs his handling of antithetical topoi, and at this thematic level of formulation the attitude becomes available for comparison with the practices of his contemporaries. An antithetical topos like Reason versus Passion, as part of the mainstream of Renaissance epic, romance, and even moral thought, appears in some form in most heroic writing of the period; it therefore provides an opportunity to assess how 'characteristic' Sidney's manipulation of antithesis actually is.

In the *New Arcadia* the nature of the Reason-Love conflict begins to crystallize in the two debates between Pyrocles and Musidorus in Book I. The close relation between the two scenes is clear even if one were unaware that they originally formed a single sequence (*OA* 13-25). The debate preceding Pyrocles' departure from Kalander's house broaches the issue of his strange behaviour in the broad terms of the contrasting claims made by the Active and Contemplative Life; the second debate, when Musidorus finds his friend disguised as an Amazon, focuses on an allied problem, the conflict between Reason and Love. Although Sidney does not employ the familiar imagery of the two paths of life, he is exploiting the full panoply of tradition that had come to be associated with Prodicus' story of Hercules choosing between Virtue and Vice.[1] The relevance of Herculean myth is unmistakable: just prior to the second debate, Sidney explicitly refers to yet another Herculean legend – the pin that fastens Pyrocles-Zelmane's mantle is a jewel bearing 'a Hercules made in little fourme, but a distaffe set within his hand as he once was by Omphales commaundement' (I, 75-6). These two legends, though unrelated in the corpus of Herculean stories, were often employed together in later literature, which saw Omphale as a version of Prodicus' Vice.[2]

Through the formal basis of the *synkrisis* (the necessity for comparison or choice; the term is Erwin Panofsky's) the motif of Hercules at the crossroads exercises unifying control over the otherwise not necessarily related conflicts between virtue and vice, the active and contemplative life, reason and love. Prodicus' fable, as Socrates relates it in the *Memorabilia*, is simple enough: Hercules, a young boy advancing to manhood, while seated in a solitary place deciding whether to enter life by the path of virtue or vice, is approached by two lofty female figures. One is sober and elegant, dressed in white; the other is plump, her fairness assisted by art, and she wears a robe 'through which her beauty would readily show itself.' The latter, whom her friends call Happiness (Εὐδαιμονία) but her enemies Vice (Κακία), offers Hercules an easy road, pleasures of the senses, and the privilege of high living on the returns of other people's labours. Virtue (Ἀρετή) reminds him of his childhood training and says that these promises of pleasure are deceptive; in reality, the gods grant nothing valuable without labour and care. Honour and love are won only through service to friends, city, and country, through studying and practising the arts of war and of bodily exercise. Virtue's notion of society is associated with the household, friendship, harmony between youth and age, the labours of peace and war. After death, she offers fame; whereas Vice, she says, is hated by the gods and her joys are fleeting.[4]

Panofsky's *Hercules am Scheidewege*, tracing the literary and pictorial representations of this fable from antiquity to the eighteenth century, suggests that in the course of its development the elements of form, content, and implication were separated and reintegrated in varying combinations.[5] The moral necessity to choose between two ways of life or between two opposing principles became firmly attached to a balanced three-figure composition (the judge standing between two pleaders), but the content of the debate might vary from virtue versus pleasure or *via vitae* versus *via mortis* to the active versus the contemplative life or heavenly versus earthly love.[6] The important substitution of the active and contemplative life as the disputing figures may be partly explained by the early identification of the Choice of Hercules with Paris' judgment among three goddesses who were commonly interpreted as representing three ways of life: Hera the active, Athena the contemplative, and Aphrodite the voluptuous. But the substitution of the active and contemplative life for the figures of Virtue and Vice encouraged by the conflation of the Paris and Hercules myths obviously complicates the issue of moral choice. Both action and contemplation are potentially aspects of Virtue, that is, aspects of the same side of the original antithesis. Once they are made to oppose each other, however, the strong moral expectation built into the form itself requires that one of them take on the negative role of Vice. In other words, the form demands that the conflicting ideas be ranked according to some moral standard. As Edgar Wind remarks about the Prodicus fable, 'it may be expected of a reliable Hercules that he will not remain suspended between them. The choice is clear because the two opposites, having been introduced in a complete disjunction, obey the logical principle of the excluded middle: *tertium non datur.*'[7]

Sidney seems perfectly willing to accept the demand for choice on the issue of the active versus the contemplative life.[8] Though the debate between the two cousins has no formal conclusion, even Pyrocles realizes that Musidorus would have won without effort; he is said to finish his defence of contemplation 'like a man unsatisfied in himselfe, though his witte might wel have served to have satisfied another' (I, 56). Sidney does not risk leaving the invention of arguments supporting the active life to the reader (who, after all, may be the 'other' whom Pyrocles would have satisfied), but instead employs this elaborate *praeteritio*:

For, having in the beginning of Pyrocles speech which defended his solitarines, framed in his minde a replie against it, in the praise of honourable action, in shewing that such a kind of contemplation is but a glorious title to idlenes; that in action a man did not onely better himself, but benefit others; that the gods would not have delivered a soule into the body, which hath armes and legges, only instruments of doing, but that it wer intended the mind should imploy them; and that the mind should best know his own good or evill, by practise: which knowledge was the onely way to increase the one, and correct the other: besides many other argumentes, which the plentifulnesse of the matter yielded to the sharpnes of his wit. (I, 58)

It is within the context of the entire *Arcadia*, however, that the victory of the active life becomes most apparent. From the donnée of the plot – Basilius' abdication of political responsibility for pastoral retirement – to sententious remarks like 'doing good [is] the only happy action of man's life' (*OA* 359), the *Arcadia* insists on the primacy of active virtue, a truth of the *Old Arcadia* that is magnified many times by the expanded 'epic' action of the *New Arcadia* in Books II and III.

The conflict between the active and contemplative ideals was an important philosophical issue of the period; it can be traced in the humanists' redefining the concept of wisdom so that it became an ethical rather than a religious virtue,

transforming it from a knowledge of divine things or of divine and human things and their causes to a code of ethical precepts, indistinguishable from prudence, on how to live well and blessedly. The result was an active, moralized wisdom more obviously in harmony with many contemporary needs and an ideal man who, as Le Caron put it, 'should excell all men in courage, intellectual subtlety, and by a careful and skillful application to his calling; who should ... consider no life higher than one devoted to great and public things.'[9]

Sidney's preference for the active ideal suggests that his allegiance is with the strongly ethical strain in Renaissance humanism, as opposed to the esoteric Neoplatonic strain represented by the Medici circle.[10] His ideas in this matter resemble those attributed to the fifteenth-century Florentine, Leonardo Bruni:

Soaked in the Ciceronian and Aristotelian ideal that the individual personality develops all its potentialities and achieves its end only by participation in the life of the *polis* or *res publica*, his image of the philosopher is not a man isolated in contemplation, but a man whose family, economic and political activity completes and perfects his intellectual work.[11]

The first debate between Pyrocles and Musidorus might therefore be said to divide and explore the nature of Virtue; the second debate works with the other half of the original antithesis, the figure of Vice or Pleasure. Through this figure the two Herculean legends are joined, for Renaissance moralists generally interpret the Omphale episode as an allegory of Passion's victory over Reason. The allegorical equation of Hercules with Reason is the result of a long history of reinterpretation which converted a basically ethical hero into an intellectual one as well – not perhaps remarkable, since Hercules was the exemplar of ideal mankind to a culture which presupposed the hegemony of the rational faculty.[12] As for Omphale, for her to become a Pleasure figure representing Passion or the lure of the senses requires only a slight abstraction or generalization of the legend, especially as it was handed down in Ovid's *Heroides* IX.

Sidney's brief reference to the myth in the *Defence* accepts and extends the Ovidian motifs: 'Hercules, painted with his great beard and furious countenance, in a woman's attire, spinning at Omphale's commandment' he considers solely as 'the representing of so strange a power in love.'[13] It is likewise in terms of this theme of the power of love that the mythographers interpret the conflict of Reason and Passion in the Omphale episode. Salutati, for example, agrees generally with Fulgentius' standard medieval interpretation: 'quod libido quamvis, etiam invictam, possit superare virtutem,' that passion can conquer any degree of virtue, even if it is invincible.[14]

Here, then, in the idea of the power of love, classical and chivalric literature seemed to agree. Even more important than Ovid, Virgil in the Dido episode sanctions the theme of the hero seduced from his more serious tasks by love; in courtly literature one has only to think of Lancelot's absolute abasement to Guinevere in Chrétien's *Knight of the Cart* or of the Petrarchan lover brooding over his love to the exclusion of all other concerns. It was therefore natural that the heir to all these traditions, the chivalric epic, would find the theme especially congenial. Ariosto, Tasso, and Spenser use the motifs surrounding the Omphale legend and the closely connected Choice of Hercules in a way that shows each shaping the mythographers' interpretation into something characteristic of his own art; more significant for our purposes, it shows all three sharing an assumption about choice that Sidney refuses to adopt. His stylistic preference for harmonizing antitheses shows even at this level of composition.

Ariosto gives extraordinary emphasis in the Ruggero-Alcina episode to the Hesiodic elements of Prodicus' fable, that is, to the idea that the path to virtue is long and arduous, whereas 'Vice it is possible to find in abundance and with ease; for the way to it is smooth, and lies very near.'[15] Ruggero, though warned, succumbs to Alcina's lure, and the motif of the road to vice is expanded into a luscious Garden of Pleasure. Ariosto does not refer explicitly to Omphale, but as clearly as Circe's presence is affirmed through the transformation of discarded lovers into beasts, so is Omphale's in the effeminizing of Ruggero:

> Di ricche gemme un splendido monile
> Gli discendea dal collo in mezzo il petto;
> E ne l'uno e ne l'altro già virile
> Braccio girava un lucido cerchietto.
> Gli avea forato un fil d'oro sottile
> Ambe l'orecchie, in forma d'annelletto;
> E due gran perle pendevano quindi,
> Qual mai non ebbon gli Arabi nè gl'Indi.[16]

A splendid collar of rich gems hung down from his neck to the midst of his breast; shining bracelets encircled both his arms once so manly. A slender thread of gold was drawn through both his ears in the form of a little ring, and two great pearls were hanging from these, such as the Arabs or other Indians never possessed.

Ruggero, aided by the magic ring that dispels enchantment, finally sees Alcina as a 'puttana vecchia,' ancient whore, and determines to travel the road to Logistilla (the equation of Reason and Virtue is automatic in Renaissance writers, though not present in Prodicus or Hesiod). After approximately forty stanzas devoted to the difficulties of his journey and the temptations to turn aside from his purpose, Ruggero arrives at Logistilla's city, where her castle is made of gems offering the onlooker self-knowledge (x.59). Ruggero's choice is made, and the separation between alternative elements is emphasized through the length and difficulty of the journey.

The dichotomy thus set up early in the poem for Ruggero by Prodicus' tale is carried out in the general handling of the Reason-Passion theme in the *Orlando furioso*: Astolfo, Rinaldo, and Orlando all have to reject their sensuality. The *synkrisis* form demands that the hero make some choice, and Ariosto accedes to the demand. So does Tasso, with greater moral fervour. In the *Gerusalemme liberata* both the Omphale and Prodicus stories are used as glosses on the episode of Rinaldo's sojourn on Armida's island: the Omphale-Iole legend[17] is carved on the gates of her castle (XVI.3), and the hermit's moral instruction of Rinaldo after his escape begins with the lesson of the two paths of life:

Signor, non sotto l'ombra in piaggia molle
tra fonti e fior, tra ninfe e tra sirene,
ma in cima a l'erto e faticoso colle
de la virtú riposto è il nostro bene. (XVII 61)[18]

Not underneath sweet shades and fountains shrill,
Among the nymphs, the fairies, leaves and flowers;
But on the steep, the rough and craggy hill
Of virtue stands this bliss, this good of ours.

In addition to being Circe, Omphale, and Prodicus' Vice rolled into one, Armida is also a pagan who believes in a false god and fights in the ranks of the infidels against Godfrey's Christian forces. The path to her pleasure garden diverges from the path of virtue and must be rejected. Armida is redeemed only when she renounces paganism, which throughout has been connected with witchcraft and enchantment. Her willingness to submit to Rinaldo is a total renunciation of her power over men's minds: 'Ecco l'ancilla tua; d'essa a tuo senno / dispon' – gli disse – e le fia legge il cenno': '"Behold your handmaid; dispose of her according to your will," she said, "and let your nod be law to her"' (XXX.136).[19] The allusion to Luke 1:38, 'Ecce ancilla Domini, fiat mihi secundum verbum tuum,' is marvelously resonant, though her own conversion is the only 'miracle' promised or wrought. Thus, Armida's acceptance of Christianity, rather than suggesting a possibility of rapprochement between pagan and Christian, affirms instead the need for choice. But the propensity of the female figures in the Prodicus story to shift their identity promotes an interesting possible bifurcation in the meaning of Armida's and Rinaldo's final reconciliation: in the moral centre of the work the problem is clearly the choice between good and evil, but allegorical overtones suggest that sensuous beauty and pleasure, if properly disciplined, may be incorporated into the Christian faith. It must have been of considerable personal importance to Tasso that this be so.

Spenser's use of the Herculean legends is morally the most uncompromising of the three because Radigund, his Omphale figure, is portrayed without sympathy. The negotiations between Radigund and Artegall and their combat define the episode in terms quite different from those of the pleasure gardens of Ariosto and Tasso. (Spenser may well have recalled that in the legend Hercules' servitude to Omphale was voluntary and contractual.) Aside from Artegall's 'wilfull' seduction by beauty, an apparent connection with the Italian enchantresses, the episode is particularly warlike and political both in its conception (she rules a city where men are forced to do female labour) and in its conclusion (Britomart defeats Radigund in combat). Jane Aptekar argues that Britomart's function here is a version of the Virtue figure in the Choice legend, Spenser making use of a variant attested to in several paintings in which Hercules has already succumbed to Pleasure and is being persuaded to leave her by Athena (Wisdom) in full armour.[20] Perhaps. It *is* clear at any rate that Artegall 'chooses' servitude to beauty,

> For though that he first victorie obtayned
> Yet after by abandoning his sword
> He wilfull lost, that he before attayned, (V.v.17)[21]

only to be dressed in women's clothes and set to work with a distaff:

> Who had him seene, imagine mote thereby,
> That whylome hath of Hercules beene told,
> How for Iolas sake he did apply
> His mightie hands, the distaffe vile to hold,
> For his huge club, which had subdew'd of old
> So many monsters, which the world annoyed;
> His Lyons skin chaungd to a pall of gold,
> In which forgetting warres, he onely joyed
> In combats of sweet love, and with his mistresse toyed. (V.v.24)

The conflation of the two Hercules stories and the Judgment of Paris is clear: Artegall chooses beauty over the Athena-like Britomart (or Vice rather than Virtue) and becomes enslaved to Omphale.

One might assume on the basis of Ariosto's, Tasso's, and Spenser's working of the Herculean motifs that a writer who used them had to assert some choice, for, as Wind notes, *tertium non datur*. But Panofsky's study of the form taken by paintings of Hercules at the Crossroads suggests that absolute choice is not mandatory, though the artist works against one's normal expectations if he refuses to choose. Raphael's 'Decision of the Young Scipio' (previously known as 'The Knight's Dream'), for example, attempts to shift the emphasis of the two female figures away from the idea of conflict or disjunction:

Der Norden und die Antike, sie beide kommen bei aller Verschiedenheit doch darin überein, dasz sie die 'Tugend' und das 'Laster' als *unversöhnliche Gegensätze* auffassen, zwischen denen ein Ausgleich nicht möglich ist. Demgegenüber gewinnen wir vor manchen südlichen Darstellungen, und eben auch schon vor der Raffaelischen, den Eindruck eines gewissen *Relativismus*: in demselben Masze, in dem die 'Virtus' sanfter wird, wird die 'Voluptas' minder gefährlich ... schlieszlich die beiden Frauen weniger zwei *ethische Grundprincipien* zu verkörpern scheinen, als zwei *verschiedene Denkungsarten und Lebensformen*, von denen zwar die eine auf einer tieferen Wertstufe steht als die andere, und insofern noch immer vom wahrhaft hochstrebenden Menschen miszbilligt zu werden verdient, die aber einander nicht mehr ganz unversöhnlich gegenüberstehen: unter der Voraussetzung, dasz die 'Voluptas' – zur bloszen Lebensfreude abgemildert – sich freiwillig der 'Virtus' unterordnet, d.h. dasz sie den moralischen Forderungen nicht hindernd in den Weg tritt, sondern im Gegenteil das, was die Tugend gebietet, durch ihre Gegenwart verschönt, läszt sich, mit Goethe zu reden, ein *'positiver Mittelzustand'* denken, der das 'Entweder-Oder' in ein 'Sowohl-Als auch' verwandelt zeigt ...[22]

Both Northern Europe and Antiquity, for all their differences, do agree in conceiving of 'Virtue' and 'Vice' as *irreconcilable opposites*, between which no accommodation is possible. On the other hand, from many Southern representations, and from that of Raphael, we obtain the impression of a certain *relativity*: to the degree that 'Virtue' becomes more gentle, 'Voluptas' becomes less dangerous ... finally the two women appear less to embody two *fundamental ethical principles* than two *different ways of thinking and kinds of life*. To be sure, one of them is of lower value than the other, and on this ground still deserves to be disapproved of by truly aspiring men, but they are no longer totally irreconcilable. On the assumption that 'Voluptas' – moderated to a mere enjoyment of life – freely subordinates herself to 'Virtus' (ie, that she does not obstruct moral demands, but on the contrary, that she beautify with her presence whatever Virtue calls for), then, as Goethe says, a *'positive middleground'* can be conceived, which shows the 'Either-Or' transformed into a 'Not only-But also.' (my translation)

It is generally to the literary tradition of the 'Sowohl-Als auch,' the 'Not only-But also,' represented by Goethe, by the allegorical implication of Armida's conversion in Tasso and by the title of Jonson's Herculean masque *Pleasure Reconciled to Virtue*,[23] as well as to the Italian pictorial tradition here suggested by Raphael, that Sidney's handling of the Hercules legends belongs. The two central topoi of the active versus the contemplative life and Reason versus Passion or Love are, as noted above, the subject of debate between the princes in Book I. Though there are two debates, the argument is essentially the same in both, and the positions are easily matched up. In each debate one side is manifestly the victor, but there is an important reservation: in the first round, action defeats contemplation; in the second, Reason naturally wins a rational debate, but the movement of the story continues to be impelled by the 'losing' force of Love.[24] What is interesting about this perhaps inevitable situation is that Sidney seems to realize its implications for his humanist theory of man and tries to incorporate this lapse from accepted virtue into a more complex view of the heroic life. The debate therefore functions by setting the attempt at reconciliation within a context that heightens one's awareness of the moral antitheses at issue. Both the nature of the conflict itself and a hint as to the means of possible resolution can be found in the reference to the Hercules-Omphale legend which precedes the second debate.

The motifs are those in other interpretations of the legend, but Sidney alone of these poets attempts to convert this universally condemned aspect of Hercules' life into a possible source of value. Zelmane's mantle bears a jewel carved with the acknowledged symbol of reason made slave to passion, of man at the mercy of lust, of nature turned upside down and justice flaunted – but the inscription over the form of Hercules dressed as a woman and carrying a distaff is 'Never more valiant' (I, 75-6). The jewel, though an emblem of Pyrocles' situation as the disguised Zelmane, points to the obvious differences as well as similarities in the two figures: Zelmane is no slave woman but an Amazon warrior, and she carries not a distaff but a sword.[25] Unlike Ruggero, Rinaldo, and Artegall, Pyrocles is not imprisoned; he retains the outward semblance of freedom and thus the capacity for heroic action (though he does not thereby escape censure for his female disguise). Sidney's is thus not just an allusion to the Hercules myth, but an attempt to reshape it into something which can more readily be moralized to suit his need to reconcile the issues contained in the original allegory. The inscription 'Never more valiant' offers a direct commentary on the debate between Reason and Love that follows;[26] it hints that some way can be found to reinterpret this standard antithesis. Reinforcing the connection already noted between the two debates, it suggests that Love need not be divorced from the Active Life, that is, that the alternatives are not offered in complete disjunction. Such a resolution has been reflected in part in the shifting terminology of this discussion. Does Reason oppose 'Love' or merely 'Passion'? Naturally it is easier to reconcile the first formulation. Tasso alone of these writers does not imply that the distinction between love and passion is a way of ending the Omphale episode; apparently we are to believe that Rinaldo has been in love with Armida all along, but has ruthlessly denied his feelings three times because of his duty to the Christian forces.[27] The use of the distinction by Ariosto and Spenser is simpler: Ruggero's attachment to Alcina is purely sensual, and the force opposing Artegall's reason or virtue cannot be termed 'love.' Sidney, on the other hand, finds the conceptual overlapping of love and passion necessary to any hope of reconciling the original conflict. He works with whichever provides his local need for antithesis, paradox, or resolution. The strategy (or is it merely the problem?) is the same in *Astrophel and Stella*, of course.

Sidney's refocusing the debate sequences around the newly conceived Hercules jewel has important repercussions for the narrative revisions of the *New Arcadia*. The idea that the hero should perform heroic actions while 'enslaved' is present to some extent even in the *Old Arcadia*, where Pyrocles slays a lion and quells the Arcadian rebellion. But as the retrospective narrative inserted into the new Book II greatly expands the content and implication of Pyrocles' earlier exploits, so must the Arcadian heroism increase in scope if it is to justify the boast that he has been 'Never more valiant.' The requisite change is potentially more significant than the additions to Books I and II, since the latter consist of material that is, strictly speaking, episodic – that is, not part of the main action or fable. But events occurring in Arcadia must alter the course of the plot despite the rigid framework provided by the oracle.[28]

Sidney's attempts to reconcile the conflicting claims of virtue and passion lean towards the solutions offered by chivalric love rather than towards the more esoteric doctrines of the Florentine Academy. Occasionally, however, he does nod in the direction of Neoplatonism, as in the opening apostrophe to Urania or in Pyrocles' half-hearted attempt to justify his passion as the initial step in achieving heavenly love: first he will become practiced in love itself and then he will 'turn it to greater matters' (I, 81). Sidney's 'solutions' to the ethical conflict are therefore not much different from those of the age. His uniqueness lies rather in his insistence both on the reality of the conflict between love and reason and on the necessity to fuse them into a unified conception of virtue, that is, in his simultaneous insistence on both the antithesis and its 'irrelevance.' The Herculean jewel and all it implies may be Sidney's attempt in the *New Arcadia* to deal with the conflict left open in the *Old*, where, just as Love governs the earlier action although Reason has won both debates, so Love conquers in the dénouement or trial scene, despite Euarchus' superior reasoning and just condemnation of the princes' behaviour.

KNOWLEDGE AND VIRTUE

The problem of Knowledge and Virtue has deeper roots in classical psychology than the conflict between Reason and Love, but undergoes important modification in the Christian era. Sidney's treatment of the topos can be related to both factors. Notwithstanding his bow to Plato and 'Tullie' in the *Defence* ('That who could see virtue would be wonderfully ravished with the love of her beauty'),[29] Sidney's more usual interpretation of the psyche's function demonstrates a post-Aristotelian awareness of the possible discrepancy between understanding and desire. Although useful distinctions can be made between Aristotle's and Plato's positions, the more important change can be found between the basic orientations of classical and Christian ethics. Aristotle objected to Socrates' equation of knowledge and virtue on the grounds that common experience proved it was possible to know the good and act otherwise, yet he explains the discrepancy in terms of the ambiguity in our use of the word 'know,' which covers both universal and particular knowledge.[30] For all his awareness that a problem may exist, Aristotle cannot believe that it creates a serious impediment to ethical action. At base, he shares with Socrates the idea that any failure to act virtuously is essentially a failure of understanding. With Christianity the emphasis shifts from the problem of knowledge to the problem of will. Sidney expresses the issue in the *Defence* when he asserts that philosophy's role in teaching virtue is superfluous: 'since in nature we know it is well to do well, and what is well, and what is evil, although not in the words of art which philosophers bestow upon us; for out of natural conceit the philosophers drew it. But to be moved to do that which we know, or to be moved with desire to know, *hoc opus, hic labor est*' (p 91).

This passage from the *Defence* offers an interesting gloss on the conflict experienced by Queen Gynecia, where the Reason-Love issue is reformulated as a problem of knowledge and virtue. The Queen is, as Jon S. Lawry says, 'one in whom desire has overpowered the will, even though reason remains urgent.'[31] This 'paradoxical' inability of knowledge to produce virtue is the basis of Gynecia's remarkable soliloquy at the opening of Book II. The passage itself remains the same in both *Arcadias*, but its impact is greater in the revision because there it offers the reader his first glimpse into Gynecia's mind. The omniscient narrator of the *Old Arcadia* summarized her state for us earlier in the story (eg, *OA* 54, 57) and even gave a brief account of the process by which her affection had grown, commenting that desire had 'reduced her whole mind to an extreme and unfortunate slavery' so that 'neither honour long maintained, nor love of husband and children, could withstand it' (*OA* 48). With the narrative technique revised, the reader discovers Gynecia's passion by 'overhearing' Pyrocles' conversation with Musidorus (I, 93-4), and the prince's account must necessarily have more limited authority and scope. Even when there is no dramatic narrator, Sidney is 'less omniscient' in his handling of Gynecia in Book I. The details are either such that a casually interested observer might have produced them, or else they echo the irony which the reader has come to associate with Pyrocles' point of view. The full depth and moral import of her emotion are left to be revealed in the soliloquy.

Gynecia's moral dilemma, perhaps because it is the most extreme experienced by the royal figures, seems meant to be emblematic.[32] Her soliloquy begins Book II (whose main plot is largely devoted to the courtship of the princesses) and it grows out of the Narrator's generalization about the nature of the love experienced by all the characters. His opening words point to the discrepancy between conventional associations (pastoral-contemplative-Neoplatonic) and the reality of their passions: 'In these pastorall pastimes a great number of dayes were sent to follow their flying predecessours, while the cup of poison (which was deeply tasted of this noble companie) had left no sinewe of theirs without mortally searching into it; yet never manifesting his venemous worke, till once ...' (I, 145) The passage having begun with this generalized statement proceeds with an account of Gynecia's 'grieved and hopeles mind':

There appeered unto the eies of her judgement the evils she was like to run into, with ougly infamie waiting upon them: she felt the terrou[r]s of her owne conscience; she was guilty of a long exercised vertue, which made this vice the fuller of deformitie. The uttermost of the good she could aspire unto, was a mortall wound to her vexed spirits: and lastly no small part of her evils was, that she was wise to see her evils. (I, 145)

The soliloquy opens with a series of apostrophes to the sun, heavens, deserts, and Virtue culminating in one to Reason:

O imperfect proportion of reason, which can too much forsee, and too little prevent. Alas, alas (said she) if there were but one hope for all my paines, or but one excuse for all my faultinesse. But wretch that I am, my torment is beyond all succour, and my evill deserving doth exceed my evill fortune ... Yet if my desire (how unjust so ever it be) might take effect, though a thousand deaths folowed it, and every death were followed with a thousand shames; yet should not my sepulcher receive me without some contentment. (I, 146)[33]

The conflict expressed here can be fully explained neither by classical ethics nor Sidney's own humanistic assumptions. It is not enough to say, as C.S. Lewis does, that Gynecia offers a study against the background of Augustinian theology,[34] though the statement itself is undeniably true. Sidney's conception of Gynecia does not ingenuously interpolate a bit of Christian theology into a pagan landscape; it severely questions the major premise of the heroic paideia, which the Arcadia is. As a work concerned with the education of the prince it expresses the humanists' faith in education, which in turn is founded on the classical belief that virtue is a state of character brought about as a result of habit: 'It makes no small difference, then, whether we form habits of one kind or of another from our very youth; it makes a very great difference, or rather all the difference.'[35] On these grounds Gynecia's 'long exercised vertue' should have some effect other than increasing the paradox of her new vice. In the *Old Arcadia* this Augustinian conception of the Queen existed side by side with an explicit formulation of Basilius' character that strongly underwrote the classical view:

> poor old Basilius, now alone ... had a sufficient eclogue in his own head betwixt honour, with the long experience he had had of the world, on the one side, and this new assault of Cleophilia's beauty on the other side. There hard by the lodge walked he, carrying this unquiet contention about him. But passion ere long had gotten the absolute masterhood, bringing with it the show of present pleasure, fortified with the authority of a prince whose power might easily satisfy his will against the far-fet (though true) reasons of the spirit – which, *in a man not trained in the way of virtue*, have but slender working. (OA 45)[36]

The *New Arcadia* omits this passage, I think, not only because of the demands of the narrative technique, but because Sidney may well have felt that his new plan called for a subtler and more interesting set of comparisons. The basic orientation of the revised material is still humanistic, however. If anything, the *New Arcadia* gives greater emphasis to the princes' education, while retaining such key statements as 'O no; he cannot be good, that knowes not why he is good, but stands so farre good, as his fortune may keep him unassaied' (I, 26).[37] Gynecia's power within the *Arcadia* is perhaps just that she is an anomaly. The Reason-Love conflict is present in many other characters, of course, but generally with the suggestion of reconciliation – even if specious – namely, that Reason might offer 'straight to prove / By reason good, good reason her to love.'[38] For Gynecia no such sophistry is possible. By her presence she points to the failure of a conventional Arcadian vision to accommodate the actualities of the world, and of classical ethics to encompass the whole of human experience as sixteenth-century men understood it. Gynecia's dilemma should prevent the reader's developing a complacent view of human perfection or perfectability, but we need not thereby exaggerate the amount of Christian pessimism it generates within the context of the work. Instead, we might see in her an expression of the darker side of Sidney's uncommon Arcadian vision, a reminder that the work is neither 'pure' pastoral nor 'pure' romance.

One peculiarity of the *Arcadia* is that it is conceived in several literary modes simultaneously.[39] Basilius, for example, is primarily a comic character, but while he and Gynecia share roles in the comic love situation, she has the additional function of 'stirring up tragedies' (I, 150). In the light of this difference, it may be misleading to compare Gynecia's and Basilius' training in the ways of virtue. A more fair comparison for the Queen would be her daughters. The majesty-humility contrast between Pamela and Philoclea is just one aspect of Sidney's balanced arrangement of these two figures in the revised *Arcadia*. The general distinction is also applied to the relation between knowledge and virtue. Pamela and Philoclea prove equally virtuous, though for opposite causes – the one through assured knowledge and the other through instinctive goodness. Gynecia may be considered a third term in this exploration, best thought of as knowledge that fails. In this connection, Philoclea and Gynecia remain largely as they were in the *Old Arcadia*. The greater attention paid to the theme in the revision stems from the elaboration of Pamela's character and from the dramatic juxtaposition of the princesses in the Captivity sequence. So intensive is exploration of this contrast in the Captivity episode that it probably makes redundant the contrast between Philoclea and Pyrocles that was central to the discussion of suicide in the *Old Arcadia*'s Book IV.[40] There, major emphasis had been given to

what small difference in the working there is betwixt a simple voidness of evil and a judicial habit of virtue. For she, not with an unshaked magnanimity, wherewith Pyrocles weighed and despised death, but with an innocent guiltlessness, not knowing why she should fear to deliver her unstained soul to God ... did almost bring her mind to as quiet attending all accidents as the unmastered virtue of Pyrocles. (*OA* 294)

This contrast is replaced in the *New Arcadia*, for example, by how the two princesses react to plans for their escape from Amphialus' castle. Clinias explains the plot,

but Philoclea (*in whose cleere minde treason could finde no hiding place*) told him, that she would be glad, if he could perswade her cosin to deliver her, and that she would never forgett his service therin: but that she desired him to lay down any such way of mischiefe, for that (for her part) she would rather yeeld to perpetuall imprisonment, then consent to the destroying her cosin, who (she knewe) loved her, though wronged her. (I, 438; my italics)

Clinias begs her for a 'promise of silence, which she perfourmed.'

But that little avayled: for Artesia having in like sort opened the device to Pamela, she (*in whose mind Vertue governed with the scepter of Knowledge*) hating so horrible a wickednes, and streight judging what was fitte to doo, Wicked woman (said she) whose unrepenting harte can find no way to amend treason, but by treason: nowe the time is come, that thy <wretched> wiles have caught thy selfe in thine owne nette: as for me, let the Gods dispose of me as shall please them; but sure it shall be no such way, nor way-leader, by which I will come to libertie. (I, 438; my italics)

Pyrocles is himself an actor in the Captivity sequence, since he has also been taken prisoner disguised as the Amazon, Zelmane. His role is minor and rather puzzling. In view of the certainty with which both the Narrator and Pamela pronounce upon the wickedness of plotting treason to escape imprisonment, how are we to interpret Pyrocles' active connivance in the plans? Pamela seems to have taken over his 'judicial habit of Virtue,' and he himself shows nothing of the 'unshaked magnanimity' that weighs and despises death (though to be fair, it is not his own death that he fails to despise). His love may be at the root of his anguish, but Sidney concentrates rather on his 'overmastered courage,'[41] at one point elaborating on his most un-Stoic state:

> But Zelmane ... was so confused withall (her courage still rebelling against her wit, desiring still with force to doo impossible matters) that as her desire was stopped with power, so her conceit was darkned with a mist of desire. For blind Love and invincible valure stil would cry out, that it could not be, Philoclea should be in so miserable estate, and she not relieve her: and so while she haled her wit to her courage, she drewe it from his owne limits. (I, 479-80)

Sidney's analysis of Pyrocles' confusion explicitly refers to the usurpation of Reason's functions by Courage or Spirit; the terminology and the conception here seem to be derived from Plato's *Republic*. The more usual dangers of the second part of the soul have always been ambition and pride (Plato's analogy is the timocratic man)[42] or perhaps even anger, but Sidney's variant is still recognizably in the same ethical tradition. Gynecia and her behaviour may not be accounted for by classical ethics,[43] but Pyrocles here offers a case that can.

Within all this shifting of roles, the part played by Philoclea remains fairly constant. Sidney appears from the beginning to have seen Philoclea in terms of innocence, and though she and Pyrocles are contrasted in the important argument concerning suicide in Book IV, her main foil in the *Old Arcadia* is her mother. The emphasis falls for both on the extent to which their virtue, however achieved, can withstand confrontation with what each acknowledges to be wrong. We have seen great stress placed on Gynecia's *true* knowledge of evil; Philoclea's is more intuitive and less sure.[44] Sidney again is quite explicit in the way he views his character's relation to virtue and knowledge:

> The sweete minded Philoclea was in their degree of well doing, to whom the not knowing of evil serveth for a ground of vertue, and hold their inward powers in better forme with an unspotted simplicitie, then many, who rather cunningly seeke to know what goodnes is, then willingly take into themselves the following of it. But as that sweet and simple breath of heavenly goodnesse, is the easier to be altered,[45] because it hath not passed through

the worldlie wickednesse, nor feelingly found the evill, that evill caries with it; so now the Ladie Philoclea (whose eyes and senses had receaved nothing, but according as the naturall course of each thing required; <whose> tender youth had obediently lived under her parents behests, without framing out of her own wil the fore-chosing of any thing) when now she came to appoint, wherin her judgement was to be practized, in knowing faultines by his first tokens, she was like a yong faune, who comming in the wind of the hunters, doth not know whether it be a thing or not to be eschewed; whereof at this time she began to get a costly experience. (I, 169)

Curiously, one ought to judge that Philoclea does indeed fall snare to evil in loving Zelmane because both her limited knowledge and her instinctive sense of virtue rebel against her feelings for the Amazon as something 'unnatural.' Her previous actions were based on obedience and natural goodness, and now that the behaviour of people whom she knows to be good (Zelmane and Gynecia) contradicts what her instinct tells her must be the good, she has no way of determining what to do.

The prelapsarian context and imagery of this passage point to the kind of problem Philoclea offers for an exploration of Knowledge and Virtue. She seems to embody 'Instinctive Virtue,' a term which fits uneasily into either Christian or classical views of man. As Milton tells us, Adam was the only man to whom it was given to know good in itself and not also by knowing evil, yet surely the clause, 'whose eyes and senses had receaved nothing, but according as the naturall course of each thing required,' implies a rapport with nature and a physical and mental perfection that were lost with the Fall. As for classical antiquity, Aristotle explicitly says that 'it is ... plain that none of the moral virtues arises in us by nature.'[46] Seneca is even more adamant. After a passage conceding the blessings and goodness of the people in the Golden Age, he continues:

Quid ergo est? Ignorantia rerum innocentes erant. Multum autem interest utrum peccare aliquis nolit an nesciat. Deerat illis iustitia, deerat prudentia, deerat temperantia ac fortitudo. Omnibus his virtutibus habebat similia quaedam rudis vita; virtus non contingit animo nisi instituto et edocto et ad summum assidua exercatione perducto. Ad hoc quidem, sed sine hoc nascimur et in optimis quoque, antequam erudias, virtutis materia, non virtus est.[47]

What, then, is the conclusion of the matter? It was by reason of their ignorance of things that the men of those days were innocent; and it makes a great deal of difference whether one wills not to sin or has not the knowledge to sin. Justice was unknown to them, unknown prudence, unknown also self-control and bravery; but their rude life possessed certain qualities akin to all these virtues. Virtue is not vouchsafed to a soul unless that soul has been trained and taught, and by unremitting practice brought to perfection. For the attainment of this boon, but not in the possession of it, were we born; and even in the best of men, before you refine them by instruction, there is but the stuff of virtue, not virtue itself.

Sidney harbours intellectual doubts about the trustworthiness of Philoclea's virtue – the Narrator of the *Old Arcadia* speaks of the contradictions which 'must needs grow in those minds which neither absolutely embrace goodness nor freely yield to evil' (*OA* 121)[48] – but because he does not give these doubts adequate dramatic expression within the work, the philosophical point is not forcefully made. This is true for the *New Arcadia* even more than for the *Old*. In the original version one could at least balance a knowledge that fails to yield virtue (Gynecia) against a virtue that requires no knowledge (Philoclea) and arrive at a tentative statement, though one requiring further qualification in the light of the other characters for whom knowledge and virtue are more conventionally related, especially the princes and Euarchus. In the revision the implicit contrast between Philoclea and Gynecia is submerged in favour of the explicit contrast between Philoclea and Pamela, where, as shown above, the emphasis falls as much on the equality of result as on the disparity of causes. Thus, in a sense, a real antithesis has given way to a formulation that can be reconciled by Sidney's sleight of hand, the vanishing distinction.

Though Sidney's basic conception of Philoclea as an example of innocence and natural virtue remains fairly constant, he reworks her character to give increased emphasis to the idea of self-knowledge. This is the focus in much of the *New Arcadia*'s additional and revised material, and indicates Sidney's deepening awareness of the moral and dramatic potentialities to be found in the education of princes.

Clear evidence of Sidney's intensified interest in self-knowledge occurs in the expansion of Philoclea's soliloquy scene, from which I have already quoted the opening moral context. The major interpolated section (roughly I, 169.17-171.39) explains in great detail how Philoclea's love for an Amazon is psychologically understandable. With its minute care for the causal links in the sequence it emphasizes the naturalness of a process that results in such an unnatural situation. The premise for Philoclea's dilemma is her initial innocence and good will. She is infected by Zelmane's passion because, admiring the Amazon, she seeks to show her admiration by emulating and responding to her gestures, 'til at the last (poore soule, ere she were aware) she accepted not onely the <badge>, but the service; not only the signe, but the passion signified' (I, 170). Though the psychological process is more accurately observed here than in the very brief corresponding passage in the *Old Arcadia* (*OA* 97-8), the effect of the psychologizing is merely to underline the earlier conception of innocence, one which would not have seemed very out of place in *Daphnis and Chloe*. Yet in context there is a difference between the two versions. In the *Old Arcadia* appearances and reality never merge for Philoclea, but remain too complicated for her simple mind to think about, even to the extent of determining what it is she feels. In the *New Arcadia*, the elaborate psychological sequence is the pathway of knowledge; through it her mind comes to distinguish between appearance and reality, and her personal experience offers a key to the outside world, making her know by her own thoughts and feelings those of other people:

For now indeed, Love puld of his maske, and shewed his face unto her, and told her plainly, that shee was his prisoner. Then needed she no more paint her face with passions; for passions shone thorow her face ... desiring she knew not what, nor how, if she knew what. Then her minde (though too late) by the smart was brought to thinke of the disease, and her owne proofe taught her to know her mothers minde ... (I, 171)

Yet Philoclea's greater self-knowledge does not lead to more virtuous action; the passage continues: 'which (as no error gives so strong assault, as that which comes armed in the authoritie of a parent, so) greatly fortified her desires, to see, that her mother had the like desires.' (In the *Old Arcadia* Philoclea knows nothing about her mother and is said to be unaware of Pamela's love.)

Perhaps the most exciting turn Sidney executes in this psychological exploration is the role he assigns to dreams. Though elsewhere quite capable of attributing occult and providential overtones to them, he limits himself here to perceptive observation. The context is Philoclea's wish that she and Zelmane might be two of Diana's nymphs, or sisters, or more boldly, that one of them could be a man: 'Then dreames by night beganne to bring more unto her, then she durst wish by day, whereout making <waking?> did make her know her selfe the better by the image of those fancies.' (I, 171) The twentieth century would consider this a creditable path towards self-knowledge.

Philoclea's self-knowledge contributes significantly to the stature she acquires in the *New Arcadia*, permitting us to believe in her behaviour during the Captivity despite the author's occasional qualms about her untried innocence. Nor does Philoclea alone show Sidney's new interest. On the whole, the characters of the revision show a greater awareness of motivation – their own and other people's – than do those of the original version, and new episodes are often studies in the kinds of self-deception that prevent one from assessing the truth of a given situation. Since many of these episodes have been designed to form part of the princes' education, it is only right that the cousins gain psychological as well as political insight from their experiences. The personal or ethical nature of Pyrocles' adventures bears specific fruit in the revision as an increased awareness of Gynecia's desires. Pyrocles' greater knowledge can be attributed to technical factors that have nothing to do with character development – for example, to the demands of first-person narrative, since he relates the plot situation to Musidorus, or to a decision to exploit the comic possibilities of an obviously ridiculous love triangle (or quadrangle) – but whatever the cause, Pyrocles' awareness helps shape Sidney's new conception of the hero. We can see the change operating in the confrontation scene between Pyrocles and Gynecia, in which the Queen implies that she knows him to be a man. The *Old Arcadia* offered amusing flat-footedness: 'Cleophila was stricken even dead with that word, finding herself discovered' (*OA* 95); the *New Arcadia* promises a battle of wits, prefacing Pyrocles' reply with 'Zelmane then knowing well at what marke she shot, yet loth to enter into it ...' (I, 148) The expanded psychological and ethical knowledge displayed by the princes in the *New Arcadia* may well be the result of reconsidering the idea of the perfect prince. Sidney's understanding of both parts of the standard topos – that he be both 'a speaker of words and a doer of deeds' – has become deeper. The more profound rhetoricism of the work perhaps suggests revision towards Aristotle's ideas of what the good rhetorician will know. The psychological and ethical knowledge demanded by the *Rhetoric* presupposes considerable familiarity with the *Ethics*, and such knowledge would be reflected more significantly in the man who achieved it than merely as an ability to manipulate audience sympathy and interests, to which the *Old Arcadia* generally limited itself. For his education of the prince, Sidney insists to a degree unparalleled in the original version on a knowledge of oneself and of others.

Self-knowledge, or rather its converse, self-deception, is a complex indicator of morality, since it sometimes functions as the cause, sometimes as the effect of moral error. For example, it seems to be inextricably at the core of Basilius' foolishness, but to be the result of Tydeus' and Telenor's refusal 'to make friendship a child, and not the father of Vertue' (I, 211). Perhaps the most sustained treatment of these and related ideas occurs in the complex of episodes surrounding Helen, Amphialus, and Cecropia, all material added to the revision. In her first appearance Helen proclaims both emblematically and by her narrative that she has little understanding of herself and other people. She stares at a portrait of Amphialus and at one point shows it to his page, Ismenus, saying, 'Here is my Lord, where is yours?' (I, 73) Helen's knowledge of Amphialus goes no deeper than this suggests: her admiration for him as a perfect knight may not stop 'this side idolatry,' but she fails to understand his feelings and loyalties. She may as well love only a picture. She knows nothing beyond her own will, not how her actions are interpreted by other people, nor whether she is in fact encouraging or discouraging her suitors. Even when she has both the knowledge and the power necessary to control events (for example, to prevent the jealous Philoxenus from confronting his friend Amphialus who he believes has betrayed him), she wilfully does no more than make sure she will be informed of what happens. In relating this to Musidorus, she both accepts and shrugs off responsibility:

> he [Philoxenus] never answered me, but pale and quaking, went straight away; and straight my heart misgave me some evill successe: and yet though I had authoritie inough to have stayed him (as in these fatall things it falles out, that the hie-working powers make second causes unwittingly accessarie to their determinations) I did no further but sent a foot-man of mine (whose faithfulnes to me I well knew) from place to place to follow him, and bring me word of his proceedings ... (I, 70)

The fault is surely not Helen's alone. The intensity of the episode lies in its multiple misunderstandings. Philoxenus recognizes neither Helen's apparently ill-disguised passion nor his best friend's loyalty. Amphialus has shared Philoxenus' lack of perception about Helen's love, but once she declares her passion, we expect him to use this knowledge to interpret Philoxenus' rage as misguided jealousy. Instead, we hear a great deal about his willingness to suffer insult from his own friend; he seems aware only of the rightness of his own conduct.[49] His outward self-control – the picture of the perfect knight – remains unimpaired, but his inner response does not have the sympathy and perceptiveness that we naturally expect of their long friendship. Forced to defend himself, he accidentally kills Philoxenus. We cannot help feeling the cosmic 'unfairness' of the event,[50] but at the same time the extraordinarily providential scheme of heroic romance suggests that Amphialus' misfortunes are external evidence for some internal imbalance or imperfection.

Amphialus' relation to his mother, Cecropia, sheds further light on the issue. He is apparently unaware of her evil nature and has no part in planning her wicked schemes, but he recognizes that by not redressing the wrongs she has committed he is in fact her accomplice. The unsound foundation on which are built his virtues of courtesy, courage, magnanimity, intelligence as a leader of men, and so on is exposed, yet without denying that the attractive edifice exists as well. Sidney manages this in part through not having Amphialus fully informed of Cecropia's actions; she continually deceives him about her intentions towards the princesses and about Philoclea's true responses to his victories in combat. One wonders, though, if Cecropia's lies and manipulations are not ultimately projections or narrative embodiments of what is after all Amphialus' *self*-deception.[51]

Cecropia presents yet another study in knowing others through self-knowledge. She is remarkably frank, and one assumes accurate, in appraising her own motivations, but the selfish arrogance of these blinds her to the possibility that others are motivated by different, virtuous, desires. Thus she fails with the princesses and does not understand the nature of her son's love for Philoclea. Her death is an ironic commentary on this aspect of her vice. She falls from the castle wall while fleeing Amphialus because she believes her son means to kill her with his unsheathed sword. Actually, he wants to kill *himself* before her eyes so that she may see the result of the evil schemes she says were designed solely for his benefit. The irony is double-edged: Amphialus, at the moment when he recognizes the heinousness of his actions, commits still another ill-fated act by unintentionally causing his mother's death.

It is difficult to summarize this discussion of Sidney's handling of the problem of Knowledge and Virtue beyond saying it indicates that the relation between them is one of the commonplaces he deliberately sets out to explore. In one phase of the examination he deals mainly with the kinds of knowledge that constitute or promote virtue. The answer Sidney seems to suggest is that there is general knowledge of what might be called ethical values and particular 'psychological' knowledge of oneself and other people, and that virtue lies in the interplay of these two factors with a third which is no more precise than an inborn goodness of character. Seen this way, the problem shows its relation to the popular antithetical topos of nature versus nurture. In a second phase of the examination Sidney explores situations in which there is no positive correlation between Knowledge and Virtue, whether because Reason has been subverted by some other faculty of the soul (by the passions or the spirited part, or in Christian terms, by the unregenerate will) or because Instinctive Goodness can bypass the need for knowledge and still be indistinguishable in practice from Virtue.

The kind and amount of schematization this reading implies is perhaps misleading, since it covers only selected examples. A sense of scheme which is neither overly neat nor pedantic is, however, thoroughly characteristic of the *Arcadia*. Though I believe Sidney created characters in order to serve thematic ends, the resulting characters most often are not merely rhetorical counters. They may not be 'rounded' novelistically, but their purposive 'second Nature' is faithful enough to Nature itself to yield complex psychological insights that transcend and complicate the purely schematic factors in their conception.

 TONAL STRUCTURE

The *Arcadia* is a highly organized, in some ways even over-organized, piece of writing. Implicit in the kinds of structure discussed so far is the idea that a narrative or dramatic work may be put together on the basis of theme as well as plot. In fact, the further one moves away from classical unity of action, the more important thematic structure becomes. The notion of 'exploring a theme or idea' is especially relevant to Renaissance literature, but it functions significantly in later writers also, for example, in the range of parent- or guardian-child relationships in Dickens' *Great Expectations* or in the idea of charity in his *Bleak House*. Within Sidney's own period this kind of exploration occurs frequently enough to be considered one of the basic principles of Renaissance composition. To cite just a few instances: it pervades *The Faerie Queene* and provides the Third Book with its major source of unity; it gives rise to several parallel examples of filial obligation and revenge in *Hamlet*; it selects and arranges the characters in Fletcher's *Faithful Shepherdess*.[1]

But there is much to be said for more traditional time-linked ideas of structure as well. As readers we are interested not only in why an author included certain material and shaped it into certain patterns; we also want to understand the sequence of these elements within the work. In the complicated, many-layered actions presented in Renaissance literature, sequence of scenes can be more significant than movement of plot. The two kinds of structure are easily differentiated. Where the latter dominates, as in Sophoclean drama, one finds a rather linear progression from cause to effect; where theme dominates, as in Elizabethan practice, the work dallies with a situation, viewing it from several perspectives before moving on. Renaissance literature offers what William Empson has called a 'system of "construction by scenes" which allows of so sharp an effect [that it] clearly makes the scenes, the incidents, stand out as objects in themselves ...'[2] This kind of form, where 'any one incident may be interesting, but the interest of their connection must depend on a sort of play of judgment between varieties of the same situation,'[3] is potentially static, existing more in space than in time, though of course it retains a temporal dimension because it is revealed sequentially. A work like the *Arcadia*, by frequently treating individual scenes and situations as vehicles for rhetorical amplification – whether this takes the form of lament, dilemma, debate, oration, or sheer pageantry – emphasizes this inherent static quality, and thus encourages structural inquiry to centre on patterns of sequence rather than plot.

In the *New Arcadia* sequence of events is often governed by a principle that I call tonal structure. Except for applying it to large elements of composition rather than more conventionally to local texture, what I mean by 'tone' is a recognizable variant on usual definitions. 'Tone' here refers to that aspect of an author's attitude towards his material which concerns its relation to an accepted system of values. This definition stresses the interpretative bias operating in most considerations of tone, since in determining whether an author is playful, serious, ironic, sentimental, and so on, we mean to isolate the distance between a given statement and what we consider to be the author's own position. For the *Arcadia*, the values and standards of judgment are public, based on the same classical-Christian-chivalric conceptions of man discussed earlier.

Sidney often constructs his sequence of narrative by means of a three-part tonal scheme comprising what may roughly be called positive, negative, and humorous (parody) elements. If the first or positive presentation is comparable to the musical statement of a theme (though the significant element may literally be an 'action'), then the next two versions are variations (reinterpretations, alternative perspectives, or possibilities) of that theme. This three-part pattern can govern structural units of different types, ranging from a series of variations on a single event to the plan of an entire Book. The simplest use of the pattern occurs in the three personal combats immediately succeeding one another in Chapters 11 to 13 of Book III.

In the first of these contests Phalantus, 'the faire man of arms,' having learned all he could about warfare from Basilius' siege tactics, becomes 'wearie of wanting cause to be wearie' (I, 412) and sends a message to Amphialus challenging combat to 'any Gentleman in youre Towne, that eyther for the love of Honour, or honour of his Love ... will winne another, or loose himselfe, to be a prisoner at discretion of the conqueror' (I, 413). The balanced calm of the phrases together with the protestations of both contestants that they bear each other no malice, 'since true valure needes no other whetstone, then desire of honour,' prepare the reader for the pageantry to follow. The combat between Phalantus and Amphialus takes place in a context totally removed from the reality of war; their encounter is hard-fought, but no blood is spilled. Phalantus, though defeated, is the key figure in the episode. It is his description, or more accurately, that of his horse, which sets the tone:

a horse, milke white, but that upon his shoulder and withers, he was <freckned> with red staines, as when a few strawberies are scattered into a dish of creame ... Phalantus-his horse young, and feeling the youth of his master, stoode corvetting; which being wel governed by Phalantus, gave such a glittering grace, as when the Sunne <in a cleare day> shines upon a waving water. (I, 415-16)[4]

The entire combat is given over to pageantry; it begins with surface brilliance and grace, proceeds through a series of movements whose resemblance to art calls forth comment on the 'perfect agreement, in so mortall disagreement: like a musick, made of cunning discords' (I, 416), and ends with gestures of courtesy and friendship between the contestants. The display is perfect for its kind, and one is not surprised to find several examples of reciprocal rhetoric in the prose.[5]

The next combat presented, between Argalus and Amphialus, works with the same nobility, honour, and courtesy, but they are distorted and finally outweighed by the concomitant realities of blood and death. Even the values themselves are questioned, for the participants' motivation is labeled a 'tyrannie of Honour' (I, 422). Sidney gives maximum emphasis to our sense of wasted life by prefacing the battle with the scene of Argalus' and Parthenia's perfect happiness. Parthenia's plea that he not fight does more than foreshadow disaster; the combat can no longer be a study in decorous gesture once she has made the stakes significant. Phalantus belongs to the world of knight-errantry: he has no ties, no obligations other than to a code of honour and his own pleasures; he wanders onto the scene from nowhere and rides off afterwards 'to seeke his adventures other-where' (I, 418). Argalus, however, belongs to the world of another kind of hero, perhaps to the world of Homer's Troy, of Hector and Andromache. Parthenia is the index of this greater complexity. Ariosto's Isabella and Doralice, for example, in their grief at their lovers' deaths, do not have the power to move us that Parthenia has at this moment of leave-taking. It is a power based as Andromache's is on the widely experienced human feelings of warmth and obligation which marriage weaves enduringly into a social fabric, of life given fulfilment without further restless seeking. The key word is 'adventure'; not chivalric 'honour' but imminent social disaster would be the only counter reality we would accept as justification for Argalus' leaving.[6] The passage underlines the sheer waste of life implied by the chivalric ethic: 'Then was it time for you to follow these adventures, when you adventured no body but your selfe, and were no bodies but your owne. But now pardon me, that now, or never, I claime my owne; mine you are, and without me you can undertake no danger ...' (I, 421).[7]

Argalus' challenge retains the earlier formula of respect for his adversary's noble virtue, but it is not issued as Phalantus' was, 'eyther for the love of Honour, or honour of his Love'; instead, Amphialus should 'disdaine not to receive a mortall chalenge' (I, 422). Once the preliminary descriptions of Argalus' furniture, horse, and the first running are over, the two fall to 'the cruellest combate, that any present eye had seene' (I, 423). The wounds are immediate and serious:

Argalus gave a great wound to Amphialus-his disarmed face ... [who] gave a cruell wounde to the right arme of Argalus, the unfaythfull armour yeelding to the swoordes strong-guided sharpenesse. But though the blood accused the hurt of Argalus, yet woulde he in no action of his confesse it: but keeping himselfe in a lower warde, stoode watching with timely thrustes to repaire his losse; which quickly he did. For Amphialus (following his fawning fortune) laid on so thicke upon Argalus, that his shield had almost fallen peece-meale to the earth, when Argalus comming in with his right foote, and something stowping to come under his armour, thrust him into the belly daungerously ... (I, 424)

Within this context gestures of courtesy, like everything else humane, must be pathetically out of place. Yet Sidney insists on the gestures anyway – and on the bitter irony of their operation once the premise of sheer spectacle is removed. In his contest with Phalantus, such gestures could win Amphialus applause and the friendship of his opponent, but not now. Here, Amphialus sees Argalus covered with blood,

and waying the small hatefulnesse of their quarrell, with the worthinesse of the Knight, desired him to take pitie of himselfe. But Argalus, the more repining, the more he founde himselfe in disadvauntage, filling his veynes with spite in steade of blood ... taking his swoorde in both handes, he stroke such a notable blowe, that he cleft his shielde, armour, and arme almost to the bone.

But then Amphialus forgat all ceremonies, and with cruell blowes made more of his blood succeed the rest ... (I, 424-5)

Parthenia enters and pleads with them to stop; Amphialus, 'his noble hart melting with compassion at so passionate a sight,' begs Argalus not to continue, but the tyranny of honour is complete:

A notable example of the woonderfull effectes of Vertue, where the conquerour, sought for friendship of the conquered, and the conquered woulde not pardon the conquerour: both indeede being of that minde to love eche other for accepting, but not for giving mercie, and neyther affected to over-live dishonour: so that Argalus not so much striving with Amphialus (for if he had him in the like sorte, in like sort he would have dealt with him) as labouring against his owne power (which he chiefly despised) set himselfe forward, stretching his strength to the uttermost. (I, 426)

Having thus presented his readers with two versions of single combat – one satisfying by its brilliance and generous nobility, the other unsettling in its pointless waste of life – Sidney proceeds to a third version which is pure parody. The 'combate of cowardes,' as it is officially dubbed (I, 434), is fought between Dametas, Basilius' chief shepherd, and Clinias, an actor-become-political agent. Step by step each element of the previous contests is turned inside out: the disinterested courtesy expressed in the letters of challenge and acceptance, the tilting furniture and imprese, the first encounter on horseback, the strategies of swordsmanship, the code of fair play, the victor's modest proffer of friendship and mercy, and the loser's single-minded concern to maintain his honour.[8] Yet in all this ridicule the values themselves are not debased. They remain intact as standards by which to measure the actions of Dametas and Clinias, who are themselves the primary butt of attack. One is again reminded of Empson's discussion of the function of the double plot: 'A clear case of "foil" is given by the play of heroic swashbucklers which has a comic cowardly swashbuckler (Parolles), not at all to parody the heroes but to stop you from doing so.'[9] The mechanism in this sequence of the *Arcadia* is complicated by the need for the parody to perform so much: it offers comic relief in the strictest sense, but it must also channel the negative feelings caused by Argalus' death away from the chivalric or heroic code. Though this code may be questioned, clearly it cannot be subverted without undermining the whole of the *Arcadia*. The parody accomplishes its task by allowing us to laugh a little at the conventions (because they are capable of being made so ridiculous), while at the same time insinuating even more strongly that life without these values would be a rather shoddy affair.

Though the existence of the three-part scheme seems firmly established by this series of jousts, the evidence is open to doubt on the grounds that Sidney describes not three single combats but five. While it is true that Amphialus' contest against Parthenia (Chapter 16) and, even more, his contest against Musidorus (Chapter 18) continue earlier motifs and the pattern of increasing ferocity, much other narrative material intervenes before they occur, changing the rhythm sufficiently to isolate the first three combats as a distinct unit. There is, however, more substantial warrant for positing a three-part scheme, in that larger units of narratives are structured in this same way, and for these instances the sum of the parts does indeed equal the whole.

Considering the entire Third Book in the *New Arcadia* as a single complex narrative unit (or to use the term loosely, a single episode), the threefold structural scheme governs the overall pattern of the parts constituting one major action of this complex episode, namely, the progression of assaults made upon Pamela and Philoclea during their captivity. There are three stages to the sisters' trial. Cecropia herself manages the first two; and as noted earlier, they move from mere physical constraint and verbal persuasion to more drastic measures of physical and mental torture in which each is scourged and forced to watch the apparent death of the other. 'Positive' and 'negative' are more relative terms here than in the series of combats, and the third stage is likewise not blatant parody but comic treatment of the motifs of courtship and sexual violation present in the previous assaults. The comic attempts are made by Anaxius and his two brothers,[10] who have taken over Amphialus' rebellion after the latter's near-fatal wounding and Cecropia's death. The result of this substitution in antagonists follows from the way Anaxius' character contrasts with his predecessors': he has Cecropia's pride but not her subtlety and Amphialus' valour without his courtesy. The difference is apparent in two parallel love situations. Just prior to Amphialus' final combat, Cecropia advises her son that he will have Philoclea only if he takes her forcibly. (The advice is a bit of black humour in itself. Cecropia's argument is that all women want to be raped in order to satisfy their desires blamelessly.) The scene seems to contain something of the psychological projection suggested earlier, so that we feel the conflict may well occur between Amphialus' passions, which are strong enough to enlist his reason's aid in rationalizing their demands, and the better part of his nature that clings to a code of honour. Anaxius and his brothers, on the other hand, are clearly conceived in the comic tradition of the *miles gloriosus* (though with skill to back up their boasting), and when they 'fall in love' their thwarted advances occasion not self-conflict on their part, but laughter on ours.

One major scene in this comic section reaches its first high point with a reminiscence of the combat motifs. Pyrocles-Zelmane challenges Anaxius to fight, calling him 'the beggerliest dastardly villaine, that dishonoureth the earth with his steppes,' but Anaxius smiles to hear a woman speak this way, replying only, 'Evill should it become the terror of the world, to fight, much <worse> to skolde with thee' (I, 506). Once a comedy based on frustration, egotism, and male-female disguise has been established, the scene focuses these same elements on matters of love. Anaxius exits after receiving a stinging rebuff for his first advance to Pamela,

leaving his brothers with them: the elder of whom, Lycurgus, liked Philoclea, and Zoilus would nedes love Zelmane; or at lest, entertain themselves with making them beleve so. Lycurgus more braggard, and nere his brothers humor, began, with setting foorth their bloud, their deedes, how many they had despised, of excellent women; how much they were bound to them, that would seek that of them. In summe, in all his speeches, more like the bestower, then the desirer of felicitie. Whom it was an excellent pastime (to those that would delight in the play of vertue) to see, with what a wittie ignorance she would not understand: and how, acknowledging his perfections, she would make, that one of his perfections, not to be injurious to Ladies. But when he knew not how to replie, then would he fall to touching and toying, still vewing his graces in no glasse but self-liking. To which, Philocleas shamefastnes, and humblenes, were as strong resisters, as choller, and disdaine. For though she yeelded not, he thought she was to be overcome: and that thought a while stayed him from further violence. But Zelmane had eye to his behaviour, and set <it> in her memorie, upon the score of Revenge, while she her selfe was no lesse attempted by Zoilus; who lesse full of bragges, was forwardest in offering (indeed) dishonourable violence. (I, 507)

Just as we noted concerning the parody combat in another of Sidney's uses of the structural scheme, the humour of this last phase does not effectively challenge the values implicit in the princesses' trial. In fact the values are on surer ground when they are vehicles for parody than when Sidney begins to prepare for the more serious business of resolving his characters' predicament; at that stage the princesses are melodramatically said to have 'now come againe to the streight she most feared for them, either of death or dishonor' (I, 512). On the whole, however, Sidney successfully interlaces the course of the narrative with humour in this last section of the revision. One result is the addition of a new dimension to Pyrocles' character: Sidney speaks of 'the Pyroclean nature, fuller of gay braverie in the midst, then in the beginning of danger' (I, 518). Although the revision breaks off during this battle in the middle of a sentence, the Captivity episode obviously has just a few more pages to run;[11] Pyrocles will defeat Anaxius in combat, and Musidorus has already arrived at the gate with an army. The lighter tone of the section, then, looks backward by completing the first two parts of the scheme in its handling of the assault on the princesses' honour and also looks forward in preparation for victory.

Sidney's most ambitious use for his three-part scheme is the disposition of the narrative material of Book I. The central subject undergoing modulation is the nature of Love, but the tone of each section encompasses other concerns as well. The Book divides into three sections on the basis of the action, even apart from considerations of tone. The opening section runs from the separation of Pyrocles and Musidorus at sea to their reunion in Kalander's house,[12] with an extra chapter in which the princes exchange accounts of their activities and the wedding of Argalus and Parthenia is celebrated. The second section (Chapters 9-14) has a parallel separation and reunion, carrying us from Pyrocles' departure from Kalander's house through his discovery by Musidorus and his account of what has occurred in the interim.[13] The action of the final section has no definable shape, unless it be in the princes' movement from ritualistic to genuine acts of heroism in behalf of their mistresses. The courtship proper may be said to begin here, the first stage encompassing the ceremony of Phalantus' tourney and the more dangerous exploit in which the cousins slay a bear and lion that have attacked the princesses in their Arcadian retreat.

The two presentations of love in the opening section – the invocation of Strephon and Claius and the story of Argalus and Parthenia – clearly view love positively, as a ground for virtue if not as a virtue in itself. The Neoplatonic context of the invocation affirms love's power to ennoble the thoughts and deeds of the lover: 'hath not the onely love of her made us (being silly ignorant shepheards) raise up our thoughts above the ordinary levell of the worlde ...?' (I, 7) Implicit in the opening apostrophe to Remembrance and their yearning for Urania, and explicit in the steward's tale of Argalus and Parthenia,[14] is love's connection with the virtue of constancy. The connection is important, for constancy supplies a link with the political concerns that also receive prominent treatment in the section. Constancy is peculiarly tied to the idea of a right order of things, thus serving as a measure of conduct. Pamela has her mother's wisdom, greatness, and nobility, but 'knit with a more constant temper' (I, 20); Philanax criticizes Basilius' decision to retire from his royal duties on the grounds that there is no reason inconstantly to change his course now when his previous thirty years' reign has been so successful (I, 24). The normative handling of politics suggested here is carried out in Kalander's disapproval of Basilius' behaviour and in the contrasts between the nations of Arcadia and Laconia and between Basilius as ruler and Pyrocles as captain of the Helots. The right order of things shows also in Sidney's attention to friendship and hospitality in these chapters, and as we saw earlier, extends even to details describing the architecture and management of Kalander's great house.

The second section opens by using constancy to comment negatively on the nature of love. Musidorus broaches the problem of Pyrocles' strange behaviour with a friendly lecture:

A mind wel trayned and long exercised in vertue (my sweete and worthy cosin) doth not easily chaunge any course it once undertakes, but upon well grounded and well wayed causes. For being witnes to it selfe of his owne inward good, it findes nothing without it of so high a price, for which it should be altered. Even the very countenaunce and behaviour of such a man doth shew forth Images of the same constancy ... (I, 55)

Love is found wanting not only from the point of view of constancy, but also when judged by the practices and aims of princely education:

I have marked in you, I will not say an alteration, but a relenting truely, and a slacking of the maine career, you had so notably begon, and almost performed ... whereas you were wont in all places you came, to give your selfe vehemently to the knowledge of those thinges which might better your minde; to seeke the familiaritye of excellent men in learning and souldiery: and lastly, to put all these thinges in practise both by continuall wise proceedinge, and worthie enterprises, as occasion fell for them; you now leave all these things undone: you let your minde fal a sleepe: beside your countenaunce troubled (which surely comes not of vertue, for vertue like the cleare heaven, is without cloudes) and lastly you subject your selfe to solitarines, the slye enimie, that doth most separate man from well doing. (I, 55)

Towards the end of the section, when Musidorus discovers his cousin dressed as an Amazon, these ideas find further expression in a debate between Reason and Love, with Musidorus putting the case against Love very strongly:

And let us see, what power is the aucthor of all these troubles: forsooth love, love, a passion, and the basest and fruitlessest of all passions ... this bastarde Love (for in deede the name of Love is most unworthylie applied to so hatefull a humour) as it is engendered betwixt lust and idlenes; as the matter it workes upon is nothing, but a certaine base weakenes, which some gentle fooles call a gentle hart; as his adjoyned companions be unquietnes, longings, fond comforts, faint discomforts, hopes, jelousies, ungrounded rages, causlesse yeeldings; so is the hiest ende it aspires unto, a litle pleasure with much paine before, and great repentaunce after. (I, 78)

Musidorus 'proves' his evaluation of Love by citing Pyrocles' own conduct: 'thus much of his worthie effects in your selfe is to be seen, that (besides your breaking lawes of hospitality with Kalander and of friendship with me) it utterly subverts the course of nature, in making reason give place to sense, and man to woman' (I, 78). Pyrocles finally admits defeat and accepts the premises of his cousin's argument:

if you seeke the victory take it; and if ye liste, <the> triumph. Have you all the reason of the world, and with me remaine all the imperfections; yet such as I can no more lay from me, then the Crow can be perswaded by the Swanne to cast of all his black fethers ... I am sicke, and sicke to the death; I am a prisoner, neither is <there> any redresse, but by her to whom I am slave. (I, 82)

Pyrocles is by no means the section's only example of Love's power to overthrow the right order of things. In the course of searching for his cousin, Musidorus comes upon Queen Helen, who tells him the story of her love for Amphialus. In addition to causing the rift in the friendship between Philoxenus and Amphialus and the dire consequences arising from it, Helen's love results in her shirking the responsibilities of sovereignty and in a reversal of the normal, that is, chivalric, male-female roles: 'For this cause have I left my country, putting in hazard how my people wil in time deale by me, adventuring what perils and dishonors might ensue, only to folow him, who proclaimeth hate against me, and to bring my neck unto him, if that may redeem my trespas and assuage his fury' (I, 72).[15]

Love's negative power displays an amusing aspect as well, for even though Pyrocles seriously despairs of the outcome, he can see the essential ludicrousness of being loved by both the King and Queen of Arcadia, while he himself loves their daughter. The situation contributes bountifully to the sense of disordered values prevalent in the section. Gynecia's and Basilius' love must overcome all kinds of normative barriers: the sanctity of marriage, for Basilius the dictates of common sense and old age, for Gynecia a previous habit of virtue and even the force of maternal love which she comes to deny through jealousy of her daughter.[16]

This jealousy, more strongly expressed in Book II, is first revealed here among other, similar disorders; Gynecia's jealousy echoes the more powerful statement of the theme contained slightly earlier in Philoxenus' behaviour towards Amphialus. The conflict between these friends also contributes to the section's exploration of another violent passion – anger. While traditionally it could be interpreted positively – as Musidorus says, it has 'power towards some good by the direction of right Reason' (I, 78) – the examples of anger on these pages are all misguided and unfortunate. Two examples from the incident framing Helen's story may indicate Sidney's concentrated handling of these ideas. Musidorus (dressed in Amphialus' discarded armour) and Kalander's son Clitophon are accosted by Helen's servants, and, indignant at the 'causeless' demand that they surrender, 'left none of them either living, or able to make his life serve to others hurt' (I, 64). Clitophon quite by accident learns that the servants had only desired to bring the man they thought to be Amphialus to their mistress and belatedly tries to undo the damage, 'framing frendly constructions of this rashly undertaken enmitie' (I, 72). But at this exact moment, 'in comes another (till that time unseene) all armed, with his bever downe, who first looking round about upon the companie, as soone as he spied Palladius [Musidorus], he drew his sword, and making no other prologue, let flie at him.' Violence is averted this time by the obvious expedient of finding out the reason for the attack, whereupon Ismenus (Amphialus' page) accepts Musidorus' acknowledgement of error for having taken the armour, and in turn desires Musidorus to 'pardon his follie, caused by extreme griefe, which easilie might bring foorth anger' (I, 73).[17] Three such examples in the course of nine pages, especially since one of them is the memorable story of Amphialus' killing of his best friend and foster father, inescapably suggest to the reader that Sidney is deliberately 'exploring' the idea of anger and give warrant for our discovery of other related thematic material in the section.

The unit from Chapters 9 through 14 thus concentrates mainly on negative aspects of the passions, but it is far from tonally monolithic. The forces of reason and virtue are strongly present in the section as well, notably through the debates and treatment of education and friendship motifs. The chapters in fact seem generally to broaden the emotional range of the work so that it includes both the humour of Pyrocles' meeting with Dametas and a hint of tragedy in Amphialus' responsibility for the deaths of Philoxenus and Timotheus.

The tonally complex Basilius-Gynecia-Zelmane-Philoclea love situation is introduced in these pages as well. The *New Arcadia*'s version is a compound of old and new material, with some of the added material being interesting both for the revisions in narrative technique and for the employment of the tonal sequence to suggest moral and psychological complexity. In the *Old Arcadia*, the Narrator first indicates Gynecia's passion towards the end of Book I, after Pyrocles has slain the lion. While promising his audience a fuller account when he can find the time, the Narrator manages in brief compass to convey a complex spectrum of responses. His tone is mostly one of moral disapproval – Gynecia is 'carried away with the violence of an inward evil' (*OA* 48), love has 'reduced her whole mind to an extreme and unfortunate slavery' – but there is room also for a gentle leer or two and a slight suggestion of pity. The gist of his account however, seems to be the more neutral assessment that her passion represents 'a perfect mark of the triumph of love' (*OA* 48) and 'a perfect demonstration of [Love's] unresistible force' (*OA* 49). Moreover, our delight at the dominantly humorous scene that occasions the stern remarks in effect counters their impact.

In the *New Arcadia* there is time to give all this greater resonance. Rather than waiting for the lion-killing scene where it must hold up the action, Gynecia's passion is revealed to Musidorus by Pyrocles, who considers it the capstone of his adventures since he vanished from Kalander's house. Pyrocles' sense of the potentially destructive aspects of her passion is consonant with the negative tonal section in which the account actually occurs; his awareness of a comic dimension in the situation helps modulate to the next section. As the final incident of section two, however, the description is weighted in the direction of its negative elements. We hear of destruction, strong-working thoughts, desperate affection, violence, even, in the next paragraph, 'tragedy.' Here is Pyrocles' summarizing picture:

Truely it were a notable dumb shew of Cupids kingdome, to see my eyes (languishing with over-vehement longing) direct themselves to Philoclea: and Basilius as busie about me as a

Bee, and indeed as cumbersome; making such <vehement> suits to me, who nether could if I would; nor would if I could, helpe him: while the terrible witte of Gynecia, carried with the beere [birr] of violent love, runnes thorow us all. (I, 94)

One page later, at the opening of section three, the *New Arcadia*'s transparent Narrator provides a similar picture of this lovers' 'quadrangle,' but transposed fully into comedy:

Zelmane returned to the Lodge, where (inflamed by Philoclea, watched by Gynecia, and tired by Basilius) she was like a horse, desirous to runne, and miserablie spurred, but so short rainde, as he cannot stirre forward: Zelmane sought occasion to speake with Philoclea; Basilius with Zelmane; and Gynecia hindered them all. If Philoclea hapned to sigh (and sigh she did often) as if that sigh were to be wayted on, Zelmane sighed also; whereto Basilius and Gynecia soone made up foure parts of sorow. (I, 95-6)

The *Arcadia*, as shown in the previous chapter, goes beyond these two perspectives on the 'meaning' of Gynecia's passion; Book II opens with a still more terrible one – an inside view of Gynecia's tormented soul. The humour of the final section does not therefore cancel out the seriousness of the moral disorder suggested by the earlier perspective. The reader's understanding is a sum of these individual, though mutually qualified, parts.

In general, it is with the theme of Love that the tonal modulations of Book I are most readily perceived. The scheme becomes clear if one studies the central 'episode' of each section; significantly, all three have been added in the revision. The first eight chapters are almost completely new material, but both its relation to the theme of Love and a fairly strict understanding of the term 'episode' make the Argalus and Parthenia story (with its treatment of constancy and of virtuous and eventually rewarded love) the key to the section. The second group of chapters contains only one added episode, Helen's tale of Amphialus, and we have just seen how fully its concerns mirror the passionate confusion of values prevailing in the section. The corresponding incident in the final chapters concerns Phalantus and Artesia. As with Argalus and Parthenia, the inception of their love is narrated for us and we are allowed to see the end ourselves. The point of the incident is, of course, humorous. When Phalantus is finally defeated after many successful defences of Artesia's beauty, she

telling him she never lookt for other, bad him seeke some other mistresse. He excusing himselfe, and turning over the fault to Fortune, Then let that be your ill Fortune too (saide she) that you have lost me.

Nay truely Madame (saide Phalantus) it shall not be so: for I thinke the losse of such a Mistresse will proove a great gaine: and so concluded; to the sporte of Basilius, to see young folkes love, that came in maskt with so great pompe, go out with so little constancie. (I, 111)

The humour of their story stems largely from its parodying the motifs previously set forth in Book I. It is a light-hearted example of inconstancy and frivolity to contrast with the constancy of Argalus and the passionate fervour of all the courtly lovers. Artesia is 'as fit to paie him in his owne monie as mighte be,' for she is the disdainful mistress of the courtly tradition, impressed into service as the parody-heroine. One notes especially the inversion of the education motif, operating even in details of Artesia's being reared in the house of a family friend (I, 98).

Unlike the humorous inversions of the love and education themes in this episode, the handling of anger and jealousy is largely without an explicitly didactic dimension. The comic agents for these explorations are Pyrocles and Musidorus, which guarantees dilution of whatever corrosive power the humour may possess. Anger receives especially flamboyant treatment in the tourney scene, where Sidney creates a miniature version of the brawl in Ariosto that results from Discord's entry into the Moorish camp (OF XXVII.40ff). Pyrocles, disguised in old and rusty armour that 'might better seeme a monument of his graundfathe[r]s courage,' challenges Phalantus to combat at almost the same moment an unknown Black Knight (Musidorus) also strikes, and breaks, the shield. Whereupon Pyrocles, 'angrie with that ... insolent injurie to himselfe,' forgets his purpose to enter the tournament and begins a sword fight in which all three participate.

The jealousy motif appears in the tournament sequence also; we are asked to smile at Pyrocles' frustration because he must either desire some rival to gain the honour of defeating Phalantus or else see Philoclea's picture placed among the conquered beauties in Artesia's triumph. The same motif is added as an amusing touch to the scene in which Musidorus explains to his cousin why he is dressed like a shepherd. At first Musidorus is the butt of the comedy for having fallen victim to the Love that he and Reason had berated, but the New Arcadia has Pyrocles' playfulness change to impatient fear that Philoclea is the one who has bewitched his cousin, since it is obvious to him as a lover that this is the inevitable effect of her beauty.[18]

Although the tone of the final section of Book I is defined primarily by the new stories concerning Phalantus, Artesia, and the tourney, the Old Arcadia itself provided much comic material to be enhanced either with further wit or sharper thematic relevance. The account of Dametas' cowardly behaviour during the bear's attack, already comic, is given greater point by being narrated in the revision by Pamela. For she, with considerable sense of the injustice being done her, notes that this Dametas is the 'governour' to whom she is 'bound' for her education (I, 123), thus tying it to the educational and political themes developed earlier. This section of the Old Arcadia was potentially rich in comic love material as well, since it provided the basic situations of Musidorus and the Eros motif and of Pyrocles' love entanglement. Indeed, this entanglement is one comic aspect of the attack by wild animals not revised away in the interest of greater heroism. In the *Old Arcadia* the incident is almost a mockery of pastoral-romance convention. The princes' single reaction to the beasts' approach is their delight in the amorous possibilities arising from the princesses' fear. Pyrocles does not disengage himself from Philoclea's embrace until the lion is almost upon them; he acts only after 'seeing how greedily the lion went after the prey she [Cleophila] herself so much desired' (*OA* 47).[19] The *New Arcadia* omits all this dalliance, but relents its sternness after the lion has been slain, keeping the *Old Arcadia*'s charming picture of Philoclea's 'light apparell being carried up with the winde, that much of those beauties she would at another time have willingly hidden, was present<ed> to the sight of the twise wounded Zelmane. Which made Zelmane not folow her over hastily, lest she should too soone deprive her selfe of that pleasure ...' (I, 120). The closing lines of the incident (like the opening lines of the section quoted on page 74) underscore the visual aspect of the humour surrounding Pyrocles' love entanglement, which may partially account for its lack of prurience, since we are continually asked to respond by visualizing a scene and not by probing motives or by bringing other 'less noble' senses into play. We are asked to view

a new sight, Fortune had prepared to those woods, to see these great personages thus runne one after the other: each carried forward with an inward violence: Philoclea with such feare, that she thought she was still in the Lions mouth: Zelmane with an eager and impatient delight, Gynecia with wings of Love, flying <she> neither knew, nor cared to know whether. (I, 120)[20]

While it is easy to demonstrate that Sidney had frequent recourse to a three-part tonal structure comprising positive, negative, and humorous perspectives in writing the *Arcadia*, it is difficult to say whether the structure in itself has meaning. If it were a purely formal element, like the octave-sestet arrangement of the Petrarchan sonnet, then the scheme would have no definable meaning. But it is not purely formal; to some degree it prescribes both content and an attitude towards that content. The question would then seem to be not whether the scheme has meaning, but what kind of meaning can it bear?

One possibility is that the scheme, with its insistence on varying perspectives and interpretations of situations and subjects, is an expression of Sidney's rhetoricism. We have discussed the rhetoricist tenet that allows alternative arguments to be constructed to account for a given action or idea, and that, in the writing of history, calls forth a plurality of arguments such as occur in the Melian dialogue of Thucydides. It is also available in the rhetorical figure *distinctio* or *paradia-*

stole, by which the same deed can be interpreted in opposing ways, for example, as either bravery or recklessness, either illiberality or diligence in family affairs.[21] It seems to be this kind of insight or predilection that Sidney has here transformed into a structural pattern that emphasizes multiplicity.

In addition to having rhetoricist ramifications, the tonal scheme also seems to echo Sidney's stylistic tendency to place ideas in maximum contrast to each other before shifting perspective to a point where the differences no longer matter. But the vanishing distinction seems valid mainly for situations where both terms are capable of 'positive' interpretation, as in the antithesis between art and nature, beauty and use, virtue and pleasure. Dealing with terms that are morally absolute complicates the issue. To say that there is no boundary between good and evil or that the boundary is fluid or irrelevant would destroy the integrity of the *Arcadia*'s moral vision.

Even in parody Sidney upholds the central values of his work. At only one point does it seem that the value structure is in jeopardy – during the combat between Argalus and Amphialus – yet I doubt if any reader has felt on a total reading of the *Arcadia* that this undeniably shattering incident finally undermines his allegiance to a code of honour and courtesy. Just because the value structure is so solid, Sidney can allow himself to probe its limitations and costs.[22] In all three phases of the tonal scheme, then, the reader is constantly aware of the values themselves. The negative and parody treatments depend on positive exposition for their meaning and do not supersede or undermine it to a point where Sidney's own evaluation of his material can be misunderstood.

In spite of these crucial differences, however, the particular movement from positive to negative to parody may well have some connection with Sidney's tendency to see the world in terms of antithetical alternatives, but not to be satisfied with the disjunction once it has been established. We have once more come upon the tension in Sidney's mind between analytical perceptions, here his complex ethical awareness, and the need for synthesis, for some assertion of harmony. Parody or humour seems to be Sidney's attempt to fulfil both these needs within a narrative frame. Parody provides a kind of transcendence because it demands that the reader hold several points of view simultaneously, yet being a form of satire it also requires that we exercise judgment in discerning the relative value of each. If we think of synthesis and analysis as alternatives on a balance scale, then stylistically in the *Arcadia* the balance tips towards synthesis, but 'tonally' towards analysis.

The third section, with its lighter perspectives (points of view from which it is possible to laugh), while not resolving anything itself, is necessary to the *Arcadia*'s mode, which in the 'mixed' Renaissance way not only combines heroic and pastoral but also is tragicomedy. The tragicomic vision is quite congenial to Renaissance writers because its major elements, paradox and wonder, are the ends they strove for both in poetry and in prose. Arthur C. Kirsch suggests that the basis of tragicomedy is the pattern of the *felix culpa*, in which the happy ending occurs not, as we might expect, in spite of the disasters which threaten the action, but actually because of them, since the happiness is increased through being tried by adversity.[23] This sort of pattern fits the *plot* of the *Arcadia* (both *Old* and *New*) very well, and the elements it calls for seem roughly analogous to those of the tonal structure. Even the lack of true resolution offered in the humour of the third section corresponds to the unsatisfying quality of most tragicomic endings. The pattern of expected comedy countered by the threat of tragedy and then resolved into comedy by literal or figurative legerdemain has its parallels in Sidney: positive views of achieved or achievable virtue are countered by images of virtue diverted into destructive channels and then the 'danger' is made to appear ludicrous.[24] Thus, while the tonal structure that organizes the sequence of much of the work is not the same as its plot structure, the emotional graph which the one embodies is consonant with the tragicomic vision shaping the other.

NARRATIVE IMPLICATIONS

The three-part scheme for separating out certain attitudes and dealing with them sequentially is a narrative device, though it might also apply to a drama conceived schematically or hierarchically, such as the morality play or plays that contain multiple plots embracing several social strata. In such cases complexity results from the interactions of discrete parts which individually may be simple, unitary views of a given theme or situation. Thus, the *Arcadia*'s understanding of love is a synthesis of what is experienced by all relevant characters in the work, not just by the heroes or individual symbolic figures like Strephon and Claius. On this level, the narrative requirement of movement in time is met by isolating single aspects of what is essentially a complex conception and arranging them so that they are read in sequence. Thus, 'movement' is in a sense only apparent, especially if understood to mean progression through causally linked elements of a plot. Or perhaps one might better say that linear movement in time is transformed into circular movement, as one would walk around a plastic form to see it whole.

At least in part, this kind of narrative projection is a function of the complexity of the character who undergoes a given experience. A 'flat' character having a relatively defined set of responses must be supplemented by others who will represent alternative or complementary positions; a highly complex character (like Hamlet) will require simpler figures who will isolate important alternatives. Either way, the problem can be solved in narrative or drama by devising parallel situations and characters. But for lyrics having a single speaker, complexity is achieved in other ways. It has often been noticed that the Reason-Passion theme connected with the two princes in the *Arcadia* is also central to the *Astrophel and Stella*; the major difference between the two treatments may be defined in the terms I have been using as a difference in tone. The narrative *Arcadia* moves through a series of discrete attitudes, leaving the synthesis to be made by the reader outside the work (his awareness is greater than any individual character's). The lyric cycle fuses all three tonal attitudes into the single personality of Astrophel, often into the brief space of fourteen lines. Synthesis is not left for the reader. Astrophel himself sees the positive and negative aspects of his behaviour, and the third element, humour, derives from this awareness. It is frequently self-irony, based on the relation of the tonal elements themselves, that is, on Astrophel's wilful distortion of positive values to make them support the negative case:

> The wisest scholler of the wight most wise
> By Phoebus' doome, with sugred sentence sayes,
> That Vertue, if it once met with our eyes,
> Strange flames of Love it in our soules would raise;
>   But for that man with paine this truth descries,
> While he each thing in sense's ballance wayes,
> And so nor will, nor can, behold those skies
> Which inward sunne to Heroicke minde displaies,
>   Vertue of late, with vertuous care to ster
> Love of her selfe, takes Stella's shape, that she
> To mortall eyes might sweetly shine in her.
> It is most true, for since I her did see,
>   Vertue's great beautie in that face I prove,
>   And find th'effect, for I do burne in love.[25]

It is noteworthy that a characteristic structure of these sonnets, in which the wit or passion of the final lines merely undercuts the affirmations of the rest of the poem without thereby denying them, is related to the tonal structure we have been defining. Moreover, as in the humorous section of the tonal scheme, one may question the efficacy of the positive values, but not their rightness:

> With what sharpe checkes I in my selfe am shent,
>   When into Reason's audite I do go:
>   And by just counts my selfe a banckrout know
> Of all those goods, which heav'n to me hath lent:
> Unable quite to pay even Nature's rent,

Which unto it by birthright I do ow:
And which is worse, no good excuse can show,
But that my wealth I have most idly spent.
My youth doth waste, my knowledge brings forth toyes,
My wit doth strive those passions to defend,
Which for reward spoile it with vaine annoyes.
I see my course to lose my selfe doth bend:
I see and yet no greater sorow take,
Then that I lose no more for Stella's sake.[26]

Though these poems might be said to express the feelings of Pyrocles and Musidorus, they could never be mistaken for the poems the two princes actually write. The reason lies in the fundamental attitude towards love displayed by the royal poetry of the *Arcadia*,[27] which, perhaps surprisingly, is less concerned with conflict and self-division than the prose narrative is. The princes' poems, as R.L. Montgomery has noted, are 'predominantly ceremonial in tone,' which he takes to be the result of the lover's quasi-religious attitude towards the ideal embodied in his beloved.[28] They are ceremonial also because they celebrate rather than examine their subject; their 'religious' feeling comes from an intense concentration on a single point of view that excludes even the hint that other attitudes may be possible. Only rarely do the princes share Astrophel's playfulness and self-irony. Pyrocles and Musidorus have no need to protest the sincerity of their verse because they have never heard of convention. Astrophel continually sees himself acting one role or another; the princes, except for their initial disguises, merely act. The prime purpose of an Arcadian or romance setting in this respect lies in its offering a place where convention *is* reality.

The *New Arcadia*'s revisions in narrative technique indicate that Sidney saw the danger of introducing a free-floating 'awareness' into his kind of romance universe. In the *Old Arcadia*, the Narrator was an independent voice outside the events of the story, outside certainly in time, and occasionally also in temperament.[29] This is a decidedly Ariostan feature of the original version; yet even in the *Old Arcadia* with its flawed heroes Sidney does not share the degree of irony in Ariosto's attitude towards love and honour. The commenting Narrator who moves freely in and out of the action, manipulating characters and chatting with his readers, is an ideal instrument for achieving Ariosto's masterful irony, but to employ the device is to invite its results. One might speculate that had Sidney allowed himself to move in and out of his story to comment upon it, he would have been forced by his own awareness of the disparity between a sophisticated point of view and Arcadian 'reality' to judge and laugh as Ariosto does. In the *New Arcadia*, which takes the integration of love and heroism much more seriously than did the *Old Arcadia*, the Narrator therefore is no longer an independent voice. Whenever possible, the characters relate their own experiences. When the Narrator does speak he has no personality outside the material or time of the story; he stands in no special relation to either actors or readers and has no power of manipulation. He has become a transparent medium.[30]

This has always seemed to critics a gain in narrative control, probably because it approximates more closely our post-Jamesian biases about fiction. It is possible to see instead that Sidney has sacrificed a special kind of compression and complexity in order to achieve the greater breadth and perspective desired by his new structure. For the Narrator of the *Old Arcadia* had a predominantly tonal function: it was he who introduced a witty or ironic perspective, who 'aerated' the linear development of a plot that unfolded largely without episodic amplification. The presence of the pastoral eclogues in the *Old Arcadia* shows that Sidney felt the need for some kind of commentary playing against the actions of his royal characters. The eclogues (presenting a rather more schematized and simplified view of some of the major themes) solve the need by means of sequence, by coming after the prose narrative; the Narrator offers a more sophisticated and complex response (often compounded of playfulness, irony, and judgment) as it were 'simultaneously.' The epically-conceived *New Arcadia* manages to subsume the Narrator's chief tonal functions in its elaborate structures, thereby allowing Sidney to dispense with his potentially dangerous free-floating awareness.

The ceremonial aspect of the narrative mode, that is, the disentanglement of a complex simultaneous perception into a sequence of unitary views, finds an analogue in one of Sidney's methods of structuring character relationships. The analogy is based on a schematic understanding of the nature and function of a fictional, especially an epic-romance, universe. A fundamental requirement of any serious fictional work is for the reader to be able to recognize that the world it represents, in however stylized or fantastic a manner, is a version of the world he lives in. Moreover, for the fictional universe to be accepted as other than trivial escape, it must encompass on some level what the reader knows of evil and misfortune. Nor can these happen only to wicked characters, for our experience cannot endorse a world governed totally by poetic justice.[31] This imposes a certain difficulty on a writer of romance. Whereas tragedy, for example, often owes its power to the hero's confrontation with an apparently inescapable malevolence, the heroes of romance, by corresponding rules of genre, are immune to whatever genuinely malignant forces operate in their universe. Even if we set up the problem as a matter of external forces to accord better with the ways of romance, the observation holds true: though confronted with storms and shipwrecks, imprisonment and risk of death in battle, the romance hero's ultimate victory or escape is never seriously in doubt. To satisfy the reader's expectations, therefore, to supply the needed depth of vision, we often find subsidiary 'heroes' – good men like Argalus and Amphialus – to whom misfortune can and does happen. In the *Epic of Gilgamesh* there is a striking example of a surrogate function in the fate of Enkidu, the hero's best friend: 'All the gods, Anu, Enlil, Ea, and Shamash sat in council and Anu said to Enlil, "Because they have killed the Bull of Heaven and killed Humbaba, one of the two must die; let it be the one [Gilgamesh] who stripped the mountains of cedar." But Enlil said, "Enkidu shall die, Gilgamesh shall not die."'[32]

The mechanism goes one step further, I think: a subsidiary hero who is *like* the primary hero becomes identified with, that is, in some way identical to, the primary hero himself. Cedric Whitman suggests, for example, that the meaning of Patroclus' death for Achilles lies in his being in some sense Achilles' double.[33] The process would be like the dream-work technique that Freud calls displacement, whereby a dreamer's own thoughts and shortcomings are attributed to other figures.[34] In narrative literature this identification occurs in response to a double need. It somehow neutralizes the reader's estrangement from the hero on account of his 'unfair' good fortune, and it makes events not merely object lessons for the hero but part of his own experience, enabling him to reach his final goal. Thus, in an epic-romance that is basically a *paedeia* or education of the prince, these intimations that the hero has undergone suffering and purification form a ritualistic substructure justifying his ultimate claim of achievement.

The appearance in older literatures of devices similar to dream mechanisms such as occur in Freud's discussion of splitting techniques and of multiple appearances of the ego,[35] or in Jung's anima and shadow archetypes,[36] suggests that these kinds of meaning are psychologically available to an author and his readers in any era even without their conscious acknowledgement. They are in a sense the way the mind works. The possibility of projecting parts of personality as independent units seems also to underlie the mechanisms involved in allegory, analogy, personification, and synecdoche. Note how easily Plato slips from the spirited part of the soul to the auxiliary class in the state to the timocratic man, or how allegorical interpretations of a figure like Hercules shift so that sometimes he apparently represents the whole soul (or even man) and sometimes a single faculty (Reason). For the purposes of the surrogate hero, what remains imperative is that somehow the reader perceives the original unity which has thus been broken apart. Kenneth Burke emphasizes this aspect of identity in discussing the dialectic of another surrogate figure, the scapegoat: 'For one must remember that a scapegoat cannot be "curative" except insofar as it represents the iniquities of those who would be cured by attacking it. In representing *their* iniquities, it performs the role of vicarious atonement ...'[37]

The relationship of Amphialus to the two princes (especially to Pyrocles) can be understood in terms of the surrogate's tendency to function as a scapegoat for the primary hero. The chief encouragement for associating Amphialus and the princes derives from the many similarities in their background, notably in the education and friendship material in the second section of Book I, although the reader has earlier been alerted for comparisons by the steward who champions Argalus' heroism, 'how soever now of late the fame flies of the two princes of Thessalia and Macedon, and hath long done of our noble prince Amphialus: who in deede, in our partes is onely accounted likely to match him ...' (I, 31)[38] Like the two princes, who were brought up in Thessalia by Musidorus' mother, Amphialus and Philoxenus are educated together under the tutelage of a single parent, Philoxenus' father, because of ties between their families.[39] Then, their friendship cemented by education, both sets of young men go out into the world seeking occasions to exercise their valour. Helen's account sounds like a résumé of the princes' history to be given in Book II, except that Pyrocles and Musidorus are more equally matched:

An endless thing it were for me to tell, how many many adventures (terrible to be spoken of) he atchieved: what monsters, what Giants, what conquest<s> of countries: sometimes using policy, some times force, but alwaies vertue, well followed, and but followed by Philoxenus: betweene whom, and him, so fast a friendship by education was knit, that at last Philoxenus having no greater matter to employ his friendship in, then to winne me, therein desired, and had his uttermost furtheraunce ... (I, 68)

Amphialus' service to his friend in wooing Helen is echoed in Musidorus' offer to do the same for Pyrocles (I, 94–5). Comparison is further encouraged when Musidorus dons Amphialus' discarded armour and we are told that 'It was something too great, but yet served well enough' (I, 64).[40]

Though his education and prowess parallel theirs, Amphialus seems to be what the princes might have become had they not been darlings of the gods; it is as though their potential weaknesses have been externalized and projected onto this other person. The dangers that merely threaten to materialize for them are the realities he must constantly deal with. His love for Philoclea is as passionately sincere as Pyrocles', but since it cannot be requited, the very absoluteness of the passion demanded by the chivalric code is assurance of disaster. It is in Amphialus, not ultimately in Pyrocles or Musidorus, that the Reason-Love controversy of Book I is substantiated, for his passion does in fact subvert his virtue. Pyrocles and Musidorus are potential dangers to the Arcadian state because they plan to run away with the heirs to the throne; Amphialus actually leads a rebellion which begins by abduction of the princesses.[41]

As with several other important additions to the *New Arcadia*, Amphialus' love for Philoclea seems conceived as the amplification of a point developed in the trial scene of the *Old Arcadia*. Amphialus' plea in his letter to Argalus, that 'Love ...

justifieth the unjustice you lay unto me' (I, 422), echoes the princes' attempt at the trial to defend their actions on the grounds of the violence of their love. The similarity in the two claims is more than a thematic bond. The problem of the split between sympathy and judgment suggestively worked out in the trial scene is again explored (in the chronology of the *New Arcadia*, 'prepared for') with Amphialus in the Captivity episode. We know that Amphialus is wrong both in his rebellion and in his pursuit of Philoclea, but we are meant to recognize also that the romance données of the work give validity to his motive and protestations as a lover. We have already, in the conspiracy of reader and hero that dominates the genre, condoned the disguises and trickery of the princes. We are invited here, by our ambivalently sympathetic response to Amphialus, to sort out the necessary evaluations and discharge our negative judgments where the fault most warrants them. We both recognize the link between Amphialus and the princes and distinguish between their cases. At the trial scene, then, if it were still the end of the *New Arcadia*, this earlier exercise in ambivalence on the reader's part might operate first to make us more aware of the split between our desires and absolute justice, and second to be more firmly (though subliminally) sympathetic to the princes. Our need that such behaviour be punished having been satisfied by the fate of Amphialus, we are free to hope that the princes will be exonerated.

The sure sign of Amphialus' being 'marked' is something we may call his ill luck, those tricks of fortune where we feel that the results of his actions are greater and more destructive than his intentions or apparent deserts. Quite the opposite is true for the princes. Even at Pyrocles' least rational moments, some force contrary to his conscious will prevents him from inflicting irreparable harm; one recalls Zelmane's jealous rage at finding a rival who begs to keep Philoclea's glove as a favour and then refuses to fight the Amazon who has saved his lady's life (a rival who will presently be revealed as Amphialus):

But Zelmane harkening to no more wordes, began with such wittie furie to pursue him with blowes and thrusts, that Nature and Vertue commanded the Gentleman to looke to his safetie. Yet stil courtesie, that seemed incorporate in his hart, would not be perswaded by daunger to offer any offence ... And so with play did he a good while fight against the fight of Zelmane, who (more spited with the curtesie, that one that did nothing should be able to resist her) burned away with choller any motions, which might grow out of her owne sweet disposition, determining to kill him if he fought no better ... But at length he found, that both in publike and private respectes, who standes onely upon defence, stands upon no defence; For Zelmane seeming to strike at his head, and he going to warde it, withall stept backe as he was accustomed, she stopt her blow in the aire, and suddenly turning the point, ranne full at his breast; so as he was driven with the pommell of his sworde (having no other weapon of defence) to beate it downe: but the thrust was so strong, that he could not

so wholy beate it awaie, but that it met with his thigh, thorow which it ranne. But Zelmane retiring her sworde, and seeing his bloud, victorious anger was conquered by the
before-conquered pittie; and hartily sorie, and even ashamed with her selfe she was, considering how little he had done, who well she found could have done more. (I, 223–4)

Compare this on the other hand with Amphialus' unintentional murder of Philoxenus and in effect of Timotheus also, or most strikingly, with the way his
conscious decision to be merciful is twisted by chance into a yet more horrible
slaughter. This last incident occurs in the opening battle between the forces of
Basilius and Amphialus; the victim, Agenor, is singled out for special attention to
make his death more moving:[42]

Among whom there was a young man, youngest brother to Philanax, whose face as yet did
not bewray his sex, with so much as shew of haire; of a minde having no limits of hope, nor
knowing why to feare; full of jollitie in conversation, and lately growne a Lover. His name
was Agenor, of all that armie the most beautifull: who having ridden in sportful conversation among the foremost, all armed saving that his beaver was up, to have his breath in
more freedome, seeing Amphialus come a pretty way before his company, neither staying
the commaundement of the captaine, nor recking whether his face were armed, or no, set
spurs to his horse, and with youthful bravery casting his staffe about his head, put it then in
his rest, as carefull of comely carying it, as if the marke had ben but a ring, and the lookers
on Ladies. But Amphialus launce was already come to the last of his descending line, and
began to make the full point of death against the head of this young Gentleman, when
Amphialus perceyving his youth and beautie, Compassion so rebated the edge of Choller,
that he spared that faire nakednesse, and let his staffe fall to Agenors vamplat: so as both
with brave breaking should hurtleslie have perfourmed that match, but that the pittilesse
launce of Amphialus (angry with being broken) with an unlucky counterbuffe full of
unsparing splinters, lighted upon that face farre fitter for the combats of Venus; geving not
onely a suddaine, but a fowle death, leaving scarsely any tokens of his former beautie ... (I,
386–7)

One cannot view the mechanism so baldly without again feeling the 'unfairness' of the primary heroes' good luck which initially created the need for a
surrogate hero. But by becoming a scapegoat – someone 'more sinned against than
sinning' – by enabling them to purify themselves vicariously through his suffering
(though a lightning rod metaphor would be more accurate: he stands beside them,
all three equally impressive in stature, but it is he who attracts the wrath of the
gods), Amphialus paradoxically takes his revenge, albeit a literary one. He is
thereby more complex, more interesting than the heroes to whom he is subordinated; he may enable them to live triumphant in a romance universe, but he does

so by evoking a tragic universe for himself. Or at least he almost does. There is something just a bit too frigidly oratorical, too abased and paralyzed about his behaviour in love for him to achieve genuine tragic stature. These factors limit response, 'flatten' character. But many elements of tragedy are present: the sense of incomprehensible forces larger than himself, of wasted potential greatness, the avoidance of neat antitheses between responsibility and fate, good and evil.[43]

It is interesting that Amphialus is new to the revision, a dominant figure in the last book that Sidney rewrote. It tempts one to think that Sidney realized that he had entered into another, perhaps richer world. The stratagems and deceits of the old Third Book must have looked thinner, even anticlimactic in comparison. Yet they are necessary to the oracle that provides the frame of the main plot. John Danby is convincing on the meaning of the romance universe and its possibility for embracing the widest range of experience, but as one can see Shakespeare settling for romance only after he has written the tragedies, so one may guess that having stumbled upon tragedy in the course of something else, the younger Sidney might have felt the need to explore the forces he had set loose. I would thus disagree with those who think that Sidney wrote 'having known' all the answers.[44] My own feeling is that the new Book III carried his vision beyond what his plot could incorporate, that having introduced tragedy on the one hand, and having demonstrated the princesses' maturity by their trial in captivity on the other, Sidney had brought the action to a point where the particular kind of comedy presented in the old Book III and first half of Book IV was no longer conceivable. I shall explore this suggestion later, in Chapter 7.

 NARRATIVE STRUCTURE:
RETROSPECTIVE HISTORY

The structural principles examined in the preceding chapters were illustrated with material taken from Books I and III or from those parts of Book II which, like them, either contribute to or do not much impede the forward movement of the action. The hundred pages of retrospective narrative in Book II bring into focus a new area of structural problems, though one already glanced at in the stories of Argalus, Parthenia, and Amphialus – namely, problems concerned with the relation between main plot and episodes. This is the general area of exploration for narrative structure, to which the rest of the book is devoted.

The two previous kinds of structures, rhetorical and tonal, because they analyse the work thematically or sequentially, have used incidents without regard to distinctions of time and place or integration with the central action. Now that I am discussing material frankly 'inserted' into the main story – since it comprises events that have happened earlier, in another part of the world (Asia Minor as opposed to Greece), and that are concerned with people who (except for the princes) have little if any relevance to the Arcadian situation – it seems necessary that some sort of distinction among narrative units be undertaken. The nature of the distinction that I believe Sidney made and the reasoning or epic theory that accounts for his understanding of the relation between main plot and episodes will be discussed in Chapter 7, which deals specifically with this relationship; for now, we need only recognize the peculiarly detachable quality of the Book II histories, and see in this independence warrant for trying to determine their organizing principles, apart from whatever functional relation or thematic unity they share with the rest of the work.

The retrospective narratives of Book II contain two sets of materials: the education and adventures of the princes and the stories of Plangus and Erona. The first set, with its narration divided between Pyrocles and Musidorus, suggests interesting possibilities for the wedding of structure to meaning. The strong differences in subject matter and narrative movement between the princes' sets of stories have previously been noticed in criticism of the *Arcadia*,[1] but without sufficient awareness that the differences are subordinated to the larger contrast Sidney wants to achieve. In broad terms, the two accounts seem to present alternative views concerning the nature and exercise of moral virtue.

Because my analysis concentrates on the inner logic determining the pattern of the episodes, I want first to acknowledge the importance of the frame in distinguishing or accounting for the material that comprises the narratives. The kind of story each prince tells is conditioned by at least two factors: his own character as it is displayed throughout the work and his particular dramatic or rhetorical situation at the moment he relates his history. Musidorus is older, more masculine, and sensible; Pyrocles more sensitive and impressionable. Though both are perfect heroes, one can see that Musidorus might emphasize the external manifestation of virtue in military and political affairs, and Pyrocles might be more alert to inner conflict and psychological motivations. Dramatically, Musidorus is wooing Pamela in the guise of a shepherd; uppermost in his mind is the need to demonstrate to her his worthiness, his claim to nobility. Moreover, he addresses his tale to a princess whose 'majesty of virtue,' wise seriousness, and relative austereness combine to create an 'audience' no rhetorician of Musidorus' ability could possibly ignore. Thus, it is not surprising that his stories should illustrate the art of good government, the nature of a princely education, acts of public chivalry, and the noble virtues of friendship, magnanimity, and justice. By his tales no less than by his horsemanship Musidorus seeks to show Pamela that he is 'no base bodie,' that is, he seeks to 'appear to her eyes, like [him] selfe' (I, 166, 165).

Pyrocles, on the other hand, has the softer and less princely Philoclea as his audience;[2] moreover, his story comes after he has revealed his true identity and they have both declared their love. In the role of Zelmane, niece of an Amazonian Queen, Pyrocles' nobility has never been questioned, but the dubious nature of his disguise and the incredible situation whereby Philoclea's mother and father are both in love with him clearly weaken his claim to integrity and ethical judgment. It is thus rhetorically fitting that the bulk of his tales should deal with just these two matters, especially as they concern love, of which he seeks to demonstrate all the knowledge possible to a heart that is both 'gentle' and chaste. This experience he offers as proof that his male-female disguise is not a symbol of his own confusion of values. Other private and political matters are included for the same general purpose of proving himself worthy of a virtuous princess' love.

In spite of the overall distinction in subject matter between the sets of stories,[3] Musidorus' account also features such private virtues as friendship and filial piety, while Pyrocles discusses such public concerns as the Iberian jousts, settling a rebellion for the King of Bithynia, and the politically ambitious plots of Plexirtus.

The inclusion of both public and private matters in each account suggests that perhaps the kind of response demanded of the princes themselves may be at least as important as the general areas in which the problems happen to lie.

The responses demanded of the princes are a function in part of the moral stability of the world they find themselves in, of the suitability of experience to be evaluated by fixed standards. Both princes, having been reared and educated together, share the same system of values, the one expounded at the beginning of Musidorus' narrative. The difference is that while Musidorus' tales are enacted within the acknowledged boundaries of these values, having reference to them at every point, Pyrocles' may almost be said to take place in another world. The nature of the difference can be established by comparing the situations opening both narratives.

Musidorus begins his history with an account of Pyrocles' father, King Euarchus of Macedon,

> Who as he was most wise to see what was best, and most just in the perfourming what he saw, and temperate in abstaining from any thing any way contrary: so thinke I, no thought can imagine a greater harte to see and contemne daunger, where daunger would offer to make any wrongfull threatning upon him. A Prince, that indeed especially measured his greatnesse by his goodnesse: and if for any thing he loved greatnesse, it was, because therein he might exercise his goodnes. (I, 185)

This virtuous man is also the ideal monarch, and Musidorus says that one can find 'the whole Arte of governement' (I, 187) in the methods by which Euarchus restored justice and prosperity to his kingdom when he assumed rule over a government that during his minority had become 'the worst kind of Oligarchie' (I, 185). The evils of this oligarchy are set forth with constant references to the ideal of monarchy which they subvert:

> For they having the power of kinges, but not the nature of kings, used the authority as men do their farms, of which they see within a yeere they shal goe out: making the Kinges sworde strike whom they hated, the Kings purse reward whom they loved: and (which is worst of all) making the Royall countenance serve to undermine the Royall soveraintie. For the Subjectes could taste no sweeter fruites of having a King, then grievous taxations to serve vain purposes; Lawes made rather to finde faults, then to prevent faultes: the Court of a Prince rather deemed as a priviledged place of unbrideled licentiousnes, then as a biding of him, who as a father, should give a fatherly example unto his people. (I, 185-6)

The same general tenor prevails in the descriptions of the friendship between Euarchus and King Dorilaus of Thessalia, the cross-marriages between their houses, and especially in the details of the education given their children Pyrocles and Musidorus (I, 189-90). This material, being preliminary to the cousins' actual adventures which comprise the rest of their narratives, may be considered a unit which sets forth positively those ideals and values the princes have learned to venerate and hope someday to realize in their own lives. It represents, to pick up a theme insisted upon in the description of their first sea voyage, the theory which they must thereafter put into practice. It is worth noting that they have been educated exclusively in these ideals, presumably on the premise that young minds brought to know and love the good will prefer it whenever they later encounter evil, which is by definition inferior to it.[4] The vision that corresponds to their education is the noble, harmonious order described at the outset of their adventures:

The winde was like a servaunt, wayting behind them so just, that they might fill the sailes as they listed; and the best saylers shewing themselves lesse covetous of his liberalitie, so tempered it, that they all kept together like a beautifull flocke, which so well could obey their maisters pipe ... while the two Princes had leasure to see the practise of that, which before they had learned by bookes: to consider the arte of catching the winde prisoner, to no other ende, but to runne away with it; to see how beautie, and use can so well agree together, that of all the trinckets, where with they are attired, there is not one but serves to some necessary purpose. And (ô Lord) to see the admirable power and noble effects of Love, whereby the seeming insensible Loadstone, with a secret beauty (holding the spirit of iron in it) can draw that hard-harted thing unto it, and (like a vertuous mistresse) not onely make it bow it selfe, but with it make it aspire to so high a Love, as of the heavenly Poles; and thereby to bring foorth the noblest deeds, that the children of the Earth can boast of. (I, 191-2).[5]

Since the chief characteristic of the stories in Pyrocles' account is their interconnectedness, it is more difficult to establish a corresponding opening segment for analysis, but I shall abide by Sidney's first editors and choose what they have marked off as Chapter 18, which runs from Anaxius' challenge to combat through the incident with Pamphilus and Dido that delays Pyrocles on his journey to that battle. Anaxius represents a blend of characteristics that the princes (chronologically)[6] have not met before: he has the bravery, 'great mind,' and ability of the hero, but his overweening pride is a mark of the villain. Admittedly, though, Sidney's conception of Anaxius is from the outset rather comic. He is one 'to whom al men would willingly have yeelded the height of praise, but that his nature was such, as to bestow it upon himselfe, before any could give it' (I, 263). Still, he is not merely to be laughed at, but represents a dangerous misuse of power potentially at the service of the good.

Having accepted Anaxius' challenge, Pyrocles must go alone to meet him. He is actually pleased at the chance to prove himself without the aid of Musidorus, whose presence he feels has been responsible for his own past achievements:

He taught me by word, and best by example, giving me in him so lively an Image of vertue, as ignorance could not cast such mist over mine eyes, as not to see, and to love it ... which made me indeed find in my selfe such a kind of depending upon him, as without him I found a weakenesse, and a mistrustfulnes of my selfe, as one strayed from his best strength, when at any time I mist him. Which humour perceiving to overrule me, I strave against it; not that I was unwilling to depend upon him in judgement, but by weakenesse I would not: which though it held me to him, made me unworthy of him. (I, 264)

One is reminded both of Guyon's separation from the Palmer and of Eve's plea to Adam that she must try her virtue alone; the passage may well be an 'allegory' along similar lines. Musidorus becomes associated with the cluster of values attached to their education, and Pyrocles' leaving him implies that he is in some sense also leaving behind the security of that education. He does not, however, repudiate it; he seeks instead to explore an area that it does not specifically chart. Pyrocles' desire to seek adventure alone, to test his personal worth, suggests that this area will have more to do with the autonomous individual than his education perhaps prepared him for.

In the context of the *Arcadia*, where the norm for evaluation is the ideal, a world that does not conform to the pattern of the ideal education (whether by direct adherence or by equally direct subversion of its tenets) is a world whose values are distorted, where one cannot be sure what is right and wrong, where the choice can no longer even be stated in these terms, where it is necessary to compromise one value for the sake of a greater one.[7] It is, in short, the world that Pyrocles encounters on the way to fight Anaxius, when he comes upon nine gentlewomen in the process of torturing a man they have tied to a tree. The situation immediately creates a problem, for a stock response is inappropriate: a man, not a woman, is in distress, and though the knight's allegiance is instinctively with the victim, using force against women would be ungentlemanly. The frustration is not permanent, however, for within a short time their male servants attack, and Pyrocles routs the whole company except Dido, who is too bent on revenge to flee. She justifies her behaviour by telling him of Pamphilus' crimes against women. The tale oscillates between comedy and a fascination with neurosis.

Pamphilus is guilty not just of idle philandering, but of deriving satisfaction from humiliating his mistresses. The account contains much psychological detail concerning the way he gains mastery by playing on the jealousy, pride, and fear which control their actions despite promptings of a Reason that seems to know better. Dido's compulsive desire for Pamphilus, even though she never thinks him 'excellent,' is 'like them I have seene play at the ball, growe extremely earnest, who should have the ball, and yet every one knew it was but a ball' (I, 269). Pamphilus impudently claims adherence to the ideal of constancy in the face of accusations by almost a dozen women he has seduced:

these constant fooles you speak of, though their Mistres grow by sicknes foule, or by fortune miserable, yet stil will love her, and so committe the absurdest inconstancie that may be, in changing their love from fairnes to foulenesse ... where I ... am ever constant; to Beautie in others; and Delight in myself. (I, 268)[8]

The comedy increases as he lists the faults that have caused him to discard each woman present, for among those we discover the true reason for Dido's unrelenting malice: not Pamphilus' deceit in seducing her, but his saying that he left her because she was not beautiful.

Pyrocles, though obviously sympathetic, must still prevent Dido from blinding the bound man with her dagger. His decision is to defend an evil man from an overly cruel punishment, a significantly more complex evaluation of right and wrong than any demanded of the princes in Musidorus' tales. To confuse matters even further, some friends of Pamphilus ride by, and the 'victim' once again becomes a tryant. He shouts to the men to kill Dido for having disgraced him. Pyrocles in turn makes the necessary shift of allegiance. The incident (and Chapter 18) closes with 'a faithfull peace promised of all sides,' but it comes as no shock to the reader when the tale erupts onto the scene again approximately two days and two pages later.

The difference suggested for these opening episodes of the narratives are reinforced by the shipwrecks appearing in each account. The two events seem by their placement to call for comparison: the first is the princes' initial adventure upon completing their formal education; the other is their last adventure before being cast ashore in Greece, where the *Arcadia* proper begins. The princes' exploits in Asia Minor are therefore framed by these two events.

The voyage to Asia Minor, as we have seen in the long quotation above (p 90), is explicitly conceived as an opportunity for the princes to translate the theory behind their education into practice; what we should expect to see demonstrated is their knowledge of political, social, and military affairs, and more importantly, their training in personal virtue. Strongest proof of this training can of course be found under conditions of adversity, and Nature dutifully 'stages' a violent storm, transforming their world into a 'tumultuous kingdome' where the winds' roar is a bid for power, the 'traiterous sea ... swells in pride' and darkness 'usurp[s] the dayes right' (I, 192). The hyperbole, as well as the metaphor, of this description is necessary to Sidney's moral point, for he means to set up the most extreme situation possible in order to test his heroes: 'Certainely there is no daunger carries with it more horror, then that which growes in those flo<t>ing kingdomes' (I, 193).[9]

The princes are adequate to the test on two counts: as leaders of men and in their personal or psychological response to danger. To their behaviour must be credited the continued functioning of the crew:

the valiantest feeling inward dismayednesse, and yet the fearefullest ashamed fully to shew it, seeing that the Princes (who were to parte from the greatest fortunes) did in their countenances accuse no point of feare, but encouraging them to doo what might be done (putting their handes to everie most painefull office) taught them at one instant to promise themselves the best, and yet not to despise the worst. (I, 193)

But the ship is dashed to pieces upon a hidden rock despite these efforts, and each man, no longer able to react as part of a crew, must draw on his personal resources of virtue. The result is summarized as 'a monstrous crie begotten of manie roaring <voices>, [which] was able to infect with feare a minde that had not prevented it with the power of reason' (I, 193-4). The princes, however, acting again in accordance with their education, use 'the passions of fearing evill, and desiring to escape, onely to serve the rule of vertue, not to abandon ones self.' The final action of the episode reaffirms the values informing their education: two brothers, whose valour had led the youthful Pyrocles and Musidorus to ransom them from prison, now save the princes by giving up their own lives in gratitude for this favour, 'perchance helped by a naturall duetie to their Princes blood' (I, 194).

The second shipwreck is as fit a culmination to the cousins' stay in Asia Minor as the first is to their formal education. The agency for the second disaster is not natural but human, and evil is present as the root of the cause, not as a metaphorical imputation to a force that is, after all, morally neutral. It offers not an example of practice moralized to fit the framework of an educational theory, but an instance of the ambiguous, unclassifiable world itself. The shipwreck is the result of a mutiny, but a mutiny directed against the captain's order to kill Pyrocles and Musidorus. Significantly, even for the mutineers the moral issue is not drawn clearly, since although the captain commanded them to murder, Plexirtus' trusted counselor (who betrayed the plot to the princes because he had come to know their virtue) commanded the contrary, promising to stand between them and the King's anger. In the general muddle the princes, too, can take only limited action. Unlike their behaviour during the first shipwreck, they do not here encourage men to realize their potential virtue through example; they no longer even function as leaders. Instead, they themselves participate in the confusion, and their only possible posture is defensive. Pyrocles is quite explicit on all these points:

> quickly it grew a most confused fight. For the narrownesse of the place, the darkenesse of the time, and the uncertainty in such a tumult how to know friends from foes, made the rage of swordes rather guide, then be guided by their maisters. For my cousin and me, truly I thinke we never perfourmed lesse in any place, doing no other hurte, then the defence of our selves, and succouring them who came for it, drave us to: for not discerning perfectlie, who were for, or against us, we thought, it lesse evill to spare a foe, then spoyle a friend. (I, 305)

Yet the princes themselves are not less virtuous in this shipwreck than they are in the first; it is merely that the virtue possible to them under the circumstances is a much less glorious and absolute quality.

The discussion of the two narratives thus far should enable us to characterize their differences more precisely. The pattern underlying Musidorus' account is composed of the two parts already indicated: the first part sets forth the ideals and values that serve as both the ends and means of a princely education, and the second provides a series of situations or problems whose solutions are to be found explicitly in this previous training. The princes view each situation 'objectively,' even when it demands the sacrifice of their own lives, for they seem to arrive unequivocally at the one answer in accord with principles of virtue. There is no indecision in these stories, no difficulty in knowing which side is right and which wrong, no uncertainty as to what ought to be done. The range of problems, however, is not extensive. The education and the episodes built upon it are concerned predominantly with military and political virtues, though they also emphasize friendship and filial piety, private virtues which strengthen the bonds of society.[10]

The princes themselves do not change in Pyrocles' account of their exploits, but the kind of situations with which they must deal shifts radically in a way that limits the effectiveness while increasing the moral difficulty of their actions. The two sets of tales move, in a sense, from the simple to the complex, from situations in which issues are clear and responses unequivocal to situations where both sides are often partially wrong and values must be ranked one above the other before response is possible. Emphasis switches from moral action to moral choice, though the two are obviously interdependent. The princes largely give up their 'objectivity' as well, for their actions and decisions often implicate them further in the problems they seek to solve. What the princes lose of the aloofness that helps to make them heroes and leaders of men, they gain in more ordinary human terms by themselves experiencing the temptations and ambiguities that can threaten abstract virtue.

Thus we find in Pyrocles' narrative a second phase of education where experience reflects the strong Sophistic and rhetoricist stress on factors of contingency or circumstance (καιρος). The problems are more difficult and require a more complex and relativistic notion of virtue, yet relativism does not mean that values are subjective. In this second phase, the principles of their education cannot be applied stringently or automatically, but they can still serve as a guide through the maze of semi-truths and partial goods. The principles remain as goals even in a complex, ambiguous world. These generalizations will become clearer as we return to the text itself.

After the shipwreck and the willingness of Leucippus and Nelsus to sacrifice themselves for the princes there remain only four episodes in Musidorus' account, centring about the King of Phrygia, the King of Pontus, the giant brothers of Pontus, and the King of Paphlagonia. The first two men are intended as examples of bad monarchs, and they are direct inversions of the good princes. In the ideal description of Euarchus only two vices are specifically listed as being absent from his character: 'he soone shewed, no baseness of suspition, nor the basest basenes of envie, could any whit rule such a Ruler' (I, 186). The key to Phrygia's political and moral troubles is that the King is melancholy and suspicious to the point of paranoia; the key to the situation in Pontus is that a tyrant utterly without standards of right beyond his own wantonly cruel will has for his chief counselor 'a man of the most envious disposition, that ... ever infected the aire with his breath' (I, 203).

The initial stages of the princes' education are relevant to the comparison Sidney later draws between them and classical heroes: the cousins will 'goe privately to seeke exercises of their vertue; thinking it not so worthy, to be brought to heroycall effects by fortune, or necessitie (like Ulysses and Aeneas) as by ones owne choice, and working' (I, 206). In the shipwreck, the agency was unquestionably 'fortune,' and in the first two Asia Minor adventures, 'necessity': the King of Phyrgia arrests Pyrocles and intends to execute him, and the King of Pontus insultingly replies to their request for their servants' liberty (Leucippus and Nelsus reached shore after all) by sending their heads. Such conditions virtually preclude the element of choice. Within this limitation, however, the princes display the same virtuous reflexes as they did during the storm and wreck at sea. This unequivocal response is in fact the point of their behaviour in the Phrygian episode, just as the inner weakness of tyranny is the political lesson. Pyrocles is to be executed, but Musidorus, knowing that the King's suspicious hatred is really directed against him because of prophecies made at his birth, offers himself in return for Pyrocles' freedom. Pyrocles naturally protests, 'But in this notable contention, (where the conquest must be the conquerers destruction, and safetie the punishment of the conquered) Musidorus prevayled' (I, 198). Such proof of the supreme value assigned to friendship must be reciprocated, and Pyrocles, intending to die with his cousin if no other remedy is possible, allows himself to be apprenticed to the executioner, 'a farre notabler proofe of his friendship, considering the height of his minde, then any death could be' (I, 199).[11]

With the demonstration of friendship completed, the episode shifts back to politics. A quarrel over the cowardice shown by a soldier in retreating from the princes who are together fighting on the scaffold starts a tumult among the men, 'which seene, and not understood by the people (used to feares but not used to be bolde in them) some began to crie treason; and that voice streight multiplying it selfe, the King (O the cowardise of a guiltie conscience) before any man set upon him, fled away' (I, 200). The spontaneous revolution turns into general mob violence against the innocent as well as the guilty until the Phrygians are persuaded to ask Musidorus to be their king. But he, 'thinking it a greater greatnes to give a kingdome, then get a kingdome,' resigns in favour of a nobleman of known virtue who is next in succession to the throne, taking care also that 'the nature of the government, should be no way apt to decline to Tyranny' (I, 202). The summary comment explicitly connects these actions with the values of their education: 'This dooing set foorth no lesse his magnificence, then the other act did his magnanimitie' (I, 202). Concerning the King of Pontus, the result of a much briefer and less richly conceived adventure in which the princes revenge the death of Leucippus and Nelsus is that Pyrocles in turn has the opportunity to refuse a throne.

Their next exploit, slaying the giant brothers of Pontus, is called a private combat (I, 204). The episode is recounted briefly, but through it we may understand the meaning of 'private' in Musidorus' stories. The term does not distinguish personal from public behaviour, but refers to matters that do not directly affect the ruler of a country or result in the establishment of a new government. The giants are suited only to war, where they show courage and 'rude faithfulnes.' Incapable of subtlety of judgment, when they are dealt with unjustly by the King, they wreak incredible havoc on the innocent people of his country in order to manifest their 'spite,' 'so that where in the time that they obeyed a master, their anger was a serviceable power of the minde to doo publike good, so now unbridled, and blinde judge of it selfe, it made wickedness violent, and praised it selfe in excellencie of mischiefe ...' (I, 205).[12] The princes, judging the giants 'so fleshed in crueltie as not to be reclaimed,' go 'secreatly' and alone to their castle and kill them.

The last of Musidorus' episodes, while it still agrees generally with the pattern established for his tales, functions also as a transition to the concerns of the next set. The Paphlagonian king is a good man and, apparently, a good ruler, except for a serious error in judgment that allowed him to be deceived and dethroned by his illegitimate son, Plexirtus. This tale of course furnished Shakespeare with the Gloucester sub-plot of *King Lear*. The princes meet the blind king and his good son Leonatus, and are moved by their story to join against the forty men who suddenly come on the scene to carry out Plexirtus' orders to kill his brother, 'so just a defence deserving as much as old friendship' (I, 211). Up to this point, and in the conclusion of the episode (which sees the old King's reinstatement and peaceful death, the defeat of Plexirtus, and the brothers' reconciliation), the tale repeats the elements of political didacticism, moral and social order, unequivocal action, and objective evaluation of good and evil noted in the rest of Musidorus' account. But other factors in the episode anticipate the situations that Pyrocles depicts. The course of action begins to take on complications and frustrations, for the princes, unable alone to save the King and Leonatus from their forty attackers, are rescued by the new King of Pontus (who has followed them because of a dream), only to have this advantage annulled by the arrival of Tydeus and Telenor with additional forces for the other side. Moreover, the princes may be able to discern good from evil, but other honest men cannot: the King chose wrongly to believe his bastard against his legitimate son, and Tydeus and Telenor are wrong in valuing their friendship with Plexirtus above virtue itself. This new element in the tale, though it has political repercussions, is at base personal and moral, with the errors being attributable largely to hypocrisy and deceit, evils which do not destroy the validity of the princes' education but make it more difficult to apply. It is in these senses that the Paphlagonian episode may be said to represent a transition between the two sets of stories. It is transitional, too, in the solution of its problems. Though the throne may be permanently in the hands of the good Leonatus as a result of the princes' efforts, the story of Plexirtus, Tydeus, and Telenor is evidently left incomplete, a narrative fact that carries moral significance.

I have treated Musidorus' narrative as though it were divided in two parts, one theory and the other application. It is also possible to see the account as divided into three, revealing an interesting parallel with Pyrocles' narrative, which obviously falls into three almost precisely equal sections. The plan of Musidorus' history would then be as follows: the first third consists in the descriptions of Euarchus, the princes' education, and the shipwreck, all prior to landing in Asia Minor; the second third in the direct application of their education to the kings of Phrygia and Pontus and to the two giants; the last third in the more complicated situation in Paphlagonia.[13] The natural divisions of Pyrocles' account give us this plan: the first third comprises Pyrocles' single encounters (the stories concerning Anaxius, Pamphilus, Dido, and her father, Chremes); in the second third the reunited princes undergo a mixed set of experiences, mostly concerned with love, that includes their captivity by Andromana, an account of the reconciliation of love and honour at Queen Helen's court, the Iberian jousts, and the plights of Palladius, Zelmane, and Leucippe (the last finishing Pamphilus' story);[14] the final third, announced by the princes' decision to return home to Thrace, immediately channels the concern with personal ethics back to the area where its political repercussions may be felt (the stories include the brief account of King of Bithynia and his brother, and the long ones of Tydeus and Telenor, Leonatus and Plexirtus, the triumphal honours given the princes by the kings they aided, and the ship-wreck). This last area is the one already noted for the Paphlagonian episode. The parallel is reinforced by having the same characters appear; the spirit and machinations of Plexirtus hover over the final third of Pyrocles' narrative, though we see more of the effects his actions have on other people than we do of the man himself. Thus the culminating section of each set of episodes affirms the inter-relatedness of public and private virtue, though the journeys are from opposite directions. This sense of mutual relevance or carry-over between the two spheres of virtue, implicit in most of the tales, becomes a key for interpreting the Arcadian experience as well.

Since it would be impracticable to consider all Pyrocles' tales in the same manner I have Musidorus', because the narrative is half again as long and the material more intertwined, I shall work with episodes whose characters have already been discussed.[15] Let us, then, test the generalizations suggested above against the complex of incidents surrounding Plexirtus.

Plexirtus re-enters the work in connection with the death of the brothers Tydeus and Telenor, whose combat while disguised from each other is witnessed by Pyrocles and Musidorus. The explanation of their battle reveals the distortions and confusions of values prevalent in the rest of Pyrocles' account. The story begins with the newly-crowned Leonatus treating his half brother Plexirtus with great favour, 'his goodnesse being as apt to be deceived, as the others crafte was to deceive' (I, 293). He uncovers Plexirtus' attempt to poison him, 'yet would [he] not suffer his kindnesse to be overcome, not by justice it selfe.' Apparently a good man acting in accordance with Christian charity does not necessarily make the correct choice. Leonatus attributes Plexirtus' crimes to 'the violence of ambition,' and gives him forces and his own claim to sovereignty over Trebizond, a city rightfully belonging to Paphlagonia, so that Plexirtus can 'with lesse unnatural-nesse glut [his] ambition' in conquering and ruling there.

Chiefly through the aid of Tydeus and Telenor, his friends since childhood, Plexirtus succeeds in conquering the territory:

Which indeede done by them, gave them such an authoritie, that though he raigned, they in effect ruled, most men honouring them, because they onely deserved honour; and many, thinking therein to please Plexirtus, considering how much he was bound unto them: while they likewise (with a certaine sincere boldenesse of selfe-warranting friendship) accepted all openly and plainely, thinking nothing should ever by Plexirtus be thought too much in them, since all they were, was his. (I, 293)

Again (though without the suggestion that the scale of values is wrong), here are good men whose virtuous assumptions fail to mesh with the reality of evil; for Plexirtus, judging all minds by his own, suddenly suspects them of self-seeking and fears their power to overthrow him. His completely cynical plan is 'to turne their owne friendship toward him to their owne destruction' (I, 294). He asks each separately to take his place in a combat against another king, swearing each to secrecy before and silence during the encounter, and relating such information about the opponent's armour that each will mistake the other for the rival king. The brothers discover the treachery only when they are about to die of their wounds. Their death is moving despite the heavy didacticism. Two points may be extracted for special notice: the brothers accuse 'their folly in having beleeved, he could faithfully love, who did not love faithfulnes: wishing us to take heed, how we placed our good wil upon any other grounds, then proofe of vertue'; and Pyrocles comments that they left 'fewe in the world behind them, their matches in any thing, if they had soone inough knowne the ground and limits of friend-ship' (I, 294-5). It is not only displaying certain virtues, then, but knowing their ground and limits that is expected of the princes in this second phase of their education. If Musidorus' episode in Phrygia was geared to express the supreme value of friendship, the death of Tydeus and Telenor and the incident growing from it are meant to qualify that supremacy.

Traveling with the princes in male disguise is Plexirtus' virtuous daughter, Zelmane, who has assumed the role of page because she is secretly in love with Pyrocles.[16] Zelmane falls ill, 'partly with the shame and sorrow she tooke of her fathers faultinesse, partly with the feare, that the hate I [Pyrocles] conceived against him, would utterly disgrace her in my opinion' (I, 205), and does not disclose her identity until she is dying, when Pyrocles' tears move her to request a favour of him. Just prior to this from a messenger seeking Tydeus and Telenor they learned (the princes with righteous pleasure) that 'Plexirtus was in pre<se>nt daunger of a cruel death, if by the valiantnesse of one of the best Knightes of the world, he were not reskewed' (I, 296). Zelmane extracts Pyrocles' promise that he will defend her father. To do this he must leave his cousin, for Musidorus has to continue the journey to Pontus, where they are to battle against three mighty warriors who threaten to usurp the crown. As the princes are parting, a messenger arrives with news of arrangements for the combat:

Now the day was so accorded, as it was impossible for me both to succour Plexirtus, and be there, where my honour was not onely <so far engaged>, but (by the straunge working of unjust fortune) I was to leave the standing by Musidorus, whom better then my selfe I loved, to go save him whom for just causes I hated. But my promise given, and given to Zelmane, and to Zelmane dying, prevailed more with me, then my friendship to Musidorus: though certainely I may affirme, nothing had so great rule in my thoughts as that. (I, 299)

The echoes of the Tydeus and Telenor scene, coming so soon after it, are probably deliberate. We are almost back in the realm of direct application of principles learned, and the insistent piling up of 'paradoxical' clauses maximizes the difficulty of the test in the same way as being aboard ship in the storm during the first adventure. But the problem here is morally more complex than in the shipwreck, and it is noteworthy that the kind of decision called for has parallels even in the few episodes examined thus far. Leonatus must decide between family loyalty (or perhaps more largely, mercy) and justice, Zelmane first between shame and love for her father and then between filial love and her love for Pyrocles. Nor is this the only kind of moral complexity. In the next part of the action we learn that Plexirtus has been captured by a good old knight who, desiring 'just' revenge, has 'condemned him to <a> death, cruell inough, if any thing may be both cruell and just' (I, 300). Pyrocles slays the fantastic beast guarding Plexirtus, but the old nobleman says (and we feel, justly) that '[his] virtue has beene imployed to save a worse monster then [he] killed' (I, 301). The problem is reminiscent of the one set up for the earlier Dido-Pamphilus episode, and again Pyrocles defends an evil man.

The princes' need to make complex decisions which in themselves pose rather than resolve moral problems seems a sign of a greater involvement or implication in events than is displayed in the unequivocal evaluations of Musidorus' account. The strongest evidence of this involvement comes in their next encounter with Plexirtus, which occurs when the people and princes of Asia Minor gather to honour Pyrocles and Musidorus as their benefactors. Plexirtus is among the most officious of these attendants. For once, the princes themselves are taken in by an act of hypocrisy, and expressly misjudge an evil:

[Plexirtus] (seeming a quite altered man) had nothing but repentance in his eies, friendship in his gesture, and vertue in his mouth: so that we who had promised the sweete Zelmane to pardon him, now not onely forgave, but began to favour; perswading our selves with a youthfull credulitie, that perchance things were not so evil as we tooke them, and as it were desiring our owne memories, that it might be so. (I, 303)

On the strength of this evaluation, they accept his gift of a royally furnished ship, the vessel of the second shipwreck. The Asia Minor episodes thus end on a note not of a triumphantly completed education, but of initiation into the full complexities of the moral life.

Dilemmas and distortions of values are emphasized in the 'private' as well as in the politically oriented episodes in Pyrocles' tale. Again selecting characters already introduced, we can explore this notion further in the material comprising the first third of the account. When we last discussed this opening group of stories, Pyrocles, having apparently secured a 'faithfull peace' between Dido and Pamphilus (I, 269), was proceeding to his combat with Anaxius. In the midst of their bloody battle, Dido rides by, chased by Pamphilus 'with the most unmanlike crueltiesᵢ beating her with wandes he had in his hande' (I, 271). Anaxius' refusal to defer their combat so that they can 'perfourme the duties of Knighthood in helping this distressed Ladie' places Pyrocles in a difficult position. He must decide either to have his name as a knight ruined by an imputation of cowardice or to refuse to answer a call for help. Our tendency may be to see no dilemma here at all, but Sidney insists on it by having Pyrocles repeatedly stress his shame and embarrassment at the catcalls from the crowd (I, 271).

Pyrocles' six-hour ride through wild terrain before overtaking Pamphilus and company is surely an emblem of the moral distance separating this sequence from the rest of the *Arcadia*. D.M. Anderson has rightly called the perversion underlying the entire Dido incident unparalleled in the work. He conjectures that it represents 'a weakened version of a rather spicy original,'[17] and indeed, the original overtones have not been excluded very rigorously. The jilted women mean eventually 'to have mangled [Pamphilus] so, as [he] should have lost his credit for ever abusing more' (I, 269), a broad hint at castration, just as the 'cruell and shamefull manner' by which Pamphilus plans 'to kill [Dido], in the sight of her owne Father' (I, 272) is undoubtedly by first handing her over to his companions to be raped.[18] (Pyrocles comes upon them as they have begun to strip her of her clothes.) The final irony suggests even greater perversion: her father would not have cared. At least this is implied by Dido's explanation of her shame at having to ask Pyrocles to lodge in her father's castle overnight (a familiar dilemma – shame versus some positive virtue, here gratitude). Chremes' fanatical miserliness will permit only wretched and grudging hospitality, since it has extended even to his own sustenance:

which extreame dealing (descending from himselfe upon her) had driven her to put her selfe with a great Lady of that countrie, by which occasion she had stumbled upon such mischance, as were little for the honour either of her, or her familie. But so wise had he shewed himselfe therein, as while he found his daughter maintained without his cost, he was content to be deafe to any noise of infamie: which though it had wronged her much more then she deserved, yet she could not denie, but she was driven thereby to receave more then decent favours. (I, 273)

The description of Chremes therefore emphasizes the distortion of all natural values for the sake of a single vicious end; he has no regard for his own comfort or honour, no paternal feeling for his only child, no responses of gratitude or hospitality. To this undisguised churlishness he adds the heavy-handed deceit needed to betray his guest for the 100,000 crown reward offered by Queen Artaxia.[19] The final outcome of the episode is a kind of cynical justice, a right action done for the wrong reasons, that may be compared with the other discrepancies between motive and effect noted for Leonatus, Tydeus, and Telenor, or in the problem of cruel but just punishment. Musidorus, who has secretly been following his cousin, joins Pyrocles to fight against the troop of soldiers which intends to arrest him, but the fray is stopped by the King of Iberia, who happens to be hunting in the area. The King sentences Chremes to be hanged primarily because he wants to offend Queen Artaxia, whom he hates for supporting his son Plangus against him (I, 277). The occasion gives rise to one of those displays of virtue despite the most aggravated circumstances. Pyrocles says of Chremes' sentencing, 'though truely for my part, I earnestly laboured for his life, because I had eaten of his bread' (I, 277). The point falls so flat, though, that one is tempted to find a more particular reason for its inclusion, which might perhaps be to link it with other confusions concerning the 'ground and limits' of virtue, or with other occasions where circumstances make good the defender of evil.

The connection between the substance or moral import of each history and the narrative style used in its relation should by now be apparent. Walter Davis describes the two styles as 'straightforward' for Musidorus and 'more complexly interwoven' for Pyrocles.[20] If all the episodes are to be read as illustrating the same point about tragedy or passion, however (as they are in his account), there would then be no functional reason for the difference in narration. Yet by exploring these terms further we can see that the formal element is significant.

'Straightforward' and 'interwoven' refer not to verbal texture, but to the sequence of characters and incidents. In Musidorus' account, each episode is discrete, though (as with the revenge for the death of Leucippus and Nelsus) there may be a causal relation between them. On the whole, the princes meet a problem, deal with it, and then go on to the next adventure and a new set of characters. Just as there is no problem in deciding the proper course of action, there is also, for the duration of Musidorus' account, no question about the permanent efficacy of these actions once taken. The straightforward manner of telling is echoed by the 'straightforward' application of theory to practice, and the result is a sense that justice and right order can be made to prevail.

The 'more complexly interwoven' style employed in Pyrocles' tales corresponds to the more difficult and exasperating lesson of his account, to the refusal of righted wrongs to remain settled. Thus Pyrocles 'solves' the dispute between Pamphilus and Dido twice, only to have it break out again a few pages later. And since Pamphilus escapes, we come upon his story once again after fifteen more pages, when towards the end of the second section the princes encounter another of his conquests, Leucippe, who tells of his marriage to Baccha, 'the most impudentlie unchaste woman of all Asia' (I, 290).[21] Thus the reconciliation between Leonatus and Plexirtus also ruptures, and the moral weakness of the latter's relationship to Tydeus and Telenor can no longer be glossed over. New episodes tend not to introduce new characters, but to reintroduce people we have already met. The princes are rescued by Plangus' father and are imprisoned and propositioned by Andromana, his stepmother and former mistress; the Iberian jousts include an account of Queen Helen's court; the disguised page turns out to be Zelmane, whom they knew in Iberia. Even when new characters appear, they are connected with the old by all sorts of family ties; Andromana is Plexirtus' half-sister and Zelmane his daughter; Anaxius is the nephew of a man Pyrocles killed in an earlier battle; and Musidorus' victim in this same battle is later revenged by his brother, who, accompanied by two giant sons of the giants slain previously, poses a threat to the new King of Pontus installed by the princes. Thus even the finality of Musidorus' episodes is undermined in Pyrocles' section. There are new threats; others, their symbolic relation made familial, arise to do the same wrongs again.

The reader's sense of complication and perhaps confusion, which is the common initial reaction to Book II, is a product of this interweaving of detail, and as a justifiable reaction, it ought to be weighed against interpretative schemes whose major strength is their simplicity. 'Interweaving' is the formal equivalent of the moral atmosphere pervading Pyrocles' tales, as it is also the direct result of the princes' more restricted power to rectify wrongs. One might push the parallel further and say that for both form and content, the confusions arise from the conflict between order and chaos.

The sequence of retrospective narrative dealing with Plangus and Erona, thus far largely omitted from this discussion, follows roughly the movement suggested for the princes' own narratives. The sequence receives special prominence in the *Arcadia* because its three relatively discrete parts are distributed among Philoclea, Pamela, and Basilius: Philoclea relates Erona's love for the base Antiphilus and the successful intervention of Pyrocles and Musidorus on their side in the war against her outraged suitor, Tiridates of Armenia; Pamela tells how Plangus' ex-mistress became his father's wife and caused him to flee to Tiridates' court as an exile from Iberia; Basilius' story concerns Antiphilus' insulting behaviour as king and husband, and the development of Plangus' noble but unrequited love for Erona. Though this complex episode begins as another event in the princes' past history, they appear in just the first instalment; the episode thus does not exist primarily for its relevance to their heroism, and has only indirect bearing on their education. The Plangus-Erona story epitomizes much of the action in the other tales, but it also functions as a part of the whole Asia Minor history.

With respect to the princes' history, incidentally, the total arrangement of the Book II episodes is chronological, providing a clear thread to follow through the maze of the five different narrations. Musidorus' account stops with their setting out to help Erona; Philoclea next fills in the background of Erona's story and recounts the princes' exploits in her behalf; the events Pamela relates concerning Plangus actually took place twelve to fifteen years before his meeting with Erona and do not advance the narrative in time; Pyrocles picks up the thread after the princes leave Erona, carrying it to their departure from Asia Minor; Basilius' final instalment overlaps this last time span, but ends at a somewhat later point with Plangus' decision to ask Euarchus to revenge the supposed drowning of Pyrocles and Musidorus, since this action will concomitantly deliver Erona from Artaxia and Plexirtus. Paralleling this chronological disposition of material, however, is the other structural movement discussed above, and the Plangus-Erona episode has a place in this pattern as well.

The stories told by Philoclea and Pamela, coming between the princes' two sets of tales, carry the transitional functions of the Paphlagonian episode still further, forming a bridge between that and the Dido incident. In Philoclea's portion this is especially evident in the actions of the princes themselves. The issue of right and wrong does not have the clarity of the previous adventures; though Tiridates is *more* wrong because he wages pitiless war in revenge for being scorned by Erona, Erona's choice of a husband nevertheless is unfortunate for both herself and her state, and the princes become Antiphilus' champions by aiding her cause. Sidney even revises the account of their exploits in Lycia to make it here that they commit their first morally ambiguous act. In the *Old Arcadia* the princes, showing their 'matchless courage,' rescue the imprisoned Antiphilus 'with a desperate camisado ... [piercing] into the midst of [the enemy's] army' (*OA* 69). In the *New Arcadia* Erona, faced with the dilemma of giving herself to Tiridates or allowing Antiphilus to be killed, sends a message agreeing to yield, then changes her mind and pleads with the princes to deliver him:[22] 'They that knew not what she had done in private, prepared that night accordingly: and as sometimes it fals out, that what is inconstancy, seemes cunning; so did this change indeed stand in as good steed as a witty dissimulation. For it made the King as reckles, as them diligent ...' (I, 236) It is difficult to assess our ethical response to this act: 'witty dissimulation' might imply approval, but one must also reckon with Artaxia's characterization of it as 'a most abominable treason' (I, 236). Sidney seems to exonerate his heroes from this latter charge only through their ignorance.

Pamela's tale of Plangus carries moral confusion even further. It is here that deceit rather than outright violence comes into its own as the major evil,[23] and our attention is drawn to the difficulty in perceiving what is right. Pamela's first sentence announces the theme: Plangus' father, the King of Iberia, is a man 'of no wicked nature, nor willingly doing evill, without [he?] himselfe mistake the evill, seeing it disguised under some forme of goodnesse' (I, 242). Plangus, caught in a compromising situation with a married woman, decides incorrectly the relative values implied in his predicament. He, 'deceived with that young opinion, that if it be ever lawfull to lie, it is for ones Lover' (I, 243), so convinces his father of Andromana's virtue that the old man falls in love with her and when she is widowed makes her his queen. Much of the story is given over to emphasizing Andromana's hypocrisy, both in snaring the old king and afterwards in taking revenge on Plangus' refusal to renew their affair. Her revenge lies in making the King fear that his son means to usurp the throne. 'Within a while, all Plangus actions began to be translated into the language of suspition':

Which though Plangus found, yet could he not avoid, even contraries being driven to draw one yoke of argument: if he were magnificent, he spent much with an aspiring intent: if he spared, he heaped much with an aspiring intent: if he spake curteously, he angled the peoples harts: if he were silent, he mused upon some daungerous plot. In summe, if he could have turned himself to as many formes as Proteus, every forme should have bene made <hideous>. (I, 247)[24]

Here then is a situation where positive virtuous action is impossible, for at one point Plangus tries merely to protest his loyalty, 'But the more he protested, the more his father thought he dissembled, accounting his integritie to be but a cunning face of falshood ...' (I, 248). In this very restricted sphere, virtue seems to reside only in the strategy of flight: Plangus goes into voluntary exile rather than take arms against his father.

Thus, by balancing public and private emphases, by progressively revealing moral dislocations and their effect in limiting virtue, and by dealing with such subjects as dissimulation, hypocrisy, adultery, and incest, these two stories form the link between the princes' own sets of tales. The narrative technique also, since a certain complication arises from distributing the parts of the episode among three people and over a hundred pages, seems to support this transitional function. The necessity that the story be told at all is in fact a result of the prime factor motivating the interwoven structure of Pyrocles' narrative – the refusal of Erona's problems, which the princes ostensibly have solved, to remain settled.

The final segment of the episode, related by Basilius at the end of Book II, appears to recapitulate rather than intensify the moral issues raised by the Asia Minor history as a whole. The account begins with the description of a bad king, Antiphilus, whose core motivation is sheer baseness: 'For in Nature not able to conceyve the <bounds> of great matters (suddenly borne into an unknowne Ocean of absolute power) he was swayed withall (he knewe not howe) as everie winde of passions puffed him' (I, 330). It moves to a display of this same unworthiness in Antiphilus' inability to face the personal matter of death, and then to a double example of the irrationality of love, which is responsible on the one hand for Erona's poor judgment and its dire consequences and on the other for spurring Plangus' loyal but self-defeating service. There is no conclusion to the episode, for the central wrong (Erona's impending execution) is still to be redressed when Basilius ends his narration. But this is appropriate to our overall sense of the Asia Minor experience and to the main action of the *Arcadia* as well, since the small rebellion just settled outside Basilius' lodge will explode into the full-scale war of Book III, entailing still another reconsideration of morality in politics and love.

If I have discussed the Plangus-Erona episode more briefly than its prominence seems to demand, it is partly because its special epitomizing function has been well handled elsewhere,[25] and partly because I want instead to focus critical attention on the whole to which it is, after all, subordinate. I believe the key to Sidney's understanding of moral virtue is to be found in the princes' own narratives, and the best way to see the other Asia Minor material is in connection with the pattern these narratives set up. The pattern has two related centres of interest: education and morality. The purport of the narratives is clearly educational, with the princes' education being devoted largely to public and private virtues. The general program is stated in the *Defence*: 'The highest end of the mistress-knowledge ... stands (as I think) in the knowledge of a man's self, in the ethic and politic consideration, with the end of well-doing and not of well-knowing only' (pp 82-3).

At the risk of oversimplifying, one might say that virtue supplies the content, education the shape or purpose of the episodes. The stories convey the sense of an initiation into princely if not merely adult responsibility, and within this the movement is from statement of principles to simple application and thence progressively to more complex application of what has been learned, a movement paralleled by the classical or Renaissance educational process itself. I have previously insisted on the alternative views of moral action implied by the two sets of stories, in the sense that Musidorus deals unequivocally with matters like self-sacrifice, friendship that overcomes fear of death or shame, overthrowing evil tyrants and establishing just governments, while Pyrocles continually confronts equivocal situations demanding choice among greater and lesser goods. If we now perceive that the two narratives are related structurally as necessary parts of a single sequence describing 'the education of a prince,' we can understand that the 'two' kinds of virtue are really one, unfolding progressively from a simple to a complex form so that the latter includes the former without rejection. This is reflected in the fact that the standards by which the princes must ultimately judge their more ambiguous experience are the same as were previously presented in an absolute form (eg, friendship remains a value even after one discovers its limits). In Musidorus' episodes, issues are encountered individually and each good can be maximally asserted without fear of encroaching upon other values, but in Pyrocles' account the problem is often to arrange a group of acknowledged values in order of their importance.

The insistence on moral choice in Pyrocles' narrative, since it represents a complex formulation of the issue, thus has the greatest bearing on our understanding of Sidney's idea of virtue. It is worth noting that Sidney, to a much greater extent than either the Italian or Greek romancers, follows Aristotle in maintaining that the essence of moral virtue lies in choice.[26] As we have seen, he significantly expands the area in which choice operates beyond problems of love in order to pose dilemmas between various sets of virtues, or else to put shame (for Aristotle not a virtue) into conflict with some positive virtue. I have also discussed more morally perplexed examples of 'right' actions done for wrong reasons, and conversely, 'wrong' actions done for right reasons. The basic morality of the *Arcadia* resides in these episodes: values and beliefs are always being challenged by other seeming goods and outside forces, and must be held actively if they are to be held at all.[27] It should be noted, however, that this dynamic conception of virtue, though inextricably related to the idea of education, is nevertheless built upon a static conception of character. The process described is not the development of virtue, but either the emergence of a virtue already potentially present, or the manifestation and exercise of one that has somehow already been achieved.[28] We may thereby by deprived of the interest provided by a genuine quest, but the account of the princes' education cannot be accused of being perfunctory in its didacticism. It is saved from this by Sidney's conviction that virtue is exposed to real danger from other goods as well as from apparent and hidden evil. It is also saved by his acute sense of discrimination, his awareness of conflict, and finally, by his practical realization that virtue in a morally ambiguous world is less absolute and potent than it is in the educational theory to which he subscribes. The ethical intuition underlying the princes' history expresses what we have earlier seen as a rhetoricist emphasis on καιρος – on circumstance, occasion, the effect of psychological and other human limitations.

It is significant that this added material, more than a hundred pages of carefully shaped and thematically crucial material, should point so strongly to a rhetoricist perception of the reality men must deal with. Yet even if the princes' history educates them to an understanding of human limitations, these limitations should not themselves be made absolute, for Sidney feels, perhaps paradoxically, that virtue is not less valuable or less to be pursued because it is precarious.

NARRATIVE EXPLORATIONS:
SCOPE

Narrative structure, as discussed in this book, is largely concerned with the relations of parts to wholes: patterns formed by episodes considered separately, relations between episodes and the fable or main plot. Such is the subject matter of Chapters 5 and 7. The present chapter, however, is an excursus into related problems which might be called matters of size and shape, that is, it offers an inquiry into the *Arcadia*'s scope and genre. Resting on the moral vision uncovered in the analysis of the princes' paideia in Chapter 5, it documents the uniqueness of Sidney's pervasive interest in society, and interprets that conscious breadth and largeness of concern as an argument that the *Arcadia* is a heroic work, attempting to present a view of man that incorporates contemplative and pastoral impulses without destroying the dominantly social and active fabric of virtue. From the perhaps unconscious implications of Sidney's rhetoricism to the apparently conscious manipulation of various intellectual and literary traditions, the *Arcadia* demonstrates an extraordinary unity of design.

To begin with the idea of social dimension or scope, the quality itself is difficult to isolate for purposes of definition. It resides in the reader's awareness that, in spite of the influence exerted by the love plot, the work unfolds within a context determined more by social than by personal ideals. The princes' heroism and education are largely directed by an idea of the ruler's function in a well-ordered state, which gives the plot a context that is 'political' in the broadest sense, a sense indistinguishable from society itself, just as Aristotle's famous dictum, ἄνθρωπος φύσει ζῶον πολίτικον, may be understood to say equally that man is by nature either a political or a social animal. What most studies overlook is the cardinal fact that Sidney's Arcadia, unlike Virgil's or Sannazaro's, exists not solely as an attitude of mind but also, and primarily, as a political construct.[1] Sidney's 'transformation of Arcadia' is even greater than the one David Kalstone documents for Sannazaro.[2]

The paradox of Sidney's title is that its primary reference is not to an Arcadia that is an idyllic pastoral retreat from responsibility, which Basilius seeks to make of it, but to Arcadia as the name of a political state.[3] The title allows both ideas to be weighed against each other, an emblem of the contest between active and contemplative ideals that is waged on its pages. Sidney's conscious evaluation of this issue favours the active life: he prefers 'doing' to 'knowing' in the *Defence*, the hunter to the shepherd in *Lady of May*.[4] There is much in both the *Old Arcadia* and *New Arcadia* that substantiates the same position, though the larger canvas of these works allows a more comprehensive view of the issue. One formulation of the active bias in the *Arcadia* opposes 'burying [one]self alive' to 'doing good, the only happy action of man's life' (*OA* 359). 'Doing good' is implicitly 'doing good for others,' and if we generalize on the basis of the princes' Asia Minor experiences, these 'others' are frequently whole nations and oppressed peoples. In this way society is the very presupposition of virtue. Moreover, the state in this conception is not an abstract entity apart from man, but something composed of men; as noted earlier concerning the 'chain of being' presented in the formal description of Arcadia, the state is the culmination of nature in this world.[5] Aristotle's evaluation of the relative merits of public and private virtue considered as the end of human action is particularly relevant: 'For even if the end is the same for a single man and for a state, that of the state seems at all events something greater and more complete whether to attain or to preserve; though it is worthwhile to attain the end merely for one man, it is finer and more godlike to attain it for a nation or for city-states.'[6]

These ideas underlying the *Arcadia's* social scope are not peculiar to Sidney, but are the common property of classical and Renaissance culture. Notwithstanding the general availability of the ideas themselves, Sidney's embodying them in his *Arcadia* is an achievement not duplicated by the works with which it is usually compared or even by the Renaissance epics with which I believe it ought to be compared. The origin of the present chapter was this perception of uniqueness, of how none of the sources generally ascribed to the *Arcadia* reminds me of Sidney's work for very long. What I attempt to do here is to validate the truth of this perception.

The route I follow to establish the uniqueness of Sidney's concern is perhaps circuitous, but it entails consideration of modes and sources that seems worth initiating. The question is, where does Sidney's sense of scope come from? One possible answer is that it is inherent in the chivalric material added in revision, so that chivalry in itself can be said to make a work 'epic.' Alternatively, pastoral might imply a framework capable of supporting Sidney's social concerns. To switch the examination to genre, the influence of a Greek romance like the *Aetheopica* might give rise to the kind of material that Sidney wants to explore, or perhaps a fictionalized historical treatise like the *Cyropaedia*. In short, can we say that Sidney's concern arises 'naturally,' if not 'automatically,' from the materials and sources of his composition? After examining these possibilities, I finally argue that rather than being the inevitable result of the component elements or sources of his work, Sidney's vision is likely to have had other origins, both temperamental and intellectual. Sidney's *Arcadia* is best seen in terms of his understanding of the nature of the heroic poem, the intellectual milieu provided by Tudor humanism, and his own preference, as shown in the *Defence*, for the moral rather than the mystical claims of poetry.

Pages 128-31 document briefly the way in which Sidney's sense of scope is articulated in the *Arcadia*. The discussion has all along not strayed very far from the *Arcadia*, but this section offers evidence in a more concentrated fashion. It is brief because the argument it supports has been carried out in earlier chapters (especially Chapter 5, but by no means confined to it) and is taken up again at length in the exploration of the final antithetical topos, public-private, in Chapter 7.

LITERARY AND INTELLECTUAL TRADITIONS

Since the *Arcadia*'s scope seems to increase appreciably because of the material added in revision (especially the Asia Minor episodes and the siege of Book III), one might tentatively attribute its greater breadth to the element of chivalry. For this hypothesis to be valid, chivalric works ought commonly to be associated with broad social perspectives. Yet we find that the prime characteristic of the most popular form of chivalric literature, the medieval romance, is its divorce from political and social reality. The most suggestive account of chivalric romance is still found in Erich Auerbach's *Mimesis*. His example is Calogrenant, from Chrétien's *Yvain*, who 'has no political or historical task, nor has any other knight of Arthur's court. Here [as opposed to the *chansons de geste*] the feudal ethos serves no political function; it serves no practical reality at all; it has become absolute. It no longer has any purpose but that of self-realization.'[7]

We tend in literary discussion not to make distinctions between the ideas of knighthood and chivalry, but the historical difference between the two is illuminating. In origin, knights were simply a warrior or arms-bearing class, with a moral obligation towards the society which supported it. By the end of the twelfth century knighthood begins to be something apart from a social and feudal status. The distinction that finally defines chivalry is that in it the ideals of the knightly class are pursued for their own sake: 'We shall hear little more of the feudal duties of the knight; henceforth chivalry is a prelude to or a distraction from those burdens. So the escapism of romance is paralleled in real life, and fantasy is increasingly chivalry's keynote.'[8] 'Knighthood' in the earlier style is the matter of the *chansons de geste*; 'chivalry' is the subject of romance, notably in the form created by the twelfth-century writer Chrétien de Troyes,[9] which influenced all subsequent versions. But at any given time 'knighthood' and its old ideals could become significant to an author's conception of his work, so that the alliterative *Morte Arthure* is, as its editor John Finlayson argues, 'heroic' rather than 'romance' literature, even though it was written in the fourteenth century.[10] Malory, in using the alliterative *Morte Arthure* for part of his work, also gives to his Arthur more political and social reality than the king has in the French cycles that are the main sources of his material,[11] but the amount is not great.

Chivalric material, then, appears to be capable of political and social exploration, but only latently so, with the trend of artistic employment in the high Middle Ages and the Renaissance being clearly towards romance. The key term in chivalric romance is *corteisie*; Auerbach's exposition of its meaning reveals the raw material that Sidney sought to reintegrate into a specifically social framework:

The values expressed in it – refinement of the laws of combat, courteous social intercourse, service of women – have undergone a striking process of change and sublimation in comparison with the *chanson de geste* and are all directed toward a personal and absolute ideal – absolute both in reference to ideal realization and in reference to the absence of any earthly and practical purpose. The personal element in the courtly virtues is not simply a gift of nature; nor is it acquired by birth; to implant them now requires, besides birth, proper training too, as preserving them requires the unforced will to renew them by constant and tireless practice and proving.[12]

Italian Renaissance romances, though superficially deriving their matter from the *chansons de geste*, do not return to the 'politico-historical context' displayed by the Roland legend. Auerbach's own example is Ariosto, and he sees 'l'audaci imprese' of the *Furioso*'s first lines as indicating the poem's attitude towards the meaning of knightly behaviour: 'The reader will understand why following Ariosto, I have chosen this term [feats of arms] rather than 'war,' for they are feats accomplished at random, in one place as well as another, which do not fit into any politically purposive pattern.'[13]

Indeed, Ariosto offers an instructive comparison to Sidney because while treating the major motifs of Renaissance heroic literature, he seems most frequently in his fable to avoid the civic and social aspects of virtue. The remarkable spare sense of social context displayed by the *Furioso* is even something of a paradox, if one recalls that it commemorates the founding of the House of Este. The very idea of allegiance – whether to a religious cause, a sovereign lord, a family, or one's comrades-in-arms – though from time to time Ariosto picks it up and weaves it seriously into his design, is one of his favoured targets for irony, being used frequently as the value that fails to tip the balance against the demands of some passion. In this respect probably more than any other Orlando is the central figure of the poem. His adventures epitomize its free-wheeling atmosphere. He is called the Lord of Anglant, though one has no sense of his being a leader or ruler of men; his passion for Angelica leads him to enmity with his own cousin, Rinaldo; he ignores his responsibility towards Charlemagne and the war both before and during his madness, which means for forty of the poem's forty-six cantos. Formally, the central action of the *Furioso* is the siege of Paris, involving large numbers of Saracen and Christian forces, but more characteristic of the work is the single combat, with the adversaries as likely to share the same religion as to be Christian against pagan. So that here, too, the larger social and political forces that dominate the *chansons de geste* are absent.[14]

Other, more socially cohesive, forces are of course also in play. If Orlando is an autonomous knight (so that his knight-errantry no less than his actual madness is associated with dereliction of duty), a second chief character, Rinaldo, reluctantly acknowledges his primary obligation to Charlemagne and twice forgoes his pursuit of Angelica in order to aid the Christian cause.[15] It seems appropriate that as Bradamante's brother he should enter the familial conflict concerning her marriage. Interestingly, this parental opposition to Bradamante's marrying Ruggero, the further complications of the Bulgarian war, and the elaborate courtesy and friendship motifs exemplified there by Ruggero and Leone were all added to the *Furioso* in the 1532 edition. Being later additions does not make them less important for the poem which the sixteenth century read, but it may suggest that Ariosto himself recognized the work's relative thinness in developing even those social themes which one could expect from his heroic genre and from his excursus into 'comedy' for the final wedding celebration.[16] Yet if we follow C.P. Brand's account of the political and social material of the more overtly epic 1532 *Furioso*, even here most of the themes catalogued are not culled from the fable, but from the Narrator's running commentary.[17] Political and social reality is part of the sixteenth-century frame of the *Furioso*, but not an aspect of the fictional chivalric world that Ariosto creates.

Sidney, like Ariosto, increases the social and thematic density of his work in revision. In so far as this is done through chivalric material, it is possible to see that his employment of it in the *Arcadia* reflects an awareness of the difference between epic and romance that distinguishes the *Arcadia* not only from the *Furioso*, but from the conflation of the two kinds implied in Sidney's own *Defence*.[18] Viewed chronologically, the Book II education in Asia Minor, which is largely in chivalry – the princes are quite like knights errant, though their exploits, especially in Musidorus' narrative, are publicly rather than privately oriented – seems to be preliminary to what is demanded of them on the Greek continent. In Greece they participate first in the Helot rebellion and then in the Book III captivity and siege, both of which incorporate chivalric motifs (prowess, loyalty, honour, courtesy, friendship, and so on) into larger social and political considerations. If Professor John Finlayson is accurate in saying that 'nothing is ever explained in the romances in terms of actual political, geographic or economic conditions,'[19] we can measure the distance from such romances to the Laconian episode, where the Helot rebellion is given elaborate documentation both in its cause and resolution.[20] 'Romance' may persist in the single combat between Pyrocles and Musidorus that ends the Laconian war, but it is giving way to greater concern with what converts heroic victories into stable political realities.

In the Book III Captivity episode the chivalric material is also given an elaborate political context, since Amphialus is rebelling against the traditional Arcadian government and its lawful king.[21] Broader issues are always being weighed against the chivalric lure of glory in single combat. Amphialus as leader of the rebellion is risking more than merely his own life and is wrong to fight; Argalus' personal honour must be measured against the human and social ties of his marriage; as already noted, Phalantus seems an anomaly because he is so completely without ties, riding in merely to observe siegecraft and wandering off 'to seeke his adventures other-where' (I, 418). Amphialus in relation to his mother is perhaps the most interesting case of this juxtaposition of values: because his chivalric ideals and prowess have been made instruments to effect Cecropia's sinister political purposes, it becomes clear that chivalric excellence by itself does not offer a sufficient human model.

The chivalry of the Captivity episode, moreover, is set against the princesses' spiritual ordeal inside the castle. Other values, other modes of endurance impinge upon our consciousness, altering the context of our response to the men's swordplay. This new material in Book III is thus appropriate for the projected ending of the *Arcadia*, which the oracle indicates was to have remained the trial scene, because there too the dominant issue is not a 'chivalric' test but the problem of justice, and there too we find the specific weighing of public and private concerns.

Chivalry may therefore contribute to a work's social scope, but it must be a chivalry consciously redefined by the author so that it no longer operates in what the Renaissance would have assumed was its conventional way. Can pastoral, a second element in the *Arcadia*'s synthesis of modes, be considered a determining factor in the work's scope? The traditional interpretation of pastoral – that it represents a sophisticated society's attempt to escape its present tensions by fleeing to another, golden, age – at first glance offers little encouragement to the social theorist. With only a slight shift in emphasis, however, flight from society becomes criticism of it, and temporal remoteness is translated into the objectivity and moral purity that validate the shepherd's role as judge.

In William Empson's view the combination of simple and complex attitudes that co-exist in a pastoral work makes it radically social in its implications.[22] Heroic and pastoral show a natural affinity in literature because hero and shepherd alike have an existence both apart from and representative of their society.[23] The tragicomic stage displays 'a sort of marriage of the myths of heroic and pastoral, a thing felt as fundamental to both and necessary to the health of society' (pp 28-9). In this relationship lies the essence of the stock double plot, which has as its basic use

to show the labour of the king or saint in the serious part and in the comic part the people, as 'popular' as possible, for whom he laboured ... This gives an impression of dealing with life completely, so that critics sometimes say that *Henry IV* deals with the whole of English life at some date, either Shakespeare's or Henry's; this is palpable nonsense, but what the device wants to make you feel. (pp 27-8)

In the light of Empson's exposition of the unsuspected ramifications of pastoral, one might be persuaded to consider the *Arcadia's* scope the result of its being a version of pastoral, though not in the more usual, restricted sense of the term.[24] But while pastoral itself, if only by implication, may have some connection with society and social ideas, it need not translate this connection into a feeling of breadth and scope. Longus' *Daphnis and Chloe* and Tasso's *Aminta* are both 'pastoral' without this extra dimension, as are the pastoral works that are Sidney's 'sources,' Sannazaro and the *Diana* of both Montemayor and Gil Polo. The English translator of Sannazaro's *Arcadia*, for example, calls attention to its 'virtual exclusion of ethics and politics.'[25] In Empson's own discussion it is pastoral not as a genre but as a 'trick of thought,' its way of putting the complex into the simple (p 23), that lends itself to the patterns of meaning he discerns. Pastoral, even in Empson's broader sense, is, I suspect, not enough either. It is perhaps rather its relation to tragicomedy and thereby to double and multiple plots that allows its potential social meanings to be realized. The relation between Tasso's *Aminta* and Guarini's *Pastor fido* may be cited as evidence here, for Guarini's complexly structured tragicomedy expresses the social conflict latent in the more simply pastoral *Aminta*.

The problem of relating these suggestions to Sidney lies partly in determining the nature and existence of pastoral in his *Arcadia*. If we apply Empson's criteria, the results are largely negative. The primary relation of heroic to pastoral in the work is not what Empson suggests generally, that of symbol to the thing symbolized (p 27); the relation seems mostly critical, with the claims of pastoral being measured against the heroic life and found wanting. Chivalry and pastoral do not co-exist in the body of the *Arcadia* as they do in Cervantes' *Don Quixote*, for example, where Renato Poggioli has seen both as alternative possibilities of embodying or arriving at justice in the social order.[26] Basilius' retirement from the responsibilities of kingship, the very reason for the story's pastoral setting, is an act condemned by every rational counselor in the work. The princes' sojourn in Arcadia is initially viewed as a straying from their true heroic mission, and the dereliction is associated with the 'values' of pastoral retreat: Musidorus accuses his cousin of subjecting himself 'to solitarines, the slye enimie, that doth most separate a man from well doing' (I, 55).

Though Musidorus' statement is by no means Sidney's final evaluation of their action, the heroic ideal remains the standard in the light of which all modifications are painfully worked out. Strephon and Claius, the only conventional pastoral figures appearing in the fable, do not command our attention beyond the symbolic prologue.[27] Dametas and his family are crude and foolish rustics, not simple people who speak more wisely than they know; their function in the plot is sometimes comic and sometimes bizarre parody, but they never represent a locus of value. One's more usual expectations of pastoral are met by the interludes between the books. Even here the shepherds' idyll is not unqualified. David Kalstone's analysis of the Arcadian poems, for example, suggests that the princes' contributions to the eclogues 'redefine the role of pastoral lover ... maintaining the hostility to *otium* [Sidney] displayed in *The Lady of May*; '[the princes] attempt to translate the experiences shared with the shepherds into attitudes and language more appropriate to their life of honor. They do not talk of the simple satisfactions of fulfilled desire, but of the hazards of desire and of that hoped-for state of virtuous love that informs the mind.'[28]

The function of pastoral in Sidney's *Arcadia* is rather more complex than this negative assessment suggests, however, for the work has some relation to what Walter Davis has defined as the basic pastoral-romance pattern (though I find each of his attempts to make the *Arcadia* fit precisely into this mould to be undermined by serious misreadings):

The action of the pastoral romance is simply the progress of the hero through the various areas of the setting: from the outer circle into the inner circle, hence to the center and out again. Since each circle of the setting encourages a certain kind of activity this progress is equivalent to entrance into Arcady in pain and turmoil and reemergence in harmony with oneself. More particularly, the standard pastoral consists of these elements in this order: disintegration in the turbulent outer circle, education in the pastoral circle, and rebirth at the sacred center.[29]

Yet this pattern of action need not be restricted to works that are pastoral themselves, but can be incorporated into larger frames. For example, it was used in epic even as early as the *Aeneid*, notably in the Arcadian material of Book VIII.

It is of primary importance for the Renaissance, which founded its understanding of the epic on the *Aeneid*, that Virgil remains open to the values and attractions of pastoral even when he writes his major work. The *Eclogues* and especially the *Georgics* temper and shape his view of heroism in the *Aeneid*. In Book VIII Aeneas, distraught because of the oncoming war with the combined peoples of Italy, is told to seek aid from the Arcadian King Evander, who has settled in Italy at a site which one day will be Rome. The experience for Aeneas is centrally 'educational.' The shrine is Evander's own small hut, which he invites Aeneas to enter:

ut ventum ad sedes, 'haec' inquit 'limina victor / Alcides subiit, haec illum regia cepit. / aude, hospes, contemnere opes et te quoque dignum / finge deo ...' (VIII.362-5)

When they come to his dwelling, he says, 'This threshold victorious Hercules entered, this house received him. Dare, my guest, to fashion yourself worthy to be a god by despising riches ...'[30]

The 'educational' point is pastoral – it has to do with humility and moral purity – but paradoxically it is also heroic, since it entails the emulation of Hercules who made himself 'worthy to be a god,' and had on that very spot slain the monster Cacus (Greek κακός, evil).[31] For Virgil's epic the point is all-important. Arcadia embodies the sort of noble primitivism which Aeneas must fuse with the hyper-civilized Phrygian attitudes he brings with him from Troy. The values are not merely rural (these he could have found in Latium itself) but also specifically heroic and Greek.

Sidney's *Arcadia* derives not from Aeneas' Arcadian adventure, however, but from the temptation that Dido (though not Carthage) offers to the ideas of the heroic mission. Hercules is crucial for both these Virgilian episodes, since Virgil himself saw the analogue between Dido and Omphale. Sidney's relation to the tradition may well be considered his attempt through the figure of Hercules to resolve the conflict between heroism and love presented in Book IV of the *Aeneid* in the same way that Virgil reconciled heroism and pastoral in Book VIII. For most critical arguments concerning pastoral in the *Arcadia* are really arguments about love and not about contemplation. Sidney's way of 'saving the structure' (ie, the pastoral pattern itself) shows the integration of Virgilian themes: the temptation becomes a means of self-clarification that will permit love to be incorporated into the heroic life. The emblem for this, as we have seen, is the Herculean jewel proclaiming the feminized hero to be 'Never more valiant.'

One should perhaps relate the *Arcadia*'s political concerns to the archetypal pastoral plot as well, for the illumination gained in pastoral retreat always makes it possible for the hero to live more effectively in the outside world to which he returns. The princes (or is it the readers?) discover other things about heroism beyond its relation to love. In the Argalus and Parthenia story, the Captivity sequence, and the imprisonment before the trial the discoveries concern responsibility, suffering, and integrity of a sort that complements the magnanimity of the Asia Minor experiences; and from the great trial in Book V[32] they learn things that are political (or if private, then concerning the moral rather than the intellectual virtues of Aristotle's terminology) and not oriented towards pastoral values.

Sidney has not, then, just 'moralized' a pastoral plot, but has used a pastoral plot for non-pastoral ends. This does not, incidentally, convert the *Arcadia* into an 'anti-pastoral' work. The total pattern projected by the revision, even more than the pattern of the *Old Arcadia*, suggests reconciliation of the central controversy concerning active and contemplative values. But it is a reconciliation which dissolves the antithesis by asserting its compatibility under a dominant active structure.

We may then leave examining the contributing elements of the *Arcadia* and turn to two particular works that Sidney probably thought belonged to the same 'genre' as his revision, those 'absolute heroical poem[s]' in prose, Xenophon's *Cyropaedia* and Heliodorus' *Aethiopica*. The context of this phrase from the *Defence* is that the essence of poetry lies not in verse, but in 'faining notable images of virtues, vices, or what else' (p 81). Xenophon's work is 'poetry' because it contains an idealized presentation of various virtues and vices; it is 'heroic' because its subject is the training and prowess of a king.

Despite a shared general subject matter and a common use of the example as a didactic device, I think most readers would be struck by the differences in vision between the *Cyropaedia* and the *Arcadia*. Their ideas of heroic virtue are alien, if not incompatible. Cyrus' life is a hyperbolic progression of victories that do not require a moment's hesitation or inner conflict.[33] The most insistently developed aspect of his character is his flamboyant generosity, but equally insistent is the paradox that he gets more by giving than he would by taking. Cyrus' motive for virtue is self-interest of the most material kind; his beneficence is a means of increasing his power.[34] Sidney's heroes, on the contrary, expect and seek no reward but glory (aside from the absolute satisfaction of having helped others and done good). E.M.W. Tillyard suggests that Cyrus is an anticipation of Aristotle's magnanimous man; it is instructive to compare Sidney's version of the same ideal as embodied in King Euarchus.[35] The contrast is suggestive even for matters of politics and society. Cyrus as king *is* the state. He arranges all administrative and political functions to suit his own needs and desires for efficiency; there is nothing to which he feels organically related or responsible.[36] As for Sidney, we have already glanced at part of the account describing Euarchus' 'whole Arte of governement' (I, 187), with its emphasis on the ruler's obligation to secure the happiness and prosperity of his people. Cyrus, being the charismatic leader, radiates a generosity that is simultaneously spontaneous and shrewd, but the overwhelming forces of love and loyalty rush centripetally towards him. Sidney's ruler is less spectacular and more hard-working, but most important, he receives the respect and love of his people in response to his own love for them:

For how could they chuse but love him, whom they found so truely to love them? He even in reason disdayning, that they that have charge of beastes, should love their charge, and care for them; and that he that was to governe the most excellent creature, should not love so noble a charge ... vertuouslie and wisely acknowledging, that he with his people made all but one politike bodie, whereof himselfe was the head; even so cared for them, as he woulde for his owne limmes: never restrayning their liberty, without it stretched to licenciousnes, nor pulling them from their goods, which they found were not imployed to the purchase of a greater good: but in all his actions shewing a delight <in> their welfare, broght that to passe, that while by force he tooke nothing, by their love he had all. (I, 187)

Thus, even when the same political ground has been covered by his predecessors, Sidney's conception of society is more organic and pervasive. In other areas that help to provide the breadth of Sidney's concern – ties of love, friendship, family, and so on – Xenophon shows only sporadic interest.

A stronger case can be made for the influence of the *Aethiopica* on the *Arcadia*, partly because as a fictional narrative rather than a quasi-historical treatise it employs means of realizing its ideas that are congenial to Sidney's own design. Heliodorus' romance contains suggestions of the *Arcadia*'s scope, but falls far short of matching Sidney's breadth and depth of vision.[37] Heliodorus' political and social interests are displayed in a variety of ways and with varying degrees of subtlety. King Hydaspes of Aethiopia is clearly conceived as the ideal monarch, proving first his wisdom and humanity in war and then his piety and justice in peace. A number of societies with differing legal and religious customs are contrasted quite naturally as the scene of the story shifts, as are a wide variety of social classes (royalty, priests, citizens, merchants, pirates, fishermen, courtesans, thieves). The scope and tone of the work are enhanced considerably by Heliodorus' opposition to human sacrifice and by his projection of a community which transcends differences in sects, being based upon the sincerity and philosophical value of each man's religious pursuits. It is especially important for the *Arcadia*, I think, that the *Aethiopica* makes structural use of its cultural and geographical scope. (See Appendix A on *in medias res* construction.)

But the importance Heliodorus ultimately attached to the political and social matters he deals with is brought sharply into question when one turns to the main plot of the *Aethiopica*. These interests exist totally apart from the hero and heroine, not even engaging their thoughts on the few occasions when such considerations would seem relevant to their predicament. Though Chariclea's goal is to be recognized as princess and heir of Aethiopia, from the action of the book one might conclude that the only qualification necessary for the office is chastity. The force motivating the hardships of Theagenes and Chariclea, and therefore the force behind the complications in the plot, is not politics, but their personal beauty. By the simple but significant decision to make his main characters aware of the moral and political complexity of their environment, Sidney dispenses with the double focus that mars Heliodorus' conception.[38]

Recent work on the Greek romances makes it clear that the *Arcadia*, though undeniably influenced by them, in fact works against their basic premises in its attempt to integrate the love and adventure motifs with social and political concerns. Two important studies of the genre emphasize its fundamentally apolitical, asocial orientation. For B.P. Reardon, the Greek romance is even further removed from the *polis* than its 'cousin-german' New Comedy, which he sees as relating a social myth: the lovers in New Comedy live in a city, undergo bourgeois tribulations having to do with inheritances and social approval; they are aided by their friends and servants and are finally rewarded by acceptance into the community.[39] Greek romance on the other hand embodies not a social myth but a personal one. The scene is now the wide Mediterranean world, and the individual is isolated in it, dependent not upon friends but upon the gods, or failing their help, upon $\tau \acute{\upsilon} \chi \eta$ or Chance.[40] For Ben Perry, Greek romance in general is 'latter-day epic for Everyman' in a non-heroic world.[41]

Sidney, in following the *Aethiopica*, chooses perhaps the best of the kind – one that seeks to express some of the heroic conception of the original epic genre while reflecting the individual and personal concerns that reach their greatest classical development in this sort of fiction. His challenge was to incorporate the material into a pattern that would reassert the proper 'ethical' alignment between public and private actions, officially subordinating the latter to the former, while still giving love the kind of primary attention that it actually demands in the individual young life. Setting the love story within the larger political concerns of his work in effect 'places' love within a more balanced or mature view of human life. The impact of love apparently cannot be overemphasized, and for long stretches of the work its effect is degrading, but the *Arcadia* as a whole resolves the issue by means of the vanishing distinction: at the end both the love of Pyrocles and Musidorus for the princesses and their training as princes were to be simultaneously triumphant. The situation is so much the expected one for romance that seeing it as an example of the vanishing distinction may seem special pleading, but I would justify the formulation by citing Sidney's energy in developing the opposing halves of his conception.

The *Arcadia*'s true relation to these Greek works will become clearer once we shift to a more theoretical perspective. What I have chosen to call aspects of political or social scope – the concern with the virtues of the good king, military exploits, the legal and administrative functions of government, and so on – are the factors whose presence in the *Cyropaedia* and the *Aethiopica* encouraged the Renaissance to consider them examples of epic. Sidney's ascription in the *Defence* obviously carries this sense: 'For Xenophon, who did imitate so excellently as to give us *effigiem iusti imperii*, the portraiture of a just empire under the name of Cyrus, (as Cicero saieth of him), made therein an absolute heroical poem (p 81).[42] Heliodorus may seem less able to meet the requirements for heroic subject matter, but the work contains much to satisfy a didactic theory built upon the notion of the example. I strongly suspect, on the basis of well-known commentaries like E.K.'s on the *Shepheards Calender* or Harington's on Ariosto, that the serious Renaissance reader would have been less disturbed than we are by the disparity between the main plot and the richer episodic material of the *Aethiopica*. The tendency in interpretation seems to have been to extract the maximum 'value' from each unit of a work, regardless of its relative importance to the work as a whole.[43] The same lack of proportion results from the medieval 'fruit and chaff' method of allegorical interpretation, of which the Renaissance technique is a later variation. By reading this way, one can amass a considerable amount of 'doctrine' without admitting that one's focus has been on less edifying matter.

The *Aethiopica*'s claim to epic status in the Renaissance, however, was probably founded not so much on its content, though its high moral tone undoubtedly helped, as on its possession of certain formal characteristics associated with the classical epic: an inverted structure, narrative résumés, dramatically presented conversation and speeches, and a highly ornamental 'grand style' or *Kunstprosa*[44] that satisfied the epic requirement of magnificence. In sum, both the *Cyropaedia* and the *Aethiopica* were considered 'epic' because they fitted prior ideas of what epic should be, ideas that governed formal as well as substantive details. They are most interesting not as 'sources' for imitation, but for what they tell us about the Renaissance's conception of the epic. The *Arcadia*'s resemblance to these works is best understood in the larger terms of the theory of epic poetry that all three were thought to illustrate.

But critical theory, because it is abstract, will not reveal the specific way ideas are to be expressed. Didactic theorizers speak only of arousing and exemplifying 'virtue'; genre requirements impose some further limitations on the content of a given work, but they are still rather broad. Finally, these general prescriptions must be interpreted in the light of the particular ideals of an author and his society. By briefly tracing these four steps for Sidney – didactic theory, genre, ideals of Tudor humanism, personal or temperamental biases – it becomes clear that the *Arcadia*'s scope is both inevitable and central to its meaning and structure.

The critical theory Sidney enunciates in his *Defence* gives to poetry a specifically didactic function. The various dicta of the treatise might be compressed into a statement something like the following: by the process of figuring forth precept and example together in a single speaking picture, which aims to be a notable image of virtue or vice, the poet both teaches and delights for the purpose of moving men to virtuous action. This describes the nature of poetry as a whole; within the whole, each genre governs a particular moral province and has its own utilitarian effect. Thus, Sidney makes the 'Elegiac' bewail 'the weakness of mankind and the wretchedness of the world,' and says that it 'surely is to be praised, either for compassionate accompanying just causes of lamentations, or for rightly painting out how weak be the passions of woefulness' (p 95). To turn to more relevant genres, Renaissance poetics requires that both tragedy and epic depict noble and illustrious actions, but discriminates further between their choice and treatment of subjects as Tasso does in his *Discorsi*:

Nor do the actions of the tragic and the epic present high matters in the same fashion; for their concern with great affairs is diverse in nature and form. In tragedy it appears in an unexpected and sudden change of fortune, and in the greatness of the happenings that produce pity and terror, but the splendid action of the heroic poem is founded on lofty military virtue and on a magnanimous resolution to die, on piety, on religion, and on actions in which these virtues are resplendent, which are in harmony with the nature of the epic and not fitting in a tragedy.[45]

Sidney is at once more general and more suggestive than Tasso in outlining the province of the heroical: it is 'the best and most accomplished kind of poetry,' for it 'doth not only teach and move to a truth, but teacheth and moveth to the most high and excellent truth' (p 98).

The *Defence* itself, both implicitly and explicitly, offers answers to the question which naturally arises at this point: what is the highest virtue or the greatest truth with which heroic poetry deals? Just as Tasso's prescription reflects the attitudes and beliefs of Counter-Reformation Italy, Sidney's ideas reflect their origin in Tudor humanism. The *Defence* says that the highest virtue is a social one, justice; the intellectual climate of Tudor England placed major emphasis on an education that was geared towards service to the state.

The specifically political and civic orientation of the New Learning in England has been well documented by Fritz Caspari in *Humanism and the Social Order in Tudor England*.[46] Under the Tudor monarchs the dominant class in England became the gentry, that is, the lower landed aristocracy comprising knights, esquires, and gentlemen. These *novi homines* had two major needs: an education that would enable them to perform the duties of an essentially civil governing class and a new social ideal that would justify their power. Humanism, with its resuscitated interest in Athens and Republican Rome, could provide both:

In some respects, conditions in sixteenth-century England resembled those of the classical states. There was a definite similarity between the functions of the Roman and the English aristocracy, of *equites* and knights; both groups tended to occupy the important judicial and administrative offices, and both preserved a certain degree of independence in their positions. The education of the Greek and Roman aristocracy could then provide a most useful example ...[47]

Classical education, centring around the needs of the court and the assembly, was dedicated to the ideal of the orator as *vir bonus peritus dicendi*. G.K. Hunter suggests that the English humanists' version of this ideal was a wistful belief that 'learning could teach a man how to live piously in the world of politics.'[48] As early as in the reign of Henry VIII the exigencies of English politics made the ideal unworkable, but 'the myth of the political effectiveness of learning,' or alternatively, 'the myth of state-service as the natural end of a training in the humanities' remained the powerful force motivating intellectuals 'from Wolsey to Milton and beyond.'[49]

Humanism, as the Elizabethans understood it, presented a goal rather like that of Castiglione's courtier. The energies of both the English gentleman and the Italian *cortegiano* were to be devoted to the service of his prince; the chance of beneficently influencing state policy was the ethical justification for whatever knowledge, charm, or skill each mastered. They were all means of gaining the confidence and respect of the ruling prince, whom he could then advise. If the prince were young, this confidence and respect would enable the courtier to educate him in conformity with humanistic principles of justice and virtue.[50]

This intellectual background suggests why much major literature of the period is concerned with educating princes and fashioning gentlemen. Yet a commitment to English humanism does not automatically require that a writer conceive his work in pervasively social terms. There is obviously room for personal or temperamental bias. Though Shakespeare in the second tetralogy and often in the tragedies does show the kind of broad political and social emphasis outlined here, Spenser does not, in spite of his aim of fashioning a noble gentleman. Whether or not Spenser could actually have realized his plan to devote twelve books to private virtues and then a second twelve to public virtues – and the overlapping of the two spheres in the completed books suggests it would have been impossible – it is significant that he could devise a scheme giving them a separate equality instead of an integral relation to each other in a hierarchy of fulfilment.[51] It tells us what we will find if we turn to the work: notwithstanding sporadic topical or political allegory and Book V in general, *The Faerie Queene* displays a rather lean sense of scope. Neither Faerie Land, the Faerie Court, nor the Faerie Queene herself for that matter has any political existence, though they do have a documented history; Prince Arthur is a ruler without a country or a function. We are occasionally told of whole peoples in distress, but even a socio-political force like democracy or equality is likely to be conceived as a single gigantic figure who can be thrown from a cliff when he proves unamenable to 'reason.' Although the uprising at the death of the Giant of Equality (V.ii.52-4) and the uprising of the Arcadian commoners in Sidney (I, 315ff.) seem to be making the same negative judgment on democracy, there is a radical difference between these episodes which can be used to measure the political and social breadth of the two works. I earlier quoted part of Sidney's description of the confusions that arise from the demands of the various groups of people (divided economically according to town and country interests, occupation, wealth, and so on) when they are asked to state their grievances to King Basilius (see above, p 39). This passage is followed by Pyrocles' long speech persuading the rebels to loyalty and peacefulness. The crowd is won over by his rhetoric, and most remain loyal in the fighting that presently breaks out among themselves (fighting no longer directed against Basilius, but stemming from confusion and insecurity about their guilt). We may if we like describe the political attitude behind this incident as anti-democratic: the people are incapable of ruling themselves because they are inconstant and cannot resolve their differences. But we should also realize that it is a view based on the recognition that society is composed of groups with legitimately opposing needs which require mediation in the interest of the greater good. It is a view based also on a belief in the inherent rationality of men that permits them to respond to reasoning as well as to coercion.[52]

The move from the Arcadian rebellion to Artegall's confrontation with the levelling Giant and the uprising that follows the Giant's death (V.ii.29 *ad fin.*) is a move away from a sense of political reality which, however schematic and simplified, is still concrete. Sidney is clearly interested in the apparent action of his story. The 'equivalent' episode in Spenser may not be equivalent at all; the Giant of Equality may be, as T.K. Dunseath suggests, the anti-Christ, a type of pride and the embodiment of the *un*-creating word, and thus not primarily a social force.[53] The bulk of the dispute between Artegall and the Giant deals with reallotting the four component elements of the world more equably and with the impossibility of weighing truth and falsehood in the same balance. Only briefly at the end of his argument does the Giant get around to mentioning tyrants or the equalization of wealth. The disjunction between the apparent social and the underlying metaphysical and theological implications of the episode is especially jarring at the conclusion, in which the Giant's audience reacts to his death by turning into a 'lawlesse multitude.' The language describing their anger is specifically political –

> They gan to gather in tumultuous rout,
> And mutining, to stirre up civill faction,
> For certaine losse of so great expectation.
> For well they hoped to have got great good,
> And wondrous riches by his innovation (v.ii.51)

– yet the moral judgment in these lines conveys no sense of the social and economic complexity due the literal context.[54]

Spenser's allegorical method reduces social interaction and complexity to the same kind of abstraction that serves for depicting psychological forces, so that Professor Dunseath can interpret these final stanzas both in terms of justice and of pride. Yet unlike the central analogy of Plato's *Republic*, for example, where the soul and the state seem equally important to Socrates, the operation of allegory in *The Faerie Queene* emphasizes the soul and the hero's spiritual confrontations. The goal, whether realized or not, is the knight's perfection, and only peripherally is this relevant to his role and organic function in the state.[55] The Tudor synthesis is thereby less complete in Spenser than in Sidney; he is less certain about the fusion of active and contemplative virtue in the civic ideal. His glorification of the poet's contemplative vision of cosmic harmony in Book VI indicates that the tension penetrated the very core of his understanding of his own vocation.

For Sidney, this particular tension did not exist, perhaps because he was temperamentally incapable of Colin Clout's vision on Mount Acidale. The *Defence* shows that Sidney attributed the highest possible value to poetry, but it is not a mystical or contemplative value. Poetry's superiority is based on its efficacy in moving men to virtuous action. If we infer the nature of the primary tensions Sidney felt from the conflicts displayed in his own work, his concern there is to reconcile the strongest irrational and personal force he has experienced (love) with what he knows with deep conviction to be man's greatest end, a rational life devoted to civic action. So firm is Sidney's acceptance of the humanists' creed that it becomes a yardstick to measure all other values.[56] This creed functions like the formal education underpinning the princes' Asia Minor adventures: it may need qualification and it is difficult to apply, but it remains the standard of judgment. Man in society, not just man, is the central object of Sidney's thought.

We can discover more about Sidney's understanding of heroic poetry by reading the *Defence*, where he defines both the 'highest truth' and 'noblest virtue' which this kind of poetry treats. The basis of the argument by which poetry emerges as the best kind of learning is itself a decision against the pre-eminence of purely speculative knowledge such as astronomy, natural philosophy, or mathematics: the highest end of learning stands 'in the knowledge of a man's self, in the ethic and politic consideration, with the end of well-doing and not of well-knowing only' (p 82). Poetry's competitors for the pedagogical laurel are history, law, and moral philosophy: 'And these four are all that any way deal in that consideration of men's manners, which being the supreme knowledge, they that best breed it deserve the best commendation' (p 85). Law is immediately dismissed, but it originally demanded consideration on grounds that shed light on Sidney's hierarchy of virtues: because '*Ius* [is] the daughter of Justice, and justice is the chief of virtues' (p 84). Sidney's emphasis on justice is pronounced; the words following his description of the heroic poet as the man who 'teacheth and moveth to the most high and excellent truth' are, 'who maketh magnanimity and justice shine through all misty fearfulness and foggy desires' (p 98).

Poetry's superiority lies partly in its ability to pre-empt the subject matter of both history and philosophy, its major rivals. Moreover, it excels history because it is not tied down to a 'bare *Was*' (p 89):

So then the best of the historian is subject to the poet; for whatsoever action, or faction, whatsoever counsel, policy, or war stratagem the historian is bound to recite, that may the poet (if he list) with his imitation make his own; beautifying it both for further teaching, and more delighting, as it pleaseth him: having all, from Dante his heaven to his hell, under the authority of his pen. (p 89)

Philosophy stands in special need of poetry's collaboration:

no doubt the philosopher with his learned definition – be it of virtue, vices, matters of public policy or private government – replenisheth the memory with many infallible grounds of wisdom, which, notwithstanding, lie dark before the imaginative and judging power, if they be not illuminated or figured forth by the speaking picture of poesy. (p 86)

The case presented by moral philosophy to prove that it deserves recognition as the chief branch of knowledge is particularly relevant to heroic poetry because Sidney sees the purpose and scope of both as identical. The philosopher asks rhetorically,

whether it be possible to find any path so ready to lead a man to virtue as that which teacheth what virtue is; and teacheth it not only by delivering forth his very being, his causes and effects, but also by making known his enemy, vice, which must be destroyed, and his cumbersome servant, passion, which must be mastered; by showing the generalities that containeth it, and the specialities that are derived from it; lastly, by plain setting down, how it extendeth it self out of the limits of a man's own little world to the government of families and maintaining of public societies. (p 83)

It is not surprising that this anatomy of virtue should offer a generally accurate groundplan of Sidney's own *Arcadia*; after all, it is the philosopher's 'Virtue' which the heroic poet makes ravishing by setting her out in holiday apparel (p 98).

Almost every aspect of Sidney's description of the content and aim of poetry, and especially of heroic poetry, thus supports the decidedly social bias of his *Arcadia*. The most high and excellent truths concern man's function in society: the chief virtue is justice, the most important knowledge encompasses on the one hand the policies and counsels of history, and on the other philosophy's precepts about a virtue that exists analogously in the individual man, in families, and in society itself. That the anatomy of virtue should move to a culmination (or fruition) in the well-ordered society suggests in retrospect that this has been its goal throughout, conditioning and directing each stage along the way. Translated into the terms of the *Arcadia*, in the notion of society lies the broadest, most significant expression of the moral and political ideas illuminated by the individual incidents of the work. We shall see in Chapter 7 that the hierarchy of personal, familial, and social virtue provides the *Arcadia* with yet another kind of structure, as well as with an end towards which all its action is directed.

Thus far among the apparent possibilities there is no single component element or work that can be considered the impetus for Sidney's pervasively social conception of his *Arcadia*; rather, the discussion has suggested that its existence owes most to his own general understanding of heroic poetry. But there *is* a work which may have been a source of encouragement and even of influence, since Sidney seems to interpret it in a manner consonant with his own practice. Though no modern reader is apt to be struck by the resemblance, Sidney probably revised the *Arcadia* to accord with his reading of the *Aeneid*. The choice of model is not surprising, for the *Aeneid* was recognized by the Renaissance as the summit of literary achievement. Sidney analyses Virgil's epic in the section of the *Defence* devoted to proving the value of heroic poetry, specifically where he demonstrates how 'the lofty image of such worthies most inflameth the mind with the desire to be worthy, and informs with counsel how to be worthy.'

Only let Aeneas be worn in the tablet of your memory; how he governeth himself in the ruin of his country; in the preserving his old father, and carrying away his religious ceremonies; in obeying God's commandment to leave Dido, though not only all passionate kindeness, but even the human consideration of virtuous gratefulness, would have craved other of him; how in storms, how in sports, how in war, how in peace, how a fugitive, how victorious, how besieged, how besieging, how to strangers, how to allies, how to enemies, how to his own; lastly, how in his inward self, and how in his outward government – and I think, in a mind not prejudiced with a prejudicating humour, he will be found in excellency fruitful ... (p 98)

What emerges from this picture of Aeneas is Sidney's conception of the best kind of hero. He is not primarily a warrior or an autonomous knight wandering over the countryside in search of battle; he is instead a good man fully engaged in the responsibilities of family, society, and country. The passage also suggests a way of viewing the action of an epic – as an obstacle course set up to try the hero's virtue. The tests would seem to be of two different kinds. He must prove himself against natural or human 'events' such as storms, wars, sieges, and he must also prove himself in relation to other men or to a complex of men who form 'institutions' such as family or country. Moreover, he must do this by knowing and remaining true to his 'inward self.'

As disparate as the two works may seem to us, using Sidney's own analysis as a guide we can see how the *Aeneid* could have encouraged both the fullness of range and the inclusion of particular kinds of incidents in the revised *Arcadia*. I do not mean therefore to offer it as a better candidate for source study than the *Aethiopica* or the *Amadis de Gaule*. As the general argument of the chapter has suggested, the *Arcadia* resembles the *Aeneid* (and works like the *Cyropaedia* and the *Aethiopica* as well) in so far as they share the themes and concerns of heroic poetry. The particular similarity it shows to the *Aeneid* is really proof of the overriding importance of genre; the Renaissance definition of epic was, after all, formed at least partially by induction from its most honoured example. And it is as significant for the English Renaissance that Sidney saw the *Aeneid* in terms of private and public virtue as it is for the Middle Ages that Macrobius saw it as an allegory of the life of the soul.

THE SOCIAL DIMENSION: SOME EXAMPLES

The argument of the previous section sought to determine both the uniqueness and the importance of Sidney's concern with society. This section illustrates how this sense of scope is manifested in the work.

Although the *Arcadia*'s social dimension is more apparent in the 1590 text and is undeniably the result of the revisions and additions, it is not totally absent from the original version. Even in the early draft we can detect Sidney's interests: Arcadia is still primarily a political entity with political problems arising first from its ruler's negligence and then from his apparent death. The love situation relies almost completely on political events for its movement and dénouement; Basilius' retirement, the Arcadian revolt, and the chaos caused by the Duke's 'death' are the wheels on which the plot moves, literally from beginning to middle to end. Despite Sidney's deprecation the Old Arcadia is not altogether 'but a trifle, and that triflinglie handled.'[57] Indeed, it is likely because he saw possibilities for expanding the public, educational, and political motifs already present in the work that Sidney decided to recast it in 'epic' form rather than to write the Arthuriad which legend says he at one time contemplated.[58]

When we turn to the New Arcadia we immediately see the broader canvas used for its design. Every addition, including even a bit of ornamentation like Phalantus' tourney, argues the operation of a freer-ranging, richer sensibility. To take examples from only Book I, one may cite the prologue with its introduction of Neoplatonic ideas, the description of Kalander's estate with its feeling for the dignity and strength of aristocratic life, the political lessons of the Helot rebellion and the princes' behaviour in conducting that war, the counterpointed theme of beauty and valour that are not guaranteed perfect success implied in both the Amphialus-Helen and the Argalus-Parthenia stories. The more strictly political aspect of the work's greater scope appears in the expanded criteria offered for evaluating a just government. It is perhaps only a matter of degree, but the revisions seem to indicate a simultaneous growth in Sidney's sense of the existence and needs of the people on the one hand, and of the extraordinary range of competence demanded by kingship on the other. We have already explored aspects of this problem in discussing the education of the prince as the unifying theme of the Book II episodes and, concerning Euarchus, in discussing the organic or reciprocal relation between ruler and subjects that determines the goal and therefore the nature of that education. The epic history probably offers the most concentrated formulation of the theme, but this new emphasis refocuses the material in the rest of the work as well.

The introduction of Laconia and the Helot rebellion into the first section of the New Arcadia immediately proclaims the work's broader political focus. Laconia is the third Greek state whose institutions are to be in any way explored; the other two, Arcadia and Euarchus' Macedon, were present also in the original version, though the extent of the exploration is much increased in the revision. The terms of the New Arcadia's three-way contrast seem to shift because of the stages of composition: Basilius and Euarchus are still to be compared as kings, but Laconia outweighs Macedon in the comparison between states. The New Arcadia virtually opens with the sharp contrast between the civil war and barren fields of Laconia and the fertility and peace of Arcadia (I, 14). The contrast is not so much between good and bad rulers (we learn almost nothing about the Lacedaemonian king, Amiclas) as between two different social orders. Arcadia's art and prosperity are both attributable to the economic independence of the Arcadian shepherd – 'Neither are our shepheards such, as (I heare) they be in other countries; but they are the verie owners of the sheepe ...' (I, 28) – whereas exploitation lies at the root of Laconia's troubles:

[the Helots] having been of old, freemen and possessioners, the Lacedemonians had conquered them, and layd, not onely tribute, but bondage upon them: which they had long borne; till of late the Lacedaemonians through greedinesse growing more heavie then they could beare, and through contempt lesse carefull how to make them beare, they had with a generall consent (rather springing by the generalnes of the cause, then of any artificiall practise) set themselves in armes ... (I, 39)

The articles of peace between King Amiclas and the rebels emphasize the idea that peace is guaranteed only by political justice: the Helots are made free citizens with equal rights in voting and education, and the second-class citizenship implied by distinctions between Lacedaemonians and Helots is avoided by establishing the single status of 'Laconian' (I, 46-7).[59]

Concerning the many-sided competence necessary for carrying out the duties of kingship, the revisions are much more suggestive than the old version, as we may see by considering the rewritten description of Euarchus printed in the 1593 text. The ostensible narrative purpose of the passage is to explain why Euarchus happens to be in Arcadia at the moment of Basilius' death, but the hypothetical situation that occurs when the second greatest power in Greece[60] suddenly abdicates political responsibility seems to take control of Sidney's imagination. For the *Old Arcadia*'s brief statement that Euarchus fears Greece's resulting vulnerability to foreign attack (*OA* 358), the revised passage substitutes three pages of diplomatic duplicity and military gestures (*OA* 355-7, variants). The contrast between Euarchus' foresight and political shrewdness and Basilius' flight into pastoral seclusion in fear of an ambiguous oracle is the point of both versions, but it is sharpened in the later text because we are made more aware of the extent and nature of Basilius' failings by the elaboration of this contrary example.[61] Independently of the contrast, we come to see that the good ruler must perform a demanding variety of roles in addition to the familiar ones of hero and magistrate. The possible criteria for evaluating good and bad rulers are thus enlarged, permitting, even encouraging, more delicate nuances of judgment.

The same political shrewdness, often expressed as a fine assessment of alternative actions or motivations, is observable in Sidney's handling of Amphialus as captain of the rebel forces in the new Third Book.

First, he dispatched privat letters to al those principall Lords and gentlemen of the country, whom he thought ether alliance, or friendship to himselfe might drawe; with speciall motions from the generall consideration of duetie: not omitting all such, whom either youthfull age, or youth-like mindes did fill with unlimited desires: besides such, whom any discontentment made hungry of change, or an over-spended wante, made want a civill warre: to each (according to the counsell of his mother) conforming himselfe after their humors. To his friends, friendlines; to the ambitious, great expectations; to the displeased, revenge; to the greedie, spoyle: wrapping their hopes with such cunning, as they rather seemed given over unto them as partakers: then promises sprong of necessitie. (I, 371)

The result is again a deeper because more convincing sense of political reality, one of the factors contributing to what has been defined here as 'scope.' The greater complexity of the material in this new Third Book – whether considered psychologically or politically – counts significantly in the reader's perception of the overall seriousness and density of the *New Arcadia*. The effect is compounded from the several elements of the action: the preparation on both sides for the siege, the movement of whole armies in addition to single combats, the tragic implications of Amphialus himself, the efficiency of having the plot machinery set into motion by an ambitious schemer like Cecropia (whose archetypal relation to the Witch-Queen of *Snow White* makes of her almost an elemental force), the accompanying confrontation between good and evil, and of course the moral stature of the princesses that emerges from their ordeal in captivity.

As Book III clearly shows, Sidney's political and social concerns in no way interfere with his interest in the moral or inner state of his characters. The trial of the princesses and the tragedy of Amphialus stand in the same relation to the scope of the private action in the *Old Arcadia* as the siege here does to the political upheavals in the earlier version. The two kinds of action – what we can perhaps call 'ethic and politic considerations' – go together in Sidney's mind, and it is probably more accurate to speak of the *New Arcadia*'s increased scope in terms of both. They go together because Sidney's social vision required that the good man fulfil himself and his purpose in life through serving his fellow men.

NARRATIVE STRUCTURE:
EPISODES AND FABLE

Discussion of the *Arcadia's* narrative structure is complicated by the existence of several versions of the work, the two primary ones each having its own dominant structure. The *Old Arcadia's* model is Terentian comedy,[1] with its five Books or 'Acts' arranged in a pattern of exposition, complication, climax, reversal, and dénouement. The *New Arcadia*, while apparently retaining a dramatic structure for its main plot, weaves into this action hundreds of pages of episodic material, with the result that its dominant structure (at least in the first two books) is thematic. For Books I and II, the added material alone exceeds the original by almost one-third, so that a discussion of the *New Arcadia* which strongly subordinates the importance of the episodic amplification to the claims of the main plot risks committing an injustice to our perception of the work as readers. The problem of the relative significance of episodes and fable is further complicated by the fact that the work is unfinished. The radical difference in tone and scope between the new and old Third Books prevents their being merely pasted together as they are in the 1593 text. Yet each Book III is integral to its own version: the new Third Book is as necessarily the outcome of the material added to Books I and II as the chicanery and intrigue of the old Third are of the original two books. Purely episodic material, which may have started as amplification of the main action, has come to demand by its inner logic a continuation that is more powerful than anything called for by the original plan, except perhaps in the events surrounding the trial. Although the new Third Book sets up particularly fruitful resonances with these final scenes, it seems ironically to do so at the expense of the credibility and aesthetic suitability of the plot intrigue that is to lead to the trial – credibility because during the siege the characters develop beyond the actions they must later perform, and aesthetic suitability because the princes' 'triumphs' in the old Third Book are anticlimactic by comparison.

The revisions of the *New Arcadia*, by both accumulation and design, have in effect made of the work something substantially new, which we are justified in considering a re-vision. The first half of this chapter is a threefold exploration of this point: theoretically, by means of defining episode and fable; textually, by determining what use one can legitimately make of the 1593 text; and substantively, by examining the differences between the two versions in handling the major subject of love.

VISION AND REVISION

The new Third Book has so frequently been called 'the Captivity Episode' that its true structural function has largely been overlooked:[2] Amphialus' rebellion and its consequences comprise no less than a major revision in the *Arcadia*'s main plot. The difficulty here is partly semantic, because the word 'episode' commonly has several meanings which blur useful distinctions. It can mean both an isolatable stage of the main action itself and a removable, digressive, or only thematically relevant unit of narrative. While this ambiguity is not crucial to twentieth-century criticism, it was to the sixteenth century, for the concepts of main plot and episode formed the basis for much of its discussion of the epic.[3]

The problem has its source in interpretations of Aristotle's *Poetics*, and since that activity goes on even today, we may follow it clearly in the footnotes of a recent exegete, Gerald F. Else:

A.H. Gilbert argues, *AJP* 70 (1949) 56-64 ... that in the *Poetics* ἐπεισόδιον always means 'any action that is a subordinate *but necessary* component of the integral action of the play.' The truth is rather the other way round: with the possible exception of 4.49ᵃ28 ... ἐπεισόδιον seems to mean everywhere in the *Poetics* a *non-essential* added scene, an 'episode' in the special sense.[4]

That ἐπεισοδιοῦν here [17.55ᵃ34-62] refers to 'episodes' in the strict sense of the word, i.e., the addition of extra scenes or speeches, and not simply to the dividing up of the plot itself into acts or scenes ('fill in the episodes,' Butcher), is proved by the particular ἐπεισόδια mentioned below, ᵇ14-15; by the specification that they are brief in the drama and bulkier in the epic; and above all by the example of the *Odyssey*, ᵇ23: everything *outside* the central plot is 'episodes.'[5]

Professor Else arrives at an interpretation of Aristotle on this point which is similar to that generally held by the sixteenth century – an episode is something outside the main plot or fable, in practice usually related by theme, but justifiable theoretically as either ornament or digression.[6] This general theory, which demands unity and necessity only for the central action while allowing great freedom for episodic elaboration, explains in part how a work like the *New Arcadia* could fulfil Renaissance formal expectations for the epic. Note, for example, Minturno's description in *L'Arte poetica* (1564) of how the *Orlando furioso* could have been organized as an epic remarkably like the *Iliad*. He implies, moreover, that Ariosto could have recast the *Furioso* in its entirety, not omitting a single incident:

for he could have undertaken to sing the amorous fury of Orlando and all that followed that madness, showing that the Moors did not have courage to undertake war ... while Orlando was sane, but when he grew mad for love they passed into France and did very great damage to the Christians. In this way he would have been able to treat the things done at that time because of love or any other cause, by knights on one side or the other, who took part in that war. And after Orlando regained his first sanity, he was able to give victory to the Christians by his valor.[7]

Sidney does not directly confront the problem of the relation between episode and fable in the *Defence*, but his remarks on drama suggest that he felt strongly about the need for a single action, with 'things done in former time or other place' being recounted by a messenger (p 114). This seems on the whole a reasonable definition of episode to apply to his own *Arcadia*, though it will not cover certain incidents that the reader feels are largely emblematic or in some way separable from the main action (eg, Phalantus' tourney, but this may be compared with the Funeral Games of classical epic, traditionally categorized as episodes).[8] Under this definition, much of the material added to Book I is episodic, though how much depends upon one's definition of the *Arcadia*'s main plot.

Sidney's habit of giving his work structures rather than a single structure extends even to the shape of his fable. Each of the several alternative ways of defining the main plot of the *New Arcadia* calls for a somewhat different assortment of episodes. Since the *Old Arcadia* began with Basilius' retirement, this original material can be equated with the fable, making 'episodes' of most of the opening material of the revision, from the prologue to Pyrocles' discovery as Zelmane. Or secondly, if we take Sidney's chronological and geographical definition as a rule of thumb ('things done in former time or other place'), we may choose our boundary for the fable as mainland Greece, where the princes are washed ashore at the outset of the work. This would parallel the structure of the *Aethiopica*. Under such a definition, the steward's tale of Argalus and Parthenia is an episode (having happened 'in former time'), but the princes' confrontation during the Helot rebellion, which results from it, is a part of the main plot.[9] As a third alternative, we can understand the geographical definition more restrictively, deciding the fable takes place in Arcadia itself, and events like the Helot rebellion and Musidorus' search for Pyrocles throughout the Greek mainland are additional episodes rather than part of an expanded fable. My own preference is for the second of these, in which the fable begins when the princes are washed ashore in Greece, because it demonstrates immediately the effects of revision: a growth in the complexity and seriousness of a work demands a larger conception of its action, not merely episodic accretion.

Early in the First Book, then, interpolated material has some repercussion on the fable, modifying it in the interest of more heroic action (here one notes Musidorus' attempt to free Argalus and Clitophon from the Helots, with the ensuing account of the battle stratagems, combat, and terms of peace). The episodes of the Second Book, being a classic example of things done in another time and place, do not directly alter the fable. Nevertheless, the cumulative impact of the experiences there helps to shape the reader's expectations of the work and its heroes. The fruition of all this material occurs in the new Third Book, which, according to Sidney's definition, must be considered part of the fable itself and not some digressive or closely related incident. It takes place in the course of the princes' sojourn in Arcadia; it opens Book III and is not framed by older material as are the other episodes; all the major characters participate in it (though Gynecia appears only momentarily); and most significantly, it is at least as important an action with respect to the princes' heroism and the threat to Arcadia's stability as are the attack by wild animals and the riot in front of the lodge, which were points in the rising crescendo of action in the *Old Arcadia*.

Some signs, however, suggest that Sidney might not have been fully aware that he was reshaping the course of his main plot. As late as three-quarters of the way through the revised Second Book, where the oracle is finally revealed, Sidney's intentions seem unchanged, since the oracle providing the knot for the central action to unravel remains substantially the same as in the *Old Arcadia*. Moreover, the characters who undergo the major experiences in the Captivity are not Pyrocles and Musidorus themselves, but Amphialus and the princesses, which may indicate that Sidney thought he was not compromising his original plans for his heroes. Then again, the Captivity is in a sense the outcome of the earlier episodes because it seems to be the way Sidney chose to end his concern with the new characters he had introduced: Argalus, Parthenia, and Cecropia are dead and Amphialus is severely wounded beyond any participation in further action.[10] Ostensibly, then, Sidney can now turn his attention from the military siege of Amphialus' castle back to the amorous siege at the royal lodges. But the question remains whether Pamela and Philoclea (and very likely the princes also) have not outgrown the roles they play in the old Third and Fourth Books: for the princes, their despair at even temporary separation and willingness to employ an army to force Basilius to give up Philoclea; for Philoclea her credulousness at Pyrocles' transfer of affections, her fainting spells, her 'wise innocency' and 'witty childhood';[11] for Pamela her helpless dependence upon Musidorus and her 'unconsidered' decision to run away with him.[12] Some of these incidents or statements could easily be omitted, but cumulatively they suggest that Sidney had changed his basic conception of their characters. We are thus entitled to question the honesty and credibility of making these new characters perform the actions originally planned for them. Rather than merely cleaning up the unfinished business created by the episodes, the new Third Book in effect takes over the central action and subordinates it to the larger concerns of the revised material.

If this set of conjectures is right, we must re-examine the claim of the 1593 text on the critic's attention. C.S. Lewis is quite correct in saying that this is the only version that can concern the literary *historian* because it was the only one known until the twentieth century,[13] but the different purposes of the literary *critic* can be better served by a more complex approach to the texts. He must hold the *Old* and *New Arcadias* distinct in his mind, but simultaneously be aware that the authorial emendations in the 1593 text of Books III-V support the relevance of much of the older material to the new design.[14]

The latest trend in Sidney criticism seems to meet only the first criterion of keeping the two *Arcadias* separate, either by studying only one of the versions, or by treating each as a distinct work even in a book concerned with both. But surely it artificially limits our understanding of the work if we assume that we know nothing of the 1590 *Arcadia* beyond its final, unfinished sentence. The *New Arcadia* is designed to find its resolution in the trial scene, and we are merely seeing *less* than we are capable of if we deliberately blind ourselves to the development of thematic materials that will find their fruition in that context. To borrow a phrase from Hugh Sanford, we do indeed have the 'conclusion [though] not the perfection' of Sidney's work – if we treat it critically enough, testing whether each action is likely to have been retained, always aware that real changes must have real consequences. This is admittedly an arbitrary procedure, because each critic's sensibility could arrive at a different conjectural text. To some extent we have such a situation already, since two important studies, by Danby and Davis, have worked with a version of the text that I do not think they would have deliberately chosen had they considered the possibility that the revisions of the 1590 text are not inherent in the main plot, or even completely harmonious with it, but that they significantly alter the character of the work. In other words, the 'testing' procedure I suggest will at least inject some awareness into the decisions which each critic is forced to make by the state of the texts.

If one is interested in discussing Sidney's alterations as 're-vision,' there are two separate questions to ask about the material contained in the old Books III, IV, and V: the first concerns consistency and the second, meaning. One remains concerned with a passage or action only after deciding that it could conceivably be incorporated into the *New Arcadia*, but Sidney's *meaning* in the passage must be determined primarily by the context of the *Old Arcadia*. The use of the 1590 *Arcadia* in this latter question is limited: it can supply resonances but it should not determine or alter meaning because that must be established by the context for which we know it was designed.[15] Applied conservatively, the only major block of material that needs rejection under the first test occurs in Book III. The important modification of Philoclea's 'seduction' by Pyrocles which Sidney made himself[16] seems to imply that, in questioning how much of every scene suits the purpose of the revision, we are following the author's own practice. The manoeuver is meant to be primarily negative: I am not trying to construct the remainder of the revision, but merely to prevent readers from the assumption that everything in the 1593 text ought to be reconciled with Sidney's revised intentions. The end product of this critical process is not a consistent revised *Arcadia*; the problem of the fable remains insuperable because the passages that most need excision are crucial to the action that is outlined and reaffirmed by the two oracles. The new Book III leaves us with a king, queen, and three rustic servants still quite capable of being duped, but with princes and princesses who are unlikely to set the plot mechanism in motion.

The second point, concerning the interpretation of those scenes from the old Books III, IV, and V which are still workable in the *New Arcadia*, perhaps calls for some illustration. The problem here arises when scenes such as the debate about suicide between Philoclea and Pyrocles or the princes' acceptance of death as they await trial are read as though they really were culminations of the 'earlier' material in the Captivity sequence. The text of the old Books III-V as it stands in the 1593 edition will simply not bear the particular freight of religion and Neo-platonism that has been thrust upon it by analogy with the expanded scope of the Captivity.[17] The difficulty is compounded by an assumption that Sidney thought of 'education' as a series of changes either in one's basic character or in one's ideals. This is debatable even for the *New Arcadia*; it is totally unjustified for the *Old*.

A closer look at the text of the two scenes from the *Old Arcadia* just mentioned will show that Sidney does not intend them to represent moments of reversal or extraordinary new insight for the princes. Instead of Pyrocles' learning Christian patience from Philoclea during the discussion in her bedchamber over his determination to commit suicide, Sidney's emphasis in the scene is on an unchanging Pyrocles – on his 'unshaked magnanimity,' 'the quiet attending all accidents ... [of his] unmastered virtue' (*OA* 294), on his being 'not so much persuaded as delighted' by her speech (*OA* 298). After their dialogue is over, in fact, Pyrocles reaches for the window bar to get on with his suicide, only to be stopped by Philoclea's passionately tearful assurance that she will kill herself as well.

Pyrocles, even overweighed with her so wisely uttered affection,[18] finding her determination so fixed that his end should but deprive them both of a present contentment, and not avoid a coming evil (as a man that ran not unto it by a sudden qualm of passion, but by a true use of reason, preferring her life to his own), now that wisdom did manifest unto him that way would not prevail, he retired himself with as much tranquillity from it as before he had gone unto it, like a man that had set the keeping or leaving of the body as a thing without himself, and so had thereof a freed and untroubled consideration. (*OA* 299)

This is surely no victory for Philoclea's superior Christian reasoning. At issue here is Pyrocles' heroism rather than Philoclea's wisdom. Sidney shows no anxiety about his didactic point. He is willing for it to be held in abeyance until Philoclea's argument that suicide falsely prejudges God's power and goodness can be affirmed by Basilius' miraculous reawakening.

Unless we approach the suicide scene with preconceptions about process, education, and change, I do not believe these ideas are to be found in it.[19] Pyrocles is not significantly altered as a result of the discussion with Philoclea. And in the second of these scenes, the 'true rampire of patience' (*OA* 370) with which the princes fortify their courage while awaiting trial is essentially the patience called for in this kind of situation by the same code of ethics they have been following all along. It is not the princes who have changed but the occasion that evokes a different kind of response. One may recall Greville's statement that Sidney's purpose 'was to limn out ... exact pictures, of every posture of the minde ...'[20] Something that might be termed 'ethical decorum' is in play: certain situations call for courage, strategy, resistance; others for undespairing acceptance. The didactic focus has shifted to the problem of dying well, and Sidney's version is not markedly different from its classical analogues. He may even have had Plato's *Phaedo* in mind, for the princes in discussing the nature of the soul's existence after the body's dissolution speak of several ideas that Socrates examines before his death.[21]

Interpretations of this pre-trial scene designed to support Neoplatonic readings of the *Arcadia* seem both wrong and unfortunate: wrong because they misread the emphasis of the argument in the text, and unfortunate because they fail to see the strong defence of the active life that underlies the princes' debate. The subject of their long dialogue is the nature of the soul's immortality, specifically the question of whether it will retain any memory of its previous existence. As I have demonstrated elsewhere, the thrust of the argument is to defend the idea of personal as opposed to impersonal immortality.[22] The defence is based on an assertion that the soul will retain some kind of memory of its own past existence; part of the blissful soul's reward is its clarified particular knowledge of its previous thoughts, deeds, and virtue.

The debate is prefaced by Musidorus' personal justification of their lives:

> We have lived, and have lived to be good to ourselves and others. Our souls (which are put into the stirring earth of our bodies) have achieved the causes of their hither coming. They have known, and honoured with knowledge, the cause of their creation. And to many men (for in this time, place, and fortune, it is lawful for us to speak gloriously) it hath been behoveful that we should live. (*OA* 371)

It continues by justifying the life of virtue itself, in its highest metaphysical context. The discussion thus moves from justification with respect to other men on earth to justification with respect to higher things – to immortality and the eternal state of the soul. And the type of life and virtue they are vindicating is manifestly the only one mentioned in the scene, the active life, characterized by the moral virtues and by helping other men. The case is very forcefully put: the princes' dedication to the active life has enabled them' [to achieve] the causes of their hither coming.'[23]

Although discussion of these two scenes has clarified Sidney's intentions in his *Arcadia*, it has not primarily offered evidence for the *New Arcadia* as a re-vision of the older material. On the contrary, the scenes point instead to the reason that Sidney felt he could compose his new, more heroic, poem on the frame of his earlier work. So much criticism of the *Old Arcadia* has centred on the princes' moral deterioration in Arcadia that we need to be reminded that this kind of positive moral evaluation was also embedded in Sidney's original conception. Sidney's treatment of his heroes there is, I suggest, more complex and sympathetic than we have recently been led to believe.

The key to the examination of the relation between episode and fable thus far has been the Captivity Episode, Book III of the *New Arcadia*. Once we see it as a revision of plot and not merely an additional episode, unconsidered use of the 1593 text becomes impossible. My further proposal is that we no longer assume the text as published in 1590 to be the only alternative to the 1593 hybrid version. There remains a need to work with whatever parts of the original Books III-V still suit the new plan because the *New Arcadia*'s two oracles show that Sidney intended the same dénouement for his revised work. We deprive ourselves of the richness of Sidney's thematic design if we do not see the new developments in relation to the form they take in the trial scene. It cannot be coincidence that these developments find fruition in the trial as we have it. Sidney revised the *Arcadia*, it seems to me, on the basis of what he had discovered in writing the trial scene: the issues it raised for him are the germs of the revision.

The first two parts of this exploration of Sidney's revisions have relied on the concept of plot as an aid in determining the text that the critic should examine. I have adduced the Captivity Episode as an example of re-vision, an alteration in the *plot* that crowns and magnifies all the alterations in episodes and form made in Books I and II, thus conditioning our acceptance of whatever will happen in the rest of the work. The earlier changes are also expressions of that new vision, of course. We shall discover, by shifting our focus from plot to theme (or more accurately, to subject), how Sidney reshapes the *Arcadia* to articulate alternative and deeper interpretations of roughly the same body of experience.[24] The subject we turn to is love, perhaps the most important touchstone of *Arcadian* criticism – *New* as well as *Old*. What a critic makes of the love story virtually determines his interpretation of the work. Emphasis on the love story has tended to count against the *New Arcadia*'s claim to heroic poetry in two ways: it has either made the work generically a romance (and so 'logically' comparable to *Rosalynde* or Montemayor's *Diana*) or it has converted it thematically to a Neoplatonic exaltation of contemplative virtue. Let us turn directly to the relative handling of love in the two versions of the *Arcadia* to see what purpose we can discover in Sidney's revisions.

Perhaps the second most peculiar aspect of the *Old Arcadia* in the light of its usual description as 'pastoral romance' – the first being the degree to which it is anti-pastoral – is the generally deprecatory attitude it displays towards love. Beyond any other of love's qualities, we are asked to contemplate its *power*. Moreover, unlike a passion such as anger, which is theoretically 'neutral' because it can be harnessed for rational purposes, love is most often seen as inherently evil because it is by nature incapable of being controlled or moderated by reason. This in a way paraphrases Musidorus' argument in his initial debate with Pyrocles, and I am sure at that point the reader suspects that the ensuing action will prove his position wrong by vindicating the vaguely Neoplatonic protest of Pyrocles' reply. Certainly the reader is predisposed to sympathize with the heroes because of the time-honoured convention that ascribes to them a virtuous and therefore properly rewarded love in the closing scenes.[25] And strangely, one continues in these expectations though the actual emotions and actions that are depicted on the pages of the *Old Arcadia* support rather than destroy Musidorus' original arguments. Apparently the conventions are so strong that they remain unimpaired by the subversive 'reality' which continually confronts them, though this reality includes a Pyrocles who would go through the demeaning intrigue of the assignations in the cave (and even contemplate Basilius' murder) for an end no nobler than spending one night in Philoclea's bed, and a Musidorus who is prevented from raping Pamela only by the intrusion of armed outlaws:

But each of these [Pamela's features] having a mighty working in his heart, all joined together did so draw his will into the nature of their confederacy that now his promise began to have but a fainting force, and each thought that rase against those desires was received but as a stranger to his counsel, well experiencing in himself that no vow is so strong as the avoiding of occasions; so that rising softly from her, overmastered with the fury of delight ... he was bent to take the advantage of the weakness of the watch [she is sleeping], and see whether at that season, he could win the bulwark before timely help might come. (OA 201-2)[26]

The didacticism is still there – 'no vow is so strong as the avoiding of occasions' – but devoted to a view of love different from the one towards which the New Arcadia seems to be working.

Of the dominant view of love expressed in the original work Richard Lanham has observed:

love in the original Arcadia is passionate love; affection has a very minor role, sentiment (in spite of common belief) almost none. And passion is described in consistently unpleasant terms by all who feel it: the Arcadian language of love is a language of attack, victory and slavery; of burning torment; wounds, poison, disease and death; of violence and compulsion, desire and appetite; above all of the folly of lust.[27]

This description is true not only for the princes, but with shifting emphasis for Basilius, Gynecia, and their daughters as well. Several incidents in the princes' Asia Minor adventures narrated among the eclogues continue the exploration of love, and as one would expect these stories reflect and clarify the thematic point of the central action. Of the approximately six tales of love offered,[28] Plangus' unrequited love for Erona and her ill-placed constancy in loving Antiphilus are the only 'noble' emotions presented, but our approbation is severely qualified. Plangus' love comes under heavy attack for being contrary to Reason and Stoic virtue (in the long poetic dialogue between Plangus and Boulon [OA 147-52]), and Erona's devotion is so emphatically undeserved as to deter any attempt to interpret it positively.

The emblem of love in the Old Arcadia may well be the picture of Cupid worn and explained by the shepherd Dicus. This Cupid is an ugly satyr with horns, long ears, an old face, and a body full of eyes. He is sitting on a gallows like a hangman: 'In his right hand, he was painted holding a crown of laurel, in his left a purse of money; and out of his mouth hung a lace which held the pictures of a goodly man and an excellent fair woman. And with such a countenance he was drawn as if he had persuaded every man by those enticements to come and be hanged there' (*OA* 64).[29] Critics who read the *Old Arcadia* with great moral fervour find much support in it for Dicus' case. Yet it is one thing to recognize the element of moral disapproval that colours the presentation of love in the *Old Arcadia* and quite another to make it the central fact of one's interpretation of the work. For the reader really bent on retribution, the 'providential' ending is cynicism, at best, and a moral outrage, at worst. But whether one takes the genre of the *Old Arcadia* to be comedy, tragicomedy, or romance – anything, that is, except tragedy or a moral treatise – the generic conventions operate to produce a reader who is sympathetic to the hero and hoping (waiting) for everything to turn out well for him. Sidney can, and does, depend on this reservoir of sympathy to counteract or mitigate the negative behaviour of the princes. He can risk making their actions so faulty because this counterforce co-exists in the reading experience.

Perhaps it would be more accurate to say that the reader makes two simultaneous responses, a critical and a sympathetic one, and that this generates part of the moral complexity of the work. In the *Old Arcadia* especially, Sidney is interested in manipulating his readers' responses both directly and indirectly; the effect is apparently one of his purposes for creating an identifiable narrative voice. The device is exceptionally clear (as we shall see later in this chapter) in the handling of Euarchus' judgment at the trial, where the reader is asked to contrast his average human response with Euarchus' 'extraordinary excellencies' (*OA* 414). Yet in spite of the Narrator's being the vehicle for most of the explicit moral judgments in the work,[30] Sidney allows him a large measure of sympathy for the princes. By doing so, he underlines the reader's complicity, even, for example, in the consummation of Pyrocles' and Philoclea's love:

he gives me occasion to leave him in so happy a plight lest my pen seem to grudge at the due bliss of these poor lovers whose loyalty had but small respite of their fiery agonies. And now Lalus' pipe doth come to my hearing, which invites me to his marriage that in this season was celebrated between him and the handsome Kala whom long he had loved; which, I hope your ears, fair ladies, be not so full of great matters that you will disdain to hear. (*OA* 243)

The narration that resumes in Book IV opens with a contrary evaluation of this same scene:

The everlasting justice (using ourselves to be the punishers of our faults, and making our own actions the beginning of our chastisement, that our shame may be the more manifest, and our repentance follow the sooner) took Dametas at this present ... to be the instrument of revealing the secretest cunning – so evil a ground doth evil stand upon, and so manifest it is that nothing remains strongly but that which hath the good foundation of goodness. (OA 265)

Sidney seems to expect us to acquiesce in both these judgments, and I think we do. Such a stance does not make Sidney less moral than the critics who see lechery and deceitfulness at the root of the princes' every action. One *must* be shocked by Musidorus' attempted rape of Pamela (though could he conceivably have done more than kiss her before she opened her eyes and put him in his place again?),[31] but Sidney surely saw it as a specific lapse rather than an indication of total moral deterioration. There is a useful distinction to be made between being moral and being judgmental.

Even if such an account of some of the moral and emotional forces in play in the Old Arcadia were acceptable, there might still be grounds for thinking that Sidney's risks in this procedure were not altogether successful. The particular romance conventions that Sidney seems to rely on are chivalric – that is, our interest in the princes depends to a great extent on their being heroes (constant in love, brave, skilled with weapons, eager to help the oppressed and do battle with evil), and the Asia Minor adventures recounted in the eclogues as well as the rescue of their ladies from marauding beasts and the quashing of a peasants' uprising are all placed in the work to substantiate their claim to heroism. The question is whether these factors have sufficient weight. Can it not be argued that making the princes' loves flawed by lust, reinforcing the theme with the desperate passion of Gynecia and Basilius' foolish desire, and then supporting only ideas of lust, incontinence, and irrationality in the Asia Minor material all ultimately have greater force in the reader's imagination than the severely limited prowess permitted in an attack by two wild animals and an uprising of tipsy peasants? I think that Sidney trusted their heroism would not be overbalanced in the Old Arcadia, but that in revising the work, he set out to be sure that the final emphasis would be unmistakable.

The New Arcadia, retaining the Old as its central action, takes over a great deal of its critical evaluation of love. The conflict between Reason and Passion remains a major theme. For the princes, love is still a disordering force that drives them to assume shameful disguises[32] and to turn aside from a life of heroic virtue. They remain flanked by the guilty passions of Basilius and Gynecia, though their own lust is now moderated, so that the act of preserving their mistresses' honour, keeping them 'still worthy to be loved' (I, 261), becomes more a sign and less a test of their virtue. But to counterbalance the largely negative valence of the fable, the New Arcadia undertakes through episodic amplification to realize the idea of virtuous love. In asserting the possible good that can come of love, Sidney uses both Neoplatonism and chivalry, but the final emphasis given to the chivalric ideal among the values inculcated by the princes' education accurately reflects the general tenor of the work:

And (ô Lord) to see the admirable power and noble effects of Love, whereby the seeming insensible Loadstone, with a secret beauty (holding the spirit of iron in it) can draw that hard-harted thing unto it, and (like a vertuous mistresse) not onely make it bow it selfe, but with it make it aspire to so high a Love, as of the heavenly Poles; and thereby to bring foorth the noblest deeds, that the children of the Earth can boast of. (I, 191-2)[33]

Significantly, the logical structure of this sentence – its 'whereby' and 'thereby' – subordinates contemplation to action, relating them as means and end or as 'power' and 'effect'.

The most salient reworking of the *Old Arcadia*'s attitude towards love is contained in the material added to Book I, notably in the opening passage on Urania and in the story of Argalus and Parthenia. The incidents gain their importance from prominent placing early in the work, for their positive evaluation of love is not echoed or elaborated until much further along, perhaps not until the princesses are captives, though there are suggestions of it in the devotion shown by Palladius and Princess Zelmane[34] and in the description of Helen's court given during the Asia Minor adventures. Until the Third Book, then, the ideals embodied in these incidents remain largely outside the experience of the major characters in the fable, at most expressing only a portion of what they are undergoing, since the violence and irrationality of the other episodes explore what love means for them as well. Taken as a whole, the episodes do not necessarily reflect aspects of the heroes' actual experiences; it would be more accurate to say that the various episodes form a spectrum that runs from Strephon and Claius' Neoplatonic striving after Divine Love to the wicked lust felt by Andromana, and that, for the princes at least, neither of these extremes represents a viable choice. The further importance of the episodes concerning Urania, Argalus, and Parthenia is that they open this spectrum in the direction of a positive evaluation of love by reconciling the antithesis between pastoral and heroism presented in the *Old Arcadia*.

The most obvious contrast between heroic and pastoral in the *Old Arcadia* stems from the juxtaposition of an aristocratic fable with the pastoral ideas contained in the eclogues. If Sidney intended to weigh the passion that ravaged his noble figures (Strephon, Claius, and Philisides among them) against the serenity that love brings to the simpler lives of the shepherds who appear in the interludes, then the significance of the contrast for Sidney's immediate readers must have seemed limited. It left them little sense of a reconciliation possible for their own aristocratic lives, and it emphasized the inaccessibility of pastoral harmony by, as it were, sealing it off from the fable. The revised plan of the *New Arcadia* substitutes integration for juxtaposition; it provides greater unity by bringing into the body of each book positive values that have some relation to the pastoral happiness of the shepherds, but that are also available to men living more complex lives. Although the *New Arcadia*'s Strephon and Claius may be shepherds, Argalus, Parthenia, Zelmane, and Palladius are not. The apparent function of this new material would then be to mediate between the opposing factors in the original scheme by bringing the concepts expounded in the eclogues into fruitful rather than merely critical relation with the story itself.

It is also possible to see the *Old Arcadia* somewhat more complexly than through the oppositions just outlined. Starting from Neil Rudenstine's fine reading of Musidorus' first discovery of Pyrocles in love (*OA* 15),[35] we can say that the love material offers some germ of reconciliation for the problem I have posed. When Pyrocles and Musidorus fall in love they begin to respond to nature with wonder and a willingness to contemplate and praise its beauty, whereas earlier they were 'acquisitive,' traveling merely to gain information about geography, government, fortifications, economics. This qualitative change in their attitude towards experience which Professor Rudenstine notes, while neither pastoral nor contemplative in any strict, doctrinal sense, is what makes love the potential link between the pastoral eclogues and the aristocratic fable. The reader can thereby recognize this love as a necessary complement to the princes' education rather than a truancy from it.

In the *New Arcadia*, the pastoral harmony is first consciously 'elevated' to a point that permits its incorporation in the heroic life. Strephon and Claius perform this function. They differ from the rest of the Arcadian shepherds, as they themselves proclaim, in that they see their love as an expression of Neoplatonism. In contrast, the vision expressed by Thyrsis and Lalus in the eclogues is a natural, innocent, springtime joy in country pleasures. The experience of Strephon and Claius is theoretically available to shepherd and aristocrat alike, but both *Arcadias* exclude aristocrats from Lalus' uncomplicated felicity.[36] Argalus and Parthenia offer an aristocratic version of harmony: felicity achieved after complications have been overcome. Here the concept of a beneficent love moves from Neoplatonism to chivalry, since the portion of their story that appears in Book I presents the victory of heroic action and constancy undertaken in the cause of love.

The significant revaluation of love and pastoral in the *New Arcadia* is suggested by the changes made in Strephon and Claius themselves. In the *Old Arcadia*, where they appear only in the Fourth Eclogues, they are gentlemen from some other nation who become shepherds in order to woo Urania, herself only supposed a shepherd's daughter. They earn their special virtue by the usual pastoral-romance means of being in reality nobly born. The *New Arcadia* makes

Strephon and Claius true Arcadian shepherds, and Urania (probably) pure allegory. A transitional state in Sidney's conception of these figures (now true shepherds, though not Arcadians) is extant in the long, unfinished poem 'A Shepherd's tale no height of stile desires' (*OP* 4), which emphasizes the very idea of love as the poisoner of peace and subverter of reason that is notably omitted from the *New Arcadia*'s prologue, where instead Urania is said to have 'throwne reason upon our desires' (I, 8).[37]

Strephon and Claius thus paradoxically give up their noble birth in order to mediate between the pastoral and chivalric matter of the *Arcadia*. The issue is even more clearly joined in the total story of Argalus and Parthenia, for Argalus is eventually forced to choose between his 'pastoral' felicity in love and a call to further heroic action. Regardless of other questions raised by this sequence concerning the ultimate compatibility of chivalric honour and fulfilled love (chivalry's viability beyond adolescence?), the love itself emerges, even after their deaths, as a triumphantly positive value. The story of Argalus and Parthenia taken as a whole, and echoed by the allied stories of Zelmane and Palladius, therefore holds out hope that the love which the princes feel, though undeniably a disruptive and violent passion, can through its association with selfless constancy be transmuted into something valuable.

The description of Queen Helen's court in Corinth given by Pyrocles in Book II offers perhaps the most optimistic statement in the *New Arcadia* of the possibility of reconciling love and virtue. The context is appropriately aristocratic and courtly, and the description is frankly of an embodied ideal:

she made her people by peace, warlike; her courtiers by sports, learned; her Ladies by Love, chast. For by continuall martiall exercises without bloud, she made them perfect in that bloudy art. Her sportes were such as caried riches of Knowledge upon the streame of Delight: and such the behaviour both of her selfe, and her Ladies, as builded their chastitie, not upon waywardnes, but by choice of worthines: So as it seemed, that court to have bene the mariage place of Love and Vertue, and that her selfe was a Diana apparelled in the garments of Venus. (I, 283)[38]

Although the additions of the 1590 text have a perceptible trend, Sidney's attitudes are not doctrinaire and his revisions are not simply programmatic. The net effect of these episodes on the Old Arcadian fable may be to suggest a broader, more ameliorative framework in which to set the largely malevolent force of love depicted by the plot, but the revision also contains episodes which tend to support the *Old Arcadia*'s theme of confusion between love and lust, the power of love to subvert internal and external order alike: one may cite, for example, Dido and Pamphilus, Erona and Antiphilus, Andromana in all her relations, Helen in the earlier Book I account. Sidney's decision to retain the *Old Arcadia* for his fable committed him to some extent to the vision it expressed; while he seemed to want to transcend its limitations for his two main characters, one assumes that he chose not to write a completely different work because he saw in the *Old Arcadia* something that reflected a view of the world and of experience that seemed to him valid. Even if the new version allowed the princes a large measure of success (though with the trial scene of the dénouement built into the oracle, the success could not be complete), it was not necessary to whitewash the negative implications of love or to minimize the difficulty of the task in order to permit their achievement. Sidney's stylistic preference for the vanishing distinction in fact required that he do the contrary.

In matters of love, therefore, no less than of politics and more public ethics, the result of Sidney's revisions is to increase the scope and moral seriousness of the work. Hardly an earth-shaking conclusion, but one that seems worth stating because these are qualities associated with heroic or epic works, and thus with the question of the *Arcadia*'s genre. The implications of this discussion run contrary to those of Walter Davis, for example, who says that 'Sidney's distribution of [non-pastoral] narrative material brings it under the control of his pastoral plot, for the chivalric and political events always parallel the action of love in Arcadia.'[39] The tendency of Sidney's revisions seems to make the emphasis misplaced here – and were they thought of literally as *re-vision* and not only as episodic elaboration, Sidney would be better served. If Professor Davis' genre is at all useful – and his analysis of the central pattern of pastoral romance plots is indeed persuasive – then what Sidney has done in the *New Arcadia* is to employ pastoral romance as the base of his heroic poem.[40] From Sidney's ethical and didactic viewpoint, there would be little reason to reconcile the heroic with a predominantly pastoral vision, but it would mean a great deal to incorporate 'pastoral' within the active life.[41]

EXTRINSIC AND INTRINSIC AMPLIFICATION

In discussing various aspects of the *Arcadia*'s structure, I have touched upon several kinds of functional relation between the episodes and fable. For example, both may participate commonly in determining tone (Chapter 4), the episodes may explore a wider range of responses to a situation presented by the fable (as in the handling of love), or the episodes may formulate the educational and ethical theory underlying the actions and judgments of the major characters in the fable (Chapter 5). Two kinds of relations are discernible among these examples. The first two listed are centripetally directed towards amplifying the plot; they clarify, emphasize, reinforce, or moderate some point expressed in the main action. The third is an instance of extrinsically guided amplification; it realizes some antecedent or absolute idea of subject matter that has as it were a doctrinal existence apart from the particular action of the fable. The doctrine may be an educational or a poetic theory; the idea may be to treat all the major forms of political constitutions or all the major forms of lyric poetry. Any one of a hundred schemes can determine the material to be selected. The only quality they share is that each arises from some impulse extrinsic to the plot itself.[42]

These two kinds of amplification – intrinsic and extrinsic – provide a useful framework for further analysis of the way the *New Arcadia* is put together. In keeping with the distinction made at the opening of this chapter, I shall emphasize not the unified narrative or dramatic structure taken over from the *Old Arcadia*, but the thematic structures that dominate the revision.

To begin with extrinsic principles, the first set exhibits what might be called encyclopedic tendencies. The suggestion that the poet is committed to dealing with a given subject comprehensively, perhaps even exhaustively, can be found in Sidney's own writing about the nature of poetry and in his friend Greville's description of the *Arcadia* itself. I have spoken of Greville's statement in connection with rhetorical devices for structuring thought;[43] more can be said about the content of the passage as well. The philosophical precepts that Sidney sought to turn into 'Images of Life' concerned both monarch and subject, a formal division meant to admit no third term. In the monarch's case, Greville includes the growth, state, and decline of princes, governments, and laws (again the topics are exhaustive), and after enumerating several vicissitudes, he concludes the tally with 'all other errors, or alterations in publique affairs' (my italics). For the subject, he enumerates nine 'states' and finishes with the same gesture of comprehensiveness: 'and all other moodes of private fortunes, or misfortunes.' With the *Arcadia* in hand, a man experiencing any good or ill fortune will know how to bear all the discountenances of adversity. Sidney's purpose, in so far as it is 'to limn out ... exact pictures, of every posture of the minde,' is encyclopedic; and incidents which are added in order to fulfil this purpose (several episodes in the epic history come to mind) are justified by some scheme extrinsic, though not of course alien, to the action of the fable.[44]

Sidney's comparable passage describing the *Aeneid* suggests that the motive Greville assigns to him stems not from Greville's own moral and political predilections, but from something more generally available, probably from the Renaissance understanding of the scope and subjects of heroic poetry. In the *Defence* passage the reader is asked to wear in the tablet of his memory how Aeneas governs himself in storms, sports, war, peace; how he acts when he is a fugitive or victorious, when he is besieged or besieging; how he behaves to strangers, allies, enemies, his own people; and finally what he is like in his inward self and out-

imitating the virtues
and vices of humankind,
their signification ...

ward government. The two descriptions match as closely as the limitations of the subject matter allow. The curious effect of Sidney's string of antitheses, moreover, is to suggest that we shall find an even larger area of experience in the *Aeneid* than is explicitly listed, a suggestion perhaps that the range between the antithetic extremes will be covered as well. We read the passage as though Sidney were offering us in Aeneas the complete model of virtue, and in fact, the *Defence* has asked earlier: 'What philosopher's counsel can so readily direct ... a virtuous man in all fortunes, as Aeneas in Virgil?' (p 86). Once one begins to see the heroes of fiction as models of behaviour for personal emulation, the commitment to a comprehensive moral spectrum follows logically: the best poem will offer the best models for the greatest number of ethically significant situations.

Another factor contributing to the same result is Sidney's definition of poetry as an imitation not of an action, but of virtues and vices. On this basis poetry claims supremacy as a teacher because it provides the strongest appreciation of such matters as love of country, anger, wisdom, temperance, friendship, remorse of conscience, pride, cruelty, ambition, revenge, 'and finally, all virtues, vices, and passions so in their own natural seats laid to the view, that we seem not to hear of them, but clearly to see through them' (p 86).[45] In addition to this list of subjects and the assumption of comprehensiveness that lies behind it, the *Defence* shows other indications that habits of looking at material according to the techniques of logical and rhetorical analysis have suggested the matter of the *Arcadia*. What is noteworthy is that once Sidney conceives a scheme or division for his *Arcadia*, he uses it completely, embodying each part somewhere in his work, often in the episodes because opportunity is lacking in the fable. The philosopher's definition of virtue (as I noted in Chapter 6) is particularly relevant. Philosophy teaches what virtue is,

not only by delivering forth his very being, his causes and effects; but also by making known his enemy, vice, which must be destroyed, and his cumbersome servant, passion, which must be mastered; by showing the generalities that containeth it, and the specialities that are derived from it; lastly, by plain setting downe, how it extendeth it self out of the limits of a man's own little world to the government of families and maintaining of public societies. (p 83)[46]

The *Old Arcadia* also is to some extent built upon this same didactic scheme, but with nothing like the *New Arcadia*'s almost methodical pursuit of comprehensiveness. The *Old Arcadia* does not give prominence to some important 'species' of vice, notably pride, avarice, hypocrisy, envy, ingratitude, inconstancy, anger, and discourtesy; it nowhere develops the idea that passions such as fear and anger may be servants of virtue (though the idea is stated on *OA* 19); it treats constancy more as a political virtue than a courtly one, and gives scant attention to pity and gratitude, or to bonds of affection between brothers, sisters, or parents and children. The absence of examples giving positive versions of filial and parental love, despite their obvious relevance to the plot itself, reminds us that some material added to the *New Arcadia* does not so much alter the original as articulate its assumptions.

The second variety of what I have called extrinsically guided amplification offers examples of comprehensiveness on a more modest scale. The schemes to be illustrated here have only a limited number of parts. For example, the three major speeches of the *Old Arcadia* cover the 'questions' involved in each of the three kinds of argument described by rhetorical manuals: the trial scene contains forensic or judicial speeches concerning justice; Pyrocles' speech to the rebels at the end of Book II is a deliberative speech concerning the advantageous or expedient course of action; the debate between Pyrocles and Musidorus in Book I concerns the honourable, and though the speeches themselves are deliberative, the inquiry is one that both epideictic and deliberative causes share.[47] The lack of a full-dress encomium is less detrimental to the inclusiveness of the scheme than one might suspect, because topics of praise and blame are so frequently used in the work in descriptions of character.[48]

If the *Rhetoric* and the *Ethics* are quarry for a poet's pen, so too is the *Politics*. The first *Arcadia* was concerned only with monarchy; the revision extends its interest to include tyranny, oligarchy, and a democracy that borders on anarchy. The forms of government are discussed by Aristotle and Plato, but Sidney's account does not seem to rely upon them for details. Unlike the Greeks, Sidney assumes that monarchy is the natural and ideal form of government, and he treats all the others as perversions of this ideal or as results of some breakdown in its functioning. Thus Macedon's oligarchy arises from a long period of regency (Euarchus' parents, grandfather, and great-grandfather all died young); the anarchic democracy of the Arcadian rebels before the Lodge obviously carries the moral that only the benevolent power of the king can restore peace among the inherently conflicting desires of various economic segments of society; the chaos following Basilius' apparent death, called 'a notable example how great dissipations monarchal governments are subject unto' (*OA* 320), is the background for a rise of factions among the aristocracy and for Tymautus' demagogic play for power. The same four variables – king, people, aristocracy, and gentlemen – are treated in Philisides' beast fable included among the eclogues, where the argument seems to concern the rise of monarchy and its transformation into tyranny. The latter transformation occurs when the king destroys the powerful nobility which, though faulty from the commons' point of view, at least stands as a potential counterforce against the king's ambitions.[49] By adding descriptions of oligarchy and democracy and by expanding the coverage of monarchy and tyranny (in the Asia Minor adventures), Sidney's New Arcadia nods in the direction of the classical treatise,[50] but he refocuses the Greeks' interest to clarify sixteenth-century European political reality, which is dominantly monarchical.

A third scheme, in addition to the oratorical and political ones, might be called psychological. The existence of the scheme is difficult to prove because it is the least explicitly presented, being concerned with three characters who need not be compared with one another in the normal course of reading. On the other hand, certain features in the portrayal of Cecropia, Gynecia, and Andromana do seem to justify comparison: all three women are strong characters, pulsating with a malevolent energy that attracts our attention; as Kenneth Myrick has noted, some balance seems to be intended between Andromana's captivity of the princes and Cecropia's of the princesses;[51] Cecropia and Andromana have only one good quality, and it is the same one, love for their sons, which apparently contrasts with Gynecia's jealous hatred of her daughter Philoclea. In discussing Gynecia earlier I suggested that basic to Sidney's conception of her was the Christian idea of the defective Will. She knows that her desire for Pyrocles-Zelmane is evil, but she cannot bring her Will to take the side of her Reason to subdue this Passion. The other two women seem to fill out the scheme: Andromana is described in terms of a complete abandonment to lust, suggesting that in her the Passions have become absolute, and Cecropia represents a perversion of Reason.

Andromana's identification with lust or Passion is encouraged by several aspects of her story. She never seems to entertain the possibility that she may be doing wrong. The moment she can no longer ignore such knowledge she commits suicide (I, 288), which suggests that Reason as an agent of moral control has not existed for her. In one case lust drives her to incest (Plangus is her stepson) and in another to the subversion of both love and friendship: 'her wordes would beginne halfe of the sentence to Musidorus, and end the other half to Pyrocles: not ashamed (seeing the friendshippe betweene us) to desire either of us to be a mediator to the other; as if we should have played <one> request at Tennis betweene us ...' (I, 279). The usurpation of Reason by the Passions that she represents is undoubtedly also symbolized (in an echo of the Hercules-Omphale motif) by the way her husband, the King of Iberia, gives her complete authority to run the affairs of his country.

Cecropia, on the other hand, though a compendium of vices, has no passions at all. She is conceived in terms of pride, envy, ambition, malice, and cruelty. Watching her machinations we are always aware of her subtlety. We may note that in traditional schemes of the vices, for example, Dante's in the Inferno and Purgatorio, those displayed by Cecropia are all associated with the higher parts of the soul, sins of the spirit rather than of the flesh. Her special connection with

Reason shows, of course, in the temptation of the princesses, which she attempts to do by casuistry and even outright lies, both perversions of the rational process. Trying to convert Pamela to atheism is an obvious tactical blunder for Cecropia, but for Sidney it is a means of making the issue absolute. Cecropia's 'godlesse minde' (I, 409) is both the cause and the logical culmination of her other vices. Further, since dividing the soul into these three faculties is traditionally hierarchical in purpose, Cecropia becomes the chief sinner in a hierarchy of vice. Her atheism achieves a symbolic function in the *Arcadia* because the God whose existence Pamela proves is the force which ratifies virtue and makes it meaningful. Cecropia's godlessness is an implicit denial of the 'perfect order, perfect beautie, perfect constancie' (I, 408) that constitute and guarantee the Arcadian cosmos. Her actions and arguments are the corresponding manifestations of that denial. Her discussions of pleasure and the nature of feminine power are materialistic reductions of beauty; her cynical assumptions about the origin and transference of love are an affront to constancy; the political rebellion itself and each of these other negations along with its supporting arguments are all sins against order.

The psychological scheme, with its traditional Christian reverberations, thus becomes instrumental in understanding the full import of the temptation scenes. Cecropia's position at the head of a hierarchy of sin adds weight and unity to the action of the *New Arcadia*, which, as I have suggested before, culminates here in the captivity sequence where the thematic concerns of the work reach their maximum intensity and fullest revelation. If the new Third Book is also a stage of the revamped plot, then this congruence in the shapes of the narrative and thematic structures is an important achievement in total design. In the *Old Arcadia*, by contrast, the thematic intensity of the trial scene far outweighs the development of thematic material in the princes' amorous success and capture, which comprise its narrative climax and turning point.

As this discussion has shown, extrinsically motivated material need not exist only in the episodes; frequently some form of unity is gained by having the fable and episodes contribute to the same scheme. The line between this sort of relation and true mutual exploration is difficult to draw. Where the themes are important to the plot – for example, the conflict between honour and love (for Argalus and in the description of Helen's court), the Reason-Passion topos (Plangus and Erona), the friendship and education motifs (Amphialus, Tydeus, and Telenor) – I should call the motive intrinsic. Of this type I have already treated in some detail the spectrum of love that Sidney creates to define the nature and potentiality of the princes' experience. Another intrinsic relation is the 'pattern of analogous plots' which Walter Davis finds to exist between the episodes and the main action of Book II: 'the plot follows the pattern shared by all the tales: *private Passion causing public chaos,* often involving the misuse of love.'[52] Although I have taken issue with the ability of this account to do justice to the complexity of the retrospective narrative, some of the episodes (especially the stories surrounding Plangus and Erona) can indeed be profitably explored as analogues to the main action.[53]

Since one can see so many patterns operating simultaneously, and even particular incidents contributing to several different schemes, it is illusory to seek the single structural principle that governs the *Arcadia*. One's discoveries must necessarily be less conclusive. Nevertheless, though the patterns discerned may amount to no more than possible alternative perspectives, some may offer helpful approaches to the work. For example, the perceptible social bias that Sidney displays in his description of a poem like the *Aeneid* encourages the critic to analyse the *Arcadia* in terms of the various significant relationships among men, that is, to analyse 'how [virtue] extendeth it self out of the limits of a mans own little world to the government of families, and maintaining of public societies.' Setting up a table of the basic relationships is a useful method of keeping the whole of the *Arcadia* at hand in units that facilitate making comparisons and perceiving degrees of Sidney's interest. Appendix B contains tables covering nine such relationships, not all of equal importance: those between friends, husbands and wives, lovers, parents and children, siblings, rulers and counselors, rulers and subjects, hosts and guests, masters and servants. The categories are self-explanatory, except that 'lovers' includes unreciprocated passion, 'parent-child' has some 'foster' parents or guardians, and 'ruler-subject' includes some instances of the more general relationship between a leader and his followers.

Since a significant example in each category occurs in the main plot, the primary function of subsequent examples is frequently intrinsic, offering some commentary or counterpoint to the 'statement' in the fable – for example, every example of friendship and love has relevance to Pyrocles and Musidorus, most examples of kings with their subjects and counselors have relevance to Basilius and Arcadia. In the minor categories all the instances seem equally important, and the exploration is directed immediately at some virtue or norm of conduct like gratitude, hospitality, or bonds of family affection, rather than mediately through some example of it in the fable. One cannot help noticing how unimportant the relationship between siblings is for Sidney in this work – and every example is a product of revision, for the bond between Pamela and Philoclea is explicitly discounted in the *Old Arcadia*[54] – when we know of his own attachment to both his sister and brother Robert. The omission is probably explained by the emphasis given to friendship, which pre-empts the characteristics of love between brothers while permitting the bond to be praised as 'virtue' rather than as arising from nature. The similarity of the bond between brothers to that between comrades is among several points Aristotle discusses in his treatment of friendship in Book VIII of the *Ethics*.[55] Aristotle's φιλία, 'friendship' is a broader concept than its English translation suggests, since it also includes the feelings between lovers, husbands and wives, brothers, business partners, parents and children, and men and gods. It thus covers the same ground as the tables I have drawn up and goes considerably beyond.

The entire account of friendship in the *Ethics*, especially VIII.ix-xii, offers an illuminating parallel to the themes and interconnections among ideas in the *Arcadia*. In these chapters Aristotle discusses the relation between friendship and justice ('the demands of justice also seem to increase with the intensity of the friendship, which implies that friendship and justice exist between the same persons and have an equal extension'), their basis in community and relation to the political community (at which point there is a summary of the three kinds of constitutions – monarchy, aristocracy, and timocracy or polity – and their perversions). He cites the resemblances and analogues to these constitutions found in the household (father as monarch, master as tyrant, the association of man and wife as aristocratic), relates kings, shepherds, and fathers analogically, and devotes special attention to friendship between comrades and kinsmen, including that between man and wife, which 'seems to exist by nature' but goes beyond reproduction to fulfil many purposes of utility and pleasure and even 'may be based also on virtue.' The section closes by repeating its initial emphasis: 'How man and wife and in general friend and friend ought mutually to behave seems to be the same question as how it is just for them to behave ...' The connections among various social and familial relations and their political context, and the further possibility of interpreting them all in terms of justice are, I believe, highly suggestive for the *Arcadia*.

Of the important relationships recorded in the tables, I want to turn now to those between parents and children and between rulers and their subjects. Both are relevant to each other and to one of the antithetical topoi I have mentioned periodically without exploring in detail: the contrast between public and private spheres of action or virtue. The kind of structural unity that can be achieved by working with these thematic relationships is best seen from an analysis of the parent-child bond as it appears in the *Old Arcadia*; in fact, its handling there presents in miniature the form of amplification these relationships undergo in revision. It is first of all a primary fact of the main plot, occurring in several different ways: in Basilius' unjust treatment of his daughters, which in turn causes the even more unjust mock-parental relationship of Dametas to Pamela; in the envy and resentment Gynecia feels against Philoclea; in the comic picture of the Dametas-Miso-Mopsa family group; and finally, in Euarchus' sentencing his own son to death. It also occurs in two of the 'episodes' related during the interludes: in the quarrel between the King of Lydia and his daughter Erona over her desire to marry Antiphilus, and in the Sesostris-Queen of Egypt-Amasis triangle (the *New Arcadia*'s King of Iberia, Andromana, and Plangus). Third, the relationship between a father and his children is a frequent metaphor for the responsibilities and duties of a king and his subjects, thus affording an important connection between the work's political and private concerns.

However extensive the *Old Arcadia*'s treatment of the parent-child relationship is, the revision, almost from its opening moments, seeks to outstrip the original. In the first twenty-five pages following the 'prologue' there are four new references to the parental theme, ranging from the description of a statue of Venus with the 'babe Aeneas' at her breast (!) to Parthenia's resistance to her mother's demand that she marry Demagoras.[56] The *New Arcadia* also magnifies Basilius' injustice to his daughters. In the original he plans merely to sequester them for one year until the oracle is fulfilled, but since the revised oracle omits all indication of time, his resolve becomes to keep them unmarried as long as he lives.[57] Philanax' attempt to dissuade Basilius from carrying out his plan invokes a concept for evaluating Basilius' action not present in the *Old Arcadia*: 'What shall I say, if the affection of a father to his owne children, cannot plead sufficiently against such fancies? once certaine it is, the God, which is God of nature, doth never teach unnaturalnes ...' (I, 25)

For it is as a powerful natural force, even more than as a virtue or a norm of conduct, that the *New Arcadia* interprets parental and filial love. Because it is primal it can plausibly be the one 'good' quality left to Andromana and Cecropia. Yet for all that, it is not inviolable. Its very potency as a force makes the turnings away from it the more shocking,[58] whether in Gynecia's jealous hatred of Philoclea, the King of Iberia's banishment of Plangus or in Chremes' cruelty towards Dido. Often the presence rather than the absence of parental or filial love can be the source of a scene's power: the King of Paphlagonia's remorse for his sins against Leonatus, the Princess Zelmane's death, and the two climaxes of error for Amphialus (the death of his foster-father Timotheus after Amphialus has killed his son and Cecropia's plunge from the castle wall as she flees from him). The purpose of this enriched development of the theme may well have been to increase the effectiveness of the final trial scene when Euarchus knowingly condemns his own son to death, 'though not only all passionate kindeness, but even ... human consideration ... would have craved other of him,'[59] because of the one absolute virtue to which all else must be subordinated, Justice.

At this trial scene the public-private topos is thrown into sharp relief, though the lack of its revised version prevents one from making a definitive statement about the resolution of any theme treated there. Nevertheless, the revisions of the *New Arcadia* suggest a deepening rather than an alteration of Sidney's opinion on

Euarchus' judgment. One sign of this is the more frequent references throughout to a hierarchy of values. Another is the greater attention paid to political matters, notably to the king-subject relationship. (Of the twelve listed in the table, only Basilius, Pamela, and a much less rich version of Euarchus are present in the *Old Arcadia*.) Especially in the light of the concentrated exploration of the bonds between parents and children, Sidney's use of the king-father analogy is never neutral (as, for example, Aristotle's is), but always contains normative overtones. Its emotional content is especially perceptible in the *New Arcadia*'s version of Pyrocles-Zelmane's speech to the rebels outside the Arcadian lodge, where the analogy operates by implication: 'And I pray you, did the Sunne ever bring you a fruitfull harvest, but that it was more hote then pleasant? Have any of you children, that be not sometimes cumbersome? Have any of you fathers, that be not sometime weerish? What, shall we curse the Sonne, hate our children, or disobey our fathers?' (I, 317)

The revised oration as a whole has a broader philosophical context than the version delivered in the *Old Arcadia*, which ventured little further than its imperative purpose of defending Basilius himself. Just as Pamela's refutation of atheism is centred on the idea of cosmological order, so Pyrocles' speech is anchored in principles of human order and government, becoming only secondarily the defence of monarchy and of Basilius that the situation demands. Pyrocles' new opening strategy – asking the rebels to submit their grievances so that the incompatibility of their interests will be exposed – leads to the display of anarchic democracy that becomes the setting, and in part, the text, for his speech. By this riot the rebels are denying the wisdom and foresight of their ancestors: 'Do you thinke them fooles, that saw you should not enjoy your vines, your cattell, no not your wives and children, without government; and that there could be no government without a Magistrate, and no Magistrate without obedience, and no obedience where every one upon his owne private passion, may interprete the doings of the rulers?' (I, 317). Government, however troublesome at times, is, like the sun, children, and fathers, necessary to the continuation of life itself. Private goods, all economic and personal prosperity, are in fact dependent upon the public good for existence, and therefore private passions must curb themselves in obedience to some greater principle of order.

The double role of king as father and ruler is the express focal point later on, when Basilius is uncertain whether to lift his siege of Amphialus' castle. Cecropia has threatened to behead Pamela, Philoclea, and Zelmane if he refuses. The king's chief counselors in the matter are Kalander and Philanax, and though Sidney apparently sides with the latter,[60] he does make Kalander's a straw argument. As Kalander sees it, the purpose of the siege is to deliver the princesses, and since that end will not be served by their execution, Basilius' only hope is to win time for further negotiation by withdrawing. The main issue for him is 'whether you will have your incomparable daughters live, or dye?' (I, 466) and he confidently sums up his argument in those terms: 'But you are wise and are a father' (I, 467).[61] Philanax introduces a second perspective, for he gives counsel 'not to these excellent Ladies father, but to my Prince.' His advice is to behave in accordance with absolute rules of virtue, to be constant in rationally determined undertakings, unswervable by fear, threats, or promises, to consider only what one's enemies might in reason be likely to do because of their own interest and to make it be in their interest to release the prisoners by offering them pardon if they do so: 'In sum, you are a Prince, and a father of <a> people, who ought with the eye of wisdome, the hand of fortitude, and the hart of justice to set downe all private conceits, in comparison of what for the publike is profitable' (I, 468).

It would seem possible to make a rational decision on either of these grounds, although it might cause Basilius some embarrassment to ignore the sententious weight of Philanax' remarks. But Sidney will allow reason no place in Basilius' decision. It is made when Gynecia 'amazed for her daughter Pamela, but mad for Zelmane' interrupts the deliberations. Unable even to speak, she pleads with 'such gestures of compassion ... that Basilius, otherwise enough tender minded, easily granted to raise the siege, which he saw dangerous to his daughters: but indeed more carefull for Zelmane ...' (I, 468). Either Kalander's or Philanax' alternative is rational and humanly dignified, though public advantage is a higher goal than private; but to set both fatherhood and kingship aside for this kind of passion suggests another order of values altogether. That the action seems to us foolish rather than monstrous is the result of Sidney's having chosen comedy and not melodrama for his conception of Basilius.[62]

In maximum contrast to Basilius lifting the siege is the exaggeratedly dispassionate Euarchus deciding the fate of the two princes. I would guess that the scene in the new Book III was conceived specifically with this contrast in mind; it shares with the other the same conflict between public and private interests, between ruler (or judge) and father. It is one of the richnesses of design we lose if we shut off our observations at the truncated last sentence of the 1590 text. But if we hold on firmly to this particular strand in Euarchus' judgment – the public-private conflict – it will resolve much of the thematic structure, if not the actual revised plot, of the Arcadia. The difficulties created by the judgment in relation to the plot, understood in a broadly Aristotelian sense to include character and purpose,[63] are legion, and have been discussed extensively in the criticism.[64] The problem, to state it rather simply, lies in the kind of justice Euarchus seems to offer; the correlative issue is what we are supposed to think of it.

In one sense, of course, the justice is absolute, and we are to approve of it. Euarchus is essentially the Stoic sage, in turn a variant of Plato's just man, whose reason has complete mastery over his passions and will. This aspect of Euarchus' conception shows up especially in his decision not to overturn his previous judgment against the defendants after he learns their identity. It is here that Sidney makes his defence of Euarchus' severity: 'the beholders ... most of them examining the matter by their own passions, thought Euarchus (as often extraordinary excellencies, not being rightly conceived, do rather offend than please) an obstinate-hearted man, and such a one, who being pitiless, his dominion must needs be insupportable' (OA 414). But it is *not* here that Euarchus' actions are most disconcerting. That point occurs earlier, and we may start examining Euarchus' 'justice' at the trial itself, where the differences between Euarchus and more ordinary mortals noted in this quotation come to the fore.

The split between the reader's emotional and Euarchus' rational response to the issues raised by the trial begins with Gynecia's confession. Her moral stature, which before this we have had to accept largely on faith, suddenly asserts itself. With genuine magnanimity she will not have Philanax wrong *himself* by delivering what the Narrator calls his 'incontinent invective':

It may be truth doth make thee deal untruly, and love of justice frames unjustice in thee ... [thou] shalt not be the oppressor of her who cannot choose but love thee for thy singular faith to thy master. I do not speak this to procure mercy, or to prolong my life. No, no, I say unto you, I will not live; but I am only loath my death should be engrieved with any wrong thou shouldst do unto me. I have been too painful a judge over myself to desire pardon in others' judgement. (OA 381-2)

Reactions to Gynecia's confession are revealing. Philanax, overcome with spiteful malice, cannot respond honourably. In bringing his charge against Pyrocles he insinuates that Gynecia has committed every conceivable moral crime in addition to Basilius' murder. Philoclea and Pamela (though without hearing Gynecia's confession) are said to be 'careful for their mother ... of whom they could never think so much evil' (OA 395). Pyrocles' response is most illuminating, for he knows the truth about her 'virtue':

And for my part, so vehemently and more like the manner of passionate than guilty folks, I see the duchess prosecute herself, that I think condemnation may go too hastily over her, considering the unlikelihood, if not impossibility, her wisdom and virtue so long nourished should in one moment throw down itself to the uttermost end of wickedness. (OA 393-4)

Pyrocles' evaluation is objectively 'right,' since it concurs with the facts and with the Narrator's own statement.[65] It will be instructive to compare Euarchus' assessment, for it is easier to discern the issue in this situation than it is in the judgment concerning the princes. With perfectly dispassionate reason, Euarchus cuts through to 'the abomination of the fact, attending more the manifest proof of so horrible a trespass, confessed by herself, and proved by others, than anything relenting to those tragical phrases of hers (apter to stir a vulgar pity than his mind which hated evil in what colours soever he found it) ...' (OA 382-3).

This idol of Justice has clay feet, and Sidney must have meant us to see them. Surely pity *is* the proper response to Gynecia at this juncture. Sidney seems to have set a trap for the reader, but only momentarily, because we examine the 'vulgarity' of our feelings only to affirm our pity as humane. Euarchus is *too much* the Stoic sage in this, and we react like Erasmus' Folly to such a figure. Euarchus' justice and reason are absolute because they are divorced not only from human passion but from particularity and even humanity itself: Euarchus sees not Gynecia but 'colored evil.' Moreover, his own warning that he is but a man, 'that is to say, a creature whose reason is often darkened with error' (OA 365), cannot be the issue because Euarchus' reason (the reasoning process itself) has not been faulty. Sidney must have had some other purpose in setting his example of absolute Justice on such a shaky foundation.

The point lies in the continuing exploration of Justice. We know Gynecia is not guilty in spite of her confession and we are encouraged to believe that a more fully humane judge might have seen it too. Such a judge might perhaps be aware of her previously honourable life and more responsive both to the nobility of her speech to Philanax at the trial and to what Pyrocles calls her 'passionate [rather] than guilty' behaviour. The principle that all these legitimate objections and qualifications invoke is equity. They are enumerated in Aristotle's classic account of the concept in the *Rhetoric*, which Sidney probably knew:

It is equity to pardon human failings, and to look to the lawgiver and not to the law; to the spirit and not to the letter; to the intention and not to the action; to the whole and not to the part; to the character of the actor in the long run and not in the present moment; to remember good rather than evil, and good that one has received rather than good that one has done; to bear being injured; to wish to settle a matter by words rather than by deeds; lastly, to prefer arbitration to judgment, for the arbitrator sees what is equitable, but the judge only the law, and for this an arbitrator was first appointed, in order that equity might flourish.[66]

Although Sidney's thematic interest at the trial seems to be an examination of the familiar antithesis between Justice (or Law) and Mercy, it is 'Law' rigorously defined by someone aware of an alternative tradition that divided the idea of Justice into the three topics of Law, Equity, and Mercy.[67] In Sidney's day law and equity were thought to be in opposition to each other: equity abated the rigour of the common law, acted according to the spirit of the rule and not to the strictness of the letter, and arose from consideration of the circumstances in every particular case.[68] It is easily confused with mercy, but they are actually different. Equity is dispensed by a regular court and aims at ethical justice, whereas mercy is a 'divine' prerogative of the ruler and has no necessary connection with merit (mercy is greater where pardon is given to the guilty). One might with some justification say that Gynecia, being innocent of the crime she is charged with, could have been saved by the proper employment of the topics of equity (the Narrator says that the charge was one that 'with her wisdom, joined to the truth, perhaps she might have refelled' [*OA* 384]), whereas the Princes, being guilty of the crimes they are finally convicted of (abduction and rape, since the princesses' consent is apparently irrelevant), can be saved only by mercy.[69]

In order to make the antithesis between law and mercy even starker, Sidney has set up his 'law' so that it specifically lacks any of the mitigating force of equity. This is of course law in its harshest and least tolerable form, which Sidney recognizes by having the Arcadian people think of Euarchus as 'one, who being pitiless, his dominion must needs be insupportable' (*OA* 414), the very terms used traditionally, from Plato onwards, to argue the *need* for equity, namely, that inflexible law is tyrannical and leads not to civil order but insurrection.[70] In *Measure for Measure* Shakespeare also sees Angelo in terms of the intolerableness of absolute law to human nature. We know that Angelo must fail to live up to his abstract conception of the law, but it is possible, because we do not share Angelo's hybris, not to recognize our own humanity in his failure. Sidney makes his readers face the issue squarely: Euarchus as judge effectively embodies absolute Justice (Sidney gives Euarchus none of the extraneous character traits that interfere with our perceiving Angelo purely in these terms), and it is *our* human nature that finds his stance unendurable. The result of Sidney's shaping the issue in this way is to point up the human limitations of Justice even before he contrasts it with divine providence.

Sidney explicitly traces the connections between Justice as Reason and Justice as Law. Euarchus announces to the Arcadians that his judgment will be made 'not by a free discourse of reason and skill of philosophy, but ... tied to the laws of Greece and the municipal statutes of this dukedom' (which 'came out of' reason and philosophy and are their 'offspring').[71] This, however, is as far as Euarchus will travel from the general to the particular, from a general concept of reason to its embodiment in specific statutes. He will not recognize, as Aristotle insists in his other important discussion of equity, that the nature of practical activity makes law, which 'is none the less correct,' still to some extent faulty because it must speak universally and take as its basis the usual case:

for the error is not in the law nor in the legislator but in the nature of the thing, since the matter of practical affairs is of this kind from the start ... Hence the equitable is just, and better than one kind of justice – not better than absolute justice but better than the error that arises from the absoluteness of the statement.[72]

I have backtracked on this material to introduce the second quotation from Aristotle because it points the direction that the concern with equity is actually taking in Sidney's mind. I am not suggesting that equity would be an answer to the impasse of the trial. Such a use of equity would indicate more optimism about the human capacity to deal with complexity and deviation from ideal patterns than Sidney probably felt. Further, the issue in the judgment against the princes is *not* the absence of equity.[73] Euarchus tries the best he can to consider the intention of the lawgivers and the spirit of the law while at the same time determining the princes' intentions and the meaning of their whole sojourn in Arcadia.[74] No, the primary emphasis falls not on equity itself but on the viability of ideals or abstract ideas, on what happens in the clash between the particular and the general.

We have met this kind of thematic interest and rhetoricist perspective earlier in our reading of the *New Arcadia*. The Asia Minor paideia especially insists on the context of human complexity that makes absolute positions untenable,[75] and the character of Amphialus as it is developed in the Captivity sequence encourages the same view of experience. This interpretation of the Euarchus material may seem indistinguishable from one that uses the 1593 text, but I am actually reading *backwards* to the *New Arcadia*. As noted earlier,[76] the trial scene crystallized certain ideas for Sidney that are easier to see in the *New* than the *Old Arcadia* because they served as the germ of the revision. The connection here between Euarchus and the princes' education in virtue is especially interesting because the two themes are similarly joined in Aristotle's definition of Justice as 'complete virtue in the fullest sense, because it is the actual exercise of complete virtue.'[77]

This sense of the limitations of reason, law, and virtue measured in a purely human context is more exciting, I think, than the second part of Sidney's contrast, which pits human reason against divine providence. If this latter were the only factor operating, the *Arcadia* would perhaps be best described as romance. But the *New Arcadia* explores more ground than is implied in the revised opening to Book IV (1593). It may indeed be Sidney's desire to demonstrate that 'the almighty wisdom' delights to act in a manner 'that human reason may be the more humbled' (OA 265, variants) – ultimately, the quotation goes on to say, so that it will 'more willingly give place to divine providence' (as Basilius' 'resurrection' demonstrates) – but he arranges matters in Euarchus' judgment so that reason first will recognize its human limitations. If Euarchus is exemplary, it is of the practical or human limitations of abstract ideals even when they are closely realized. We are asked simultaneously to appreciate the necessity of Euarchus' judgment and to rejoice in the romance world's providence, and Sidney would have it, in Divine Providence itself, that allows the decision to be overturned.

Euarchus' judgment is legally necessary because of the security offered by living in a community which promulgates and obeys just laws: 'the laws, applying themselves to the necessary use, fold us within assured bounds, which once broken, man's nature infinitely rangeth' (*OA* 404). His judgments are logically 'necessary' also because they follow from his explicitly stated premises, which subordinate all concerns to notions of society, community, and the public good. Gynecia, in confessing to Basilius' murder, is said to have offended 'both in private and public respects,' but 'private' does not imply 'individual.' The two in fact sound equally steeped in ideas of community:

in private, because marriage being the most holy conjunction that falls to mankind, out of which all families, and so consequently all societies, do proceed, which not only by community of goods but community of children is to knit the minds in a most perfect union which whoso breaks dissolves all humanity ... in public respect, the prince's person being in all monarchal governments the very knot of the people's welfare and light of all their doings, to which they are not only in conscience but in necessity bound to be loyal ... (*OA* 383)

Justice is absolute and never-changing, but should it be interpreted to accord with convenience, it had better be with that of society itself:

For if the governors of justice shall take such a scope as to measure the foot of the law by a show of conveniency, and measure that conveniency not by the public society, but by that which is fittest for them which offend, young men, strong men, and rich men, shall ever find private conveniences how to palliate such committed disorders as to the public shall not only be inconvenient but pestilent.[78]

Given such premises, there is no alternative but to sentence the princes to death for abducting Philoclea and Pamela from their father: 'for if they must die who steal from us our goods, how much more they who steal from us that for which we gather our goods. And if our laws have it so in the private persons, much more forcible are they to be in princes' children, where one steals as it were the whole state and well being of that people ...' (*OA* 406).

Euarchus' judgment, given 'without passion or partiality' (*OA* 405) and weighed on a scale of public rather than private convenience, depicts Justice as a function of the state. The situation shifts for his second decision, after he learns that the defendants are his own son and nephew. The princes are now to die as an example of his personal justice, that is, Justice is here a function of the individual man. Although public and private 'conveniency' have been developed as an antithesis, Sidney insists that public and personal justice are not. Both demand the same sentence. In a paradox that is only apparent, 'personal' justice invokes for its criterion not specific circumstances, but the abstract principle of Justice itself, a universal that transcends persons, the state, all particular facts and contingencies:

But, alas, shall justice halt, or shall she wink in one's cause which had lynx's eyes in another's? Or rather, shall all private respects give place to that holy name? Be it so, be it so. Let my grey hairs be laid in the dust with sorrow. Let the small remnant of my life be to me an inward and outward desolation, and to the world a gazing stock of wretched misery. But never, never, let sacred rightfulness fall. It is immortal, and immortally ought to be preserved. If rightly I have judged, then rightly have I judged mine own children ... (OA 411)

Considering the reader's recalcitrance to the original judgment, this is a masterly stroke on Sidney's part. For there is no doubt whatever that once Euarchus has decided that the defendants are to be executed, he cannot rescind the sentence merely because they turn out to be his own children. Moreover, he has specifically stated that mercy can form no part of his function: 'But since among yourselves you have taken him away in whom was the only power to have mercy, you must now ... look for no other than that which the dead pitiless laws may allot unto you' (OA 304). Since the maximum emotional intensity of the trial is focused on this one dramatic moment (during the entire Fifth Book the reader has been anticipating the shock of recognition), Sidney can make us believe in and admire Euarchus and Justice in a way that is necessary to the thematic structure of the work – for he is the ideal monarch and it is the chief virtue, the one in which all other virtues are comprehended – but not satisfying to us as readers of comedy or romance. In this last moment when the antithetical tension between sympathy and judgment is greatest for the reader (we accede intellectually and even with admiration to the necessity of the princes' deaths although emotionally we desire their freedom), Basilius' reawakening makes the antithesis disappear. We are to be left with both the satisfaction of Euarchus' nobility and the joyous marriages of the princes. We are to have both Justice and Mercy.

Perhaps the continuous use of the rhetoric of reciprocity in the New Arcadia would have made this sleight of hand more acceptable than it has proved to readers of the Old Arcadia. In its final gesture of dissolving distinctions as well as in its preliminary subordination of private to public demands, the trial scene is a fitting culmination of actions, attitudes, and themes central to Sidney's revision.[79]

CONCLUSION

Eight

The principal difference between the *Old* and *New Arcadias* has always been considered the latter's greater complexity. It is an accurate perception, as long as we recognize that the difference *is* complexity and not merely complication. The revised *Arcadia* is literally a re-vision when compared to the original one; Sidney's larger conception of what he wanted to do and greater grasp on the reality that a serious work must treat led him to find structures that could articulate his new vision. The burden of this book has been the complexity of Sidney's vision and the multiplicity of structures he invented to convey it. We have discovered that beyond the variety and number, even beyond the drive for meeting complexity that is their most general characteristic, there is a resemblance or compatibility among these structures because they reflect the same habits of thought and temperament.

Sidney's complex vision is expressed on one level in rhetorical figures which emphasize difference and range, such as antithesis and paradox, and in similar rhetorical concepts such as the antithetical topos. The pattern of tonal structure, which in effect communicates a single, complex evaluation as a sequential or narrative movement, reflects the same kind of vision. The humorous and parodic elements of this scheme are especially significant because by their very nature they demand that the reader consider more than one aspect of a given experience. (Parody necessarily evokes the 'straight' ideal which is its subject.) Sidney employs other structures that resemble the tonal scheme in attempting to achieve a multiple perspective. For example, incidents may be designed to form a spectrum of possibilities, as in the treatment of love, or the various examples may be arranged hierarchically on the basis of the analogical relation controlling personal, familial, and political virtue. That the virtue exemplified by heroic poetry was hierarchical for Sidney (as the *Defence* suggests) is an additional guarantee of complexity, for in a hierarchy lower forms are subsumed and fulfilled by higher ones, and every stage is to be analysed in terms of its multiple relations to the whole. A similar hierarchy, based on a movement from simple to more complex, also organizes the princes' education in Book II, where the principles that effectively solve the problems offered in the first set of experiences can provide no more than standards for the greater moral difficulties of the second set.

The end result of this emphasis on complexity and multiplicity is to undermine the 'neatness' of the patterns imposed by calling attention to them as attempts to make order out of experience which is too miscellaneous to allow itself to be so arranged. The net effect, therefore, is profoundly rhetoricist, since it throws into relief not only the contingent and variable nature of reality but also the rhetor's role as mediator or shaper of this welter into forms that can be understood. Sidney's stylistic preference for the vanishing distinction is an interesting example of how this rhetoricism works. It is a figure more flamboyant than plain antithesis, or even than paradox, because it makes us watch the sharpest possible distinctions disappear before our eyes, like a magician's sleight-of-hand. As a device, it calls attention to itself, yet the results, like the magician's, do not convince us that what we have seen is 'real'; we admire instead the skill of the conjurer. Ideality is one such marvelous trick for Sidney: a fragile victory won by fusing antithetical ideas that threaten to fly off in opposing directions. Experience, on the other hand, is not so neat to begin with – the pulls are perhaps in all directions – but Sidney's desire to conquer it in some way, this time to give it some form which will be less like 'magic' and more like the thing itself, still dominates. What emerges are large 'forms,' humanist concepts like education and justice, that are explored and examined so that they fit contingent reality as well as possible; but 'as well as possible' turns out to be inadequate to the task. It is only the best one can do.

The resolutions achieved are triumphs of art, and in a work as artificial as the Arcadia, the simultaneously temperamental and technical need for form dominates over the knowledge that experience is intractable. For some of the key thematic conflicts the resolution comes not by means of the vanishing distinction (perfection, after all, is a rare commodity), but by the more ordinary means of subordination within a hierarchy. Thus the important antithetical topoi of action and contemplation, public and private, even reason and passion, prove reconcilable by having one of the terms fulfilled in the realization of the higher term.

The principle of hierarchy need not be reserved for ideas that are originally antithetical. We saw that the two stages of the princes' education could be so conceived. The similarity in the way contingent reality limits both the effectiveness of absolute virtue in their paedeia and the effectiveness of Euarchus' absolute justice at the trial suggests some formal relation between the two actions, and the relevant one is this principle of hierarchy. It is an argument for the integrity and pervasiveness of the re-vision of the Arcadia that such a large and serious conceptual framework stemming from the resolution of the fable should determine the creation of episodic material and eventually, in the Captivity sequence, the nature of the fable itself.

The subjects of these major actions, virtue and justice, can be seen as specific examples of the public-private topos, allowing the education to be subsumed and fulfilled by the justice established at the trial. What the princes have learned in preparation for the greatest test of their education, the adventure in Arcadia, was to culminate in the final lesson that this kind of 'formal' training in virtue can teach, the lesson in Justice, which would then offer a thematic resolution to all this material. Euarchus' double decision considers public and private aspects of the same action and proclaims their identity; Aristotle in the *Ethics* suggests the identity of virtue and justice as well. Education in virtue (by definition 'private' because virtue is a disposition or habit of the mind) has its final flowering in justice (by definition a public concept), for, says Aristotle, the certain kind of disposition that is virtue, considered in relation to others, is justice.[1] The princes' education has been based on this very point: Pyrocles and Musidorus demonstrate and exercise their virtue by helping others, so that the education has been directed at justice throughout.[2] The Captivity sequence, seen in this context, is another level of that education, one where the internal stresses of virtue are given the necessary emphasis.

However 'heroic' Sidney's intentions are in the *Arcadia*, the work retains enough of its romance basis to prevent the human and practical limitations on virtue from thwarting the princes' success. Circumstances may force them to begin their love by assuming disguises that run contrary to the dictates of reason and virtue, but we are to believe that the continuation of their lives after marriage will be virtuous in the sense that their education has taught. Marriage is not merely the conventional and convenient final action of the *Arcadia*, but the thematically necessary one. It resolves the conflict between reason and passion by enabling love (including sexual desire) and virtue (that is, a more rationally conceived view of obligations and loyalties than is possible under the prompting of unfulfilled desire) to be compatible with each other and with the larger needs of society.

Sidney ensures that the reader will not gloss over the potential hazards merely because the princes are successful by including heroic characters such as Argalus and Amphialus who are defeated by the evil and misfortune that the princes manage to escape. If the mechanism of the surrogate hero is at base ritualistic, so that the princes are felt in some way to experience the sufferings of Argalus and Amphialus, then the meaning of their education is enhanced by overtones of purification and initiation, all of which colour our acceptance of their final triumph.

Initiation, even without ritual overtones, offers a useful perspective on the total action of the *Arcadia*. The education presented in the Asia Minor adventures moves from automatic to more complicated processes of choice. At this stage of initiation and in this 'sphere of human imperfection, political and passionate,'[3] it is fitting that conflict and the need for choice predominate. The arrival on the Greek mainland represents still another phase of the princes' initiation into the full responsibilities of the active life, and the chief problem they confront at this stage, the conflict between reason and passion, between action and *otium*, occasioned by their falling in love, is to be solved not by disjunction and choice but by reconciliation. This at least is the goal for which they strive. It is partly because the princes have already proved themselves in the exercise of moral choice that we are willing to follow them and Sidney to a level of experience which calls for harmony rather than rejection.

For Arcadia is potentially, though not actually, the geographical site for the sphere of perfection, just as Asia Minor is a geographical projection of Danby's psychological sphere of human imperfection. Perfection, as we have seen, is characterized for Sidney by reciprocity or harmonious interchange. It is a higher state than mere opposition. Perfection resolves – no, dissolves – all contraries, superseding elements originally worked out as some sort of antithesis. Sidney insists on the conflict before he makes it disappear. Disjunction before resolution, choice and rejection before harmony: the rhetorical and moral patterns are consistent. It may be a fragile triumph, but 'the best one can do' turns out to be impressive nonetheless.

APPENDIXES

NOTES

INDEX

IN MEDIAS RES
CONSTRUCTION

The cultural and geographical variety of the *Aethiopica* is important especially in so far as it is articulated structurally in the work: 'The scene of the action lies almost entirely in Egypt with a shift to Ethiopia for the final climax ... The exceptions are in the subplot presented in Cnemon's narrative of his life history which is laid in Athens, and in Calasiris' long account of his visit to Delphi. These however are clearly set off as insets in the unity of the Egyptian scene.'[1] The connection implied here between unity of place and *in medias res* construction is interesting beyond its relevance to the *Arcadia*. One might argue plausibly that epic does not start 'in the middle' of its action any more than Greek tragedy does when it begins at a point close to the catastrophe and fills in background events while the play unfolds. The *Iliad* undertakes to relate the anger of Achilles and begins with the causes of that anger. Gerald Else argues persuasively that the single action of the *Odyssey* is not all the hero's wanderings but specifically his return to Ithaca, so that the poem's action begins at the lowest point of his fortunes when he is furthest from home and ends as comedy would with his triumphant reinstatement.[2] The *Aeneid*, whose action is the founding of Rome, begins chronologically just after Aeneas' father has died – a symbolic death of the Trojan past, leaving Aeneas with only Ascanius, that is, his mission and his future. Or more positively, it begins with Dido's temptation, the first major threat to the possibility of Aeneas' achieving that mission. Likewise, the *Aethiopica* opens when the chief characters first arrive in Egypt, where the entire main plot unfolds, except for the last scene in which Chariclea is recognized as the princess of Aethiopia. Again, as in the *Aeneid*, there is a tacit realization that previous adventures are preliminary, less important than the major phase begun when, having lost the guidance of Calasiris, they must act on their own. This major phase alone comprises the work's action or plot.

How spurious the effect of plunging *in medias res* is can be seen very clearly in the 1590 *Arcadia*. Critics speak of the new, 'inverted' epic structure as though Sidney had rearranged the plot of the earlier work. Yet the action of both versions begins when the princes arrive in Arcadia. The revision postpones only the precise wording of the oracle that has caused Basilius' retirement, for we still know the general nature of his motive from the outset. The total action, though considerably expanded, follows the same plot sequence as the *Old Arcadia* except for the 'epic history' inserted in Book II, which clearly has no power to reshape the main action of the work. The distinction may be clarified in the following formulation: in 'epic' structure, the writer begins in the middle of the story (total material used) but at the beginning of the plot (structure of the action).[3] Sidney and Heliodorus thus find similar ways to handle the tension between epic techniques and logical narrative requirements: both define their actions spatially or geographically, thereby emphasizing the subordinate status of previous temporal events.

TABLES OF
RELATIONSHIPS

LOVERS

Strephon
          Urania
Claius
Argalus-Parthenia ← Demagoras
Philoxenus → Helen → Amphialus
Amphialus → Philoclea → Pyrocles
Gynecia ↘
          ⊃ Pyrocles-Philoclea
Basilius ↗
Musidorus-Pamela ← Anaxius
Tiridates ↘
          ⊃ Erona → Antiphilus → Artaxia
Plangus ↗
King of Iberia → Andromana → Plangus
                              ↗ Pyrocles
King of Iberia → Andromana ⊂
                              ↘ Musidorus
Palladius → Zelmane → Pyrocles
Plexirtus-Artaxia
Artesia → Amphialus
Clitophon → Helen
Phalantus-Artesia
Dido
Leucippe
          Pamphilus
Baccha
et al.
Dorus-Mopsa

KEY

arrows: direction of unrequited love
⊃: unequal relationship
~: foster relationship

HUSBAND-WIFE

Basilius-Gynecia
Dametas-Miso
Argalus-Parthenia
King of Iberia-Andromana
Antiphilus-Erona
Basilius' brother-Cecropia

PARENT-CHILD

Basilius ⟨ Pamela / Philoclea
Kalander-Clitophon
P's mother-Parthenia
Timotheus ⟨ Philoxenus / Amphialus
Cecropia-Amphialus
Dametas ∿ Pamela
Cecropia ∿ Artesia
Gynecia ⟨ Philoclea / Pamela
Musidorus' Mother ⟨ Musidorus / Pyrocles
Dametas ⟩ Mopsa / Miso
Euarchus-Pyrocles
King of Paphlagonia ⟨ Leonatus / Plexirtus
King of Lycia-Erona
King of Iberia ⟨ Plangus / Palladius
Chremes-Dido
Plexirtus-Zelmane
Andromana-Palladius

SIBLINGS

Pamela-Philoclea
Kalander-Parthenia's Mother
Phalantus-Helen
Artesia-Ismenus
Leucippus-Nelsus
2 Giants of Pontus
Leonatus-Plexirtus
Tydeus-Telenor
Tiridates-Artaxia
Andromana-Plexirtus
King of Bythynia-Brother
Otaves-Barzanes
Philanax-Agenor
Anaxius ⟨ Lycurgus / Zoilus

FRIENDS

Strephon-Claius
Musidorus-Pyrocles
Argalus ⊃ Clitophon
Pyrocles ⊃ Clitophon
Amphialus-Philoxenus
Plexirtus ⟨ Tydeus / Telenor
Agenor-Leontius
Anaxius-Amphialus

KEY

arrows: direction of unrequited love
⊃: unequal relationship
∿: foster relationship

175 Tables of Relationships

RULER-COUNSELLOR

Basilius-Kalander
Basilius-Dametas
Basilius-Philanax
Basilius-Oracle
Pyrocles-Musidorus (parody)
King of Phrygia-Adviser
King of Paphlagonia-Plexirtus
King of Iberia-Andromana
Cecropia-Clinias
Anaxius-Servant
Musidorus-Pamela (OA)

MASTER-SERVANT

Basilius-Clitophon
Kalander-Steward
Amphialus-Ismenus
Musidorus-Calodoulus
Dametas-Dorus
Pamela-Dorus
Gynecia-Miso

Pyrocles and Musidorus $<$ Leucippus / Nelsus

Pyrocles-Zelmane (Diaphantus)

'RULER'-SUBJECT

Basilius-Arcadians
Lacedaemonians-Helots
Demagoras-Helots
Pyrocles-Helots
Helen-Corinthians
Euarchus-Macedonians
King-Phrygians
King-Iberians
Plangus-Iberians
Antiphilus-Lycians
Amphialus-Arcadian rebels
Pamela-Arcadians (OA)

HOST-GUEST

Strephon / Claius $>$ Musidorus

Kalander $<$ Musidorus (Palladius) / Pyrocles (Diaphantus)

Basilius-Zelmane
Menalcas-Musidorus
Chremes-Pyrocles

King of Iberia $<$ Pyrocles / Musidorus

NOTES

CHAPTER ONE: INTRODUCTION

1 E.M.W. Tillyard, *The English Renaissance: Fact or Fiction?* (Baltimore and Cambridge 1952)

2 John F. Danby, *Poets on Fortune's Hill: Studies in Sidney, Shakespeare, Beaumont and Fletcher* (London 1952) 73

3 See Jean Robertson, ed., *The Countess of Pembroke's Arcadia*, by Sir Philip Sidney (Oxford 1973) xv-xvii for the dating. This edition, cited as *OA*, will be used for quotations from the *Old Arcadia* and the 1593 alterations.

4 *The Works of Sir Philip Sidney*, ed. Albert Feuillerat, 4 vols (Cambridge, Eng. 1912-26). I shall quote from the 1962 reprint, published as *The Prose Works of Sir Philip Sidney*. Vol I contains the 1590 text. Hereafter cited as *Works*.

5 The ms copy of the 1590 *Arcadia*, Cm, is dated 1584; Robertson conjectures that it represents the year of transcription (*OA* xlviin). The dates 1582-4 are A.C. Hamilton's sensible suggestion: *Sir Philip Sidney: A Study of His Life and Works* (Cambridge, Eng. 1977) 126.

6 See John Buxton's review of Ringler's edition, *RES* 15 (1964) 200, supporting the case made for Florio's editorship in Frances Yates, *John Florio* (Cambridge, Eng. 1934) 203-6. Robertson agrees (*OA* lvi). The reference to Ringler is to William A. Ringler, jr, ed., *The Poems of Sir Philip Sidney* (Oxford 1962) 532. This edition will be cited hereafter as *Poems*.

7 See Robertson, *OA* lviii-lxii and Ringler, *Poems* 375-8.

8 Sir William Alexander's bridge between the two actions was printed first in 1621 and frequently thereafter.

9 Bertram Dobell, 'New Light on Sidney's "Arcadia",' *Quarterly Review* 211 (1909) 74-100, is the important article, but Dobell announced his discovery first in *Athenaeum*, 7 Sept. 1907.

10 Danby, *Poets on Fortune's Hill*, and Walter R. Davis, 'A Map of Arcadia: Sidney's Romance in Its Tradition,' in *Sidney's Arcadia* by Walter R. Davis and Richard A. Lanham (New Haven 1965)

11 Of books, Arthur K. Amos, jr, discusses only the 1590 *Arcadia* in *Time, Space and Value: The Narrative Structure of the New Arcadia* (Lewisburg, Ohio: Bucknell University Press 1976); Lanham in *Sidney's Arcadia* and Andrew D. Weiner, *Sir Philip Sidney and the Poetics of Protestantism: A Study of Contexts* (Minneapolis 1978), discuss only the *Old Arcadia*. Hamilton treats both works separately, as do Jon S. Lawry, *Sidney's Two Arcadias: Pattern and Proceeding* (Ithaca, NY 1972) and Richard C. McCoy, *Sir Philip Sidney: Rebellion in Arcadia* (New Brunswick, NJ: Rutgers University Press 1979). Valuable comparisons are made in sections of Dorothy Connell, *Sir Philip Sidney: The Maker's Mind* (Oxford 1975) and Josephine A. Roberts, *Architectonic Knowledge in the New Arcadia (1590): Sidney's Use of the Heroic Journey*, Elizabethan Studies 69 (Salzburg 1978). See also the comparisons in Elizabeth Dipple, 'Metamorphosis in Sidney's Arcadias,' *PQ* 50 (1971) 47-62.

12 The term is from Heinrich Wölfflin, *Principles of Art History: The Problem of the Development of Style in Later Art*, trans. M.D. Hottinger, 7th ed. (New York: Dover nd) 166.

13 *Poems* lvii, lix. The ideas expressed in these passages are corroborated by Robert L. Montgomery, jr, *Symmetry and Sense: The Poetry of Sir Philip Sidney* (Austin, Texas 1961) eg, 30, 119.

14 On oratory see Lorna Challis, 'The Use of Oratory in Sidney's Arcadia,' *SP* 62 (1965) 561-76; on moving the will, see Kenneth O. Myrick, *Sir Philip Sidney as a Literary Craftsman* (Cambridge, MA 1935).

15 Nancy S. Struever, *The Language of History in the Renaissance: Rhetoric and Historical Consciousness in Florentine Humanism* (Princeton 1970)

16 Struever, *The Language of History* 10, for both these quotations

17 Mario Untersteiner, *The Sophists*, trans. K. Freeman (Oxford 1954)

18 Difficulties are based both on the paucity of extant texts and on the particular interpretations and translations offered. The best English translations available are in *The Older Sophists*, ed. Rosamund Kent Sprague, trans. from Diels-Kranz, eds, *Die Fragmente die Vorsokratiker*, 7th ed., Berlin 1951-4 (Columbia, SC 1972).

19 On antilogy, see Struever, *The Language of History* 18-19 and 219, on irony, 32; fuller, very useful discussions of antilogy, antithesis, and irony occur on pp 128-36. On *enargeia*, see pp 25, 76, and Heinrich Lausberg, *Handbuch der Literarischen Rhetorik: Eine Grundlegung der Literaturwissenschaft* (Munich 1960) I, paras. 810-11, 'evidentia.'

20 Friedrich Solmsen, 'The Aristotelian Tradition in Ancient Rhetoric,' *AJPh* 62 (1941) 40-1

21 Struever thus describes the debasement of Sophistic rhetorical aims in the practice of Hellenistic rhetorical history: 'The importance of form is exaggerated in a theory

of artificial intensification; the goal of persuasion of will becomes translated into a narrow didacticism; the creative spontaneity of the improvisation which considers individual and particular circumstances is dimmed to a slavish imitation of models of decorum; the semantic self-consciousness of the earlier rhetoric is transformed into an emphasis on pure mnemonic – of rhetoric as a closed list of arguments and figures' (p 27). It is a list of Renaissance literary vices as well.

22 See Jerrold E. Seigel, *Rhetoric and Philosophy in Renaissance Humanism: The Union of Eloquence and Wisdom, Petrarch to Valla* (Princeton 1968) Chap. 1.

23 See Struever, *The Language of History* p 29 for this and the next quotation. Her whole discussion of this matter is valuable.

24 In *Ad familiares* 1, 9, 23 Cicero intimates that the *De oratore* embodies both the *ratio Aristotelia* and the *ratio Isocratia*; cited by F. Solmsen, 'Aristotle and Cicero on the Orator's Playing upon the Feelings,' *CPh* 33 (1938) 387n.

25 See Seigel, *Rhetoric and Philosophy in Renaissance Humanism* 12-15. On Aristotle and Gorgias see Solmsen, 'Aristotelian Tradition,' 40-1 and Struever, *The Language of History* 22.

26 Cf. *The Rhetoric of Aristotle*, trans. Sir Richard C. Jebb, ed. John E. Sandys (Cambridge, Eng. 1909) 1, 4, 1359^b on the limited competence of rhetoric, with Cicero, *De oratore*, III.xxxi.122f in *De oratore, De fato, Paradoxa stoicorum, De partitione oratoriae*, ed. H. Rackham, Loeb Classical Library (London 1942). The emphases are quite different: for Aristotle rhetoric is one of the arts an educated man must employ, but it is not the chief kind or crown of knowledge.

27 *De orat.* I.viii.32f in *De oratore*, Vol. I, ed. E.W. Sutton and H. Rackham, Loeb Classical Library. Speech is *the* civilizing power. Solmsen considers the exaltation of the logos a standard Sophistic topos, which Cicero brought back to life, *AJPh* 59 (1938) rev. art., 106-7.

28 John Hoskins, *Directions for Speech and Style*, ed. Hoyt H. Hudson (Princeton 1935) 41

29 See Struever, *The Language of History* 38f.

30 Dorothy Connell seems to support my anti-Platonist position (*The Maker's Mind* 21); on the other hand, Weiner (*Poetics of Protestantism*) places great emphasis on Sidney's Calvinism, both in the *Defence* and in the *Old Arcadia*.

31 On Augustine, see Marcia Colish, *The Mirror of Language: A Study in the Medieval Theory of Knowledge* (New Haven 1968) 8-9; and Joseph A. Mazzeo, *Renaissance and Seventeenth-Century Studies* (New York 1964) Chap. 1, especially the section on theory of styles, pp 12-23.

32 Homer's ideal of being a 'speaker of words and doer of deeds' (*Iliad* ix.443) is the basis of Sidney's conception of his heroes; there is little of Plato's Philosopher King about them. Curtius discusses the Homeric topos extensively: Ernst Robert Curtius, *European Literature and the Latin Middle Ages*, trans. Willard R. Trask, Bollingen Series XXXVI (New York 1953) 170-9.

33 In the light of the discussion in chap. 7 (pp 159ff), it is interesting to note the Sophists' concern with equity (τὸ ἐπιεικές), with its obvious link to particulars and circumstance (καιρός). See Untersteiner, *The Sophists* 177-8.

34 Sidney's *Defence of Poesie* is quoted from *Miscellaneous Prose of Sir Philip Sidney*, ed. Katherine Duncan-Jones and Jan Van Dorsten (Oxford 1973) 89. In the classical tradition the crucial contamination is thought to be of history by tragedy. See B.L. Ullman, 'History and Tragedy,' *TAPA* 73 (1942) 25-53.

35 F.J. Levy, *Tudor Historical Thought* (San Marino 1967), and his 'Sir Philip Sidney and the Idea of History,' *Bibliothèque d'humanisme et renaissance'* 26 (1964) 608-17. See also F. Smith Fussner, *The Historical Revolution: English Historical Writing and Thought 1580-1640* (New York 1962).

36 Struever, *The Language of History* 43, 96. The relevant discussion of Salutati occurs on pp 75-7.

37 *Works* III, 131. See the letter to Edward Denny for a further assessment of history's importance and an indication of Sidney's wide acquaintance with historical literature, in James M. Osborn, *Young Philip Sidney, 1572-1577* (New Haven 1972) 537-40. This 'encyclopedic' quality of history is traditionally assigned to poetry, and by Aristotle also to rhetoric. Sidney does assign it to poetry in the *Defence*, so that the matter of philosophy as well as of history becomes grist for the poet's mill. In fact, the poet has 'all, from Dante's heaven to his hell, under the authority of his pen' (89).

38 *Enargeia* is of course the hallmark of rhetorical history, specifically praised in this context by Polybius (see Struever, *The Language of History* 25). It is also a dominant figure in Hellenistic romances such as the *Aethiopica*, which in turn are related in their development to the historical writing of their time (see below, p 205 n41).

39 Mark Rose, *Heroic Love: Studies in Sidney and Spenser* (Cambridge, MA 1968) 57ff., makes a similar comparison, though he links it to what I think is an overemphasis on Stoic doctrine.

CHAPTER TWO: RHETORICAL STRUCTURE – THE TOPICAL TRADITION

1 Cf. Walter J. Ong, 'Oral Residue in Tudor Prose Style,' in *Rhetoric, Romance and Technology: Studies in the Interaction of Expression and Culture* (Ithaca, NY 1971) Chap. 2.

2 Fulke Greville, *Life of Sir Philip Sidney*, ed. Nowell Smith (Oxford 1907) 15-16. As in all quotations, I have regularized the printing of u and v, i and j, expanded contractions and abbreviations, and normalized the usage of italics.

3 There seems to be a further division in the passage into subject and purpose, but it is hard to tell in Greville's style whether 'intent and scope' is merely a doublet or whether it means to set up a partition.

4 Heinrich Lausberg, *Handbuch der Literarischen Rhetorik: Eine Grundlegung der Literaturwissenschaft* (Munich 1960) para. 262, offers a table comparing the names and parts of various theorists. All paragraph references are to the first of the two volumes of this work, since the second is the index.

5 M. Fabius Quintilian, *Institutio oratoria*, ed. H.E. Butler, Loeb Classical Library, III.ix.3. Thomas Wilson similarly considers it one of the four 'offices' of logic, mandatory in all discourse (*Rule of Reason*, 1551, B3ᵛ). See also Brian Vickers, *Francis Bacon and Renaissance Prose* (Cambridge, Eng. 1968) Chap. 2, 'Organisation and Structure.'

6 *Rhetorica ad Herennium*, ed. Harry Caplan, Loeb Classical Library, IV.xl.52 and IV.xxxv.47; George Puttenham, *The Arte of English Poesie*, ed. Gladys Willock and Alice Walker (Cambridge, Eng. 1936) 221ff.

7 Aristotle, *Rhetoric*, 1398ᵇ, 1399ᵃ (the ninth and twelfth topics for demonstrative enthymemes); Cicero, *Topica*, in *De inventione, De optimo genere oratorum, Topica*, ed. H.M. Hubbell, Loeb Classical Library, v.28-viii.34 on definition and genus. See Walter J. Ong, SJ, *Ramus, Method, and the Decay of Dialogue: From the Art of Discourse to the Art of Reason* (Cambridge, MA 1958) 104, 121-2 for various lists of loci.

8 *Ad Her.* I.x.17. Caplan cites Cicero's mockery of Hortensius for counting his points on his fingers (Quint. IV.v.24), which suggests his general agreement. The 'pedagogical dictum' is from Ong, *Ramus* 199.

9 Ong, *Ramus* 199. See N.W. Gilbert, *Renaissance Concepts of Method* (New York: Columbia University Press 1960), for the many versions of division based on Plato's *diaíresis* prevalent in the period.

10 *Ad Her.*, p li (analysis of III.ii-vii). Cf. Sidney's 'sometimes using policy, some times force' (*Works* I, 68).

11 Cf. Cicero's distinction between enumeration and analysis in *Topica* viii.33-4. The same distinction can be made between *division* (analysis into component members) and *partition* into any number of headings.

12 I.M. Bochenski says, 'Aristotle never defined them [topoi], and so far no-one has succeeded in saying briefly and clearly what they are' (*A History of Formal Logic*, trans. Ivo Thomas [Notre Dame, Ind. 1961] 51).

13 Sister Joan Marie Lechner, OSV, *Renaissance Concepts of the Commonplaces* (New York: Pageant Press 1962) 229-30. See also Ong, *Ramus* 211, on the subject topos.

14 Karl R. Wallace, *Francis Bacon on Communication and Rhetoric, or The Art of Applying Reason to Imagination for the Better Moving of the Will* (Chapel Hill 1943) 56, citing *Advancement of Learning, Works*, ed. Spedding, Ellis, and Heath, III, 389ff. and *De augmentis scientiarum* v.3.

15 The same distinction can be made between the Erasmus-Veltkirchius concept of the commonplaces (from Veltkirchius' commentary on the 1536 edition of *De Copia*) and the Aphthonius-Cicero-Quintilian forensic commonplace (Lechner,

Renaissance Concepts of the Commonplace 178). The distinction is elaborated usefully in Friedrich Solmsen, 'The Aristotelian Tradition in Ancient Rhetoric,' *AJPh* 62 (1941) 40-1 and Nancy S. Struever, *The Language of History in the Renaissance: Rhetoric and Historical Consciousness in Florentine Humanism* (Princeton 1970) 125-6 and notes.

16 Wallace, *Francis Bacon on Communication* 64. See also pp 72-6. All topoi are in a sense 'mnemonic' because each is an aid for inventing arguments that was intended to be memorized. Cf. Sidney's letter to his brother Robert about constructing tables for historical study (*Works* III, 131-2). The connection between the topics and mnemonics is discussed in Frances A. Yates, *The Art of Memory* (Chicago 1966) 31.

17 Greville, *Life of Sir Philip Sidney* 18.

18 Ong notes that because the rhetoric student was only fourteen years old, he needed a system such as the topics, commonplace book, and traditional formulations offered in order to give him something worth saying with the complex and subtle technique provided by his rhetoric (Walter J. Ong, SJ, 'Tudor Writings on Rhetoric, Poetic, and Literary Theory,' in *Rhetoric, Romance and Technology* 59-60). In 'Oral Residue,' 40, Ong speaks of the commonplaces as providing 'structure' for parts of oration other than the proof because of 'the commonplace frame of mind.'

19 They are related only to the discussion in the chapter on heroes and rulers, where, however, Curtius oscillates between considering the contrast between experience and youth, *sapientia* and *fortitudo*, to be the reflection of a primal or archaic polarity (p 171) when used by Homer and Virgil and a mere 'topos' (in the sense of cliché?) when used afterwards (p 174; cf. p 70). Further, Curtius seems more interested in making the conflict account for surface details than for organization or structure.

20 See also, for example, 'Poetry ever sets virtue so out in her best colours, making Fortune her well-waiting handmaid, that one must needs be enamoured of her. Well may you see Ulysses in a storm, and in other hard plights; but they are but exercises of patience and magnanimity to make them shine the more in the near-following prosperity' (p 90); and the description of the *Aeneid* (p 98), quoted pp 127-8. Cf. also the antithetical form of Elyot's treatment of the study of history in *The Book Named The Governor*, ed. S.E. Lehmberg, Everyman's Library (London 1962) 38.

21 William W. Ryding, *Structure in Medieval Narrative* (The Hague 1971) discusses narrative motifs as extensions of rhetorical procedures. See, for example, p 98n for *commutatio* and *digressio* in interlaced narrative.

22 See Myron Turner, 'The Disfigured Face of Nature: Image and Metaphor in the Revised *Arcadia*,' *English Literary Renaissance* 2 (1972) 116-18, for a discussion of the opening passage of the *NA*, and the whole article for an attractive statement of

the Neoplatonic-Christian core of the *Arcadia*. Davis, *Sidney's Arcadia* 84-6, offers a more programmatic account of the passage's embodiment of Neoplatonic ideas.

Sidney's handling of the figure of Urania seems problematic. Her *NA* meaning *may* be based on the *OA* sestina, 'Yee Gote-herd Gods,' but her effect on the lovers Strephon and Claius is vastly different in the two passages. The long unfinished poem, 'A Shepheard's tale no height of stile desires' (*OP* 4; see *Poems* 494, for the dating), represents a transitional state. One notes that in both the *OA* and *OP* 4 Urania's symbolic value as 'Heavenly Love' is curiously independent of her actions. In *OA* she is said to 'hate' Strephon and Claius (p 328), and in *OP* 4 her name (and that of the other characters such as Nous and Cosma) suggests allegory, but as a character in a narrative she is alternately frisky and tearful, and the love she evokes is 'likerous, poison'd' and part of Cupid's 'triumph badd' (ll 165, 131). Her other appearance in *NA*, in Artesia's triumph, suggests by its tenderness and vulnerability a still different conception (see discussion below, p 24 and n31).

23 Eyes are of course as 'physical' as eyelids, but the pressure of the form gives them spiritual valence. Sidney may have felt that the content of his comparisons called for a distinction in figurative language between 'sensuous' physical meanings and relatively 'non-sensory' spiritual meanings. The critical bias operating in my analysis, that ideas made concrete are more effective (affecting) than those not realized imagistically or metaphorically, may thus run counter to the theoretical content of the passage and to Sidney's conscious poetic intention, but I think it is faithful to the poetic impression made by the passage. The critical position is expressed elsewhere by Sidney himself in his understanding of the term $\dot{\epsilon}\nu\dot{\epsilon}\rho\gamma\epsilon\iota\alpha$. See Neil L. Rudenstine, *Sidney's Poetic Development* (Cambridge, MA 1967) 150-8. In spite of Rudenstine's technically correct distinction between this term and $\dot{\epsilon}\nu\dot{\alpha}\rho\gamma\epsilon\iota\alpha$ (p 305n13), techniques for achieving $\dot{\epsilon}\nu\dot{\epsilon}\rho\gamma\epsilon\iota\alpha$ (forcibleness, a sense of active energy) are similar to those required for $\dot{\epsilon}\nu\dot{\alpha}\rho\gamma\epsilon\iota\alpha$ (vividness, a sense of reality) because both aim at 'setting things before the eyes' of an audience. Lausberg, s.v. $\dot{\epsilon}\nu\dot{\epsilon}\rho\gamma\epsilon\iota\alpha$ (index), notes that Aristotle's discussion of this term even occurs in the course of explaining the other one. See also Forrest G. Robinson, *The Shape of Things Known: Sidney's 'Apology' in Its Philosophical Tradition* (Cambridge, MA 1972) 130-5.

24 *Works* I, 49; the folios all read 'disfigured.' Feuillerat includes the variant readings of Folios A through M (1593-1674), which I have occasionally used in the text to correct the quarto.

25 The new version extends the possibility that love is not merely a form of adversity but itself provides a legitimate end for action, and therefore indicates the revised vision of the *New Arcadia* as much as the opening invocation. See Chap. 7.

26 William K. Wimsatt, jr, *The Prose Style of Samuel Johnson* (New Haven 1941) 22, has a discussion of illustrative range and emphasis as motives for word pairs. Cf. also Lausberg's treatment of 'alpha to omega' statements as an attempt to express

the wholeness of a three-part enumeration in the more tense two-unit or antithetical form (para. 433 1a).

27 Renaissance interest in the problem is shown in Pico's *Commentary* on Benivieni's
Canzone d'amore, stanza 6. The following account is given in John Charles Nelson,
Renaissance Theory of Love: The Context of Giordano Bruno's Eroici furori (New
York 1958) 60:

> The sixth stanza describes how the particular beauty of an individual body
> kindles the fire of love in another's soul. In explanation of this process, Pico first
> expounds the nature of corporeal beauty, in the manner of the Florentine
> humanists, including Ficino and Lorenzo de' Medici. Two things are apparent:
> the 'material disposition of the body,' consisting in the proper 'quantity,' or pro-
> portion and position of parts, and quality, which is in figure and color; and a
> certain 'grace' (*gratia*), which alone inflames the lover's heart. Common opinion
> holds that the second component of beauty has its origin in the first; not so
> Pico, who declares that we frequently see a body perfect in the first respect, but
> utterly lacking in the second, and vice versa. He therefore attributes the second
> 'effect' – that which alone excites love – not to the body, but to the soul.

See also Robert Ellrodt, *Neoplatonism in the Poetry of Spenser* (Geneva 1960) 26,
for the relevant passages from the *Enneads*.

28 *Works* I, 102; 'most' is supplied from the folio variants. These emendations appear
within broken brackets, and will not be cited in future notes unless further comment is needed. Words in square brackets are my own editorial queries and additions.

29 I would compare with this the play of implication in Sidney's statement in the
Defence about poets' making the 'too much loved earth more lovely' (p 78) and
my remarks above about the 'Canticles' description of Urania. The specific details
in the portraits of Helen and Parthenia suggest mythological allegory. Parthenia's
grey eyes, broad forehead, and great-mindedness sound to me like Athena, while
Helen's hair entwined with pearl ropes strongly suggests pictorial representations of
Venus. See Erwin Panofsky, *Hercules am Scheidewege: Studien der Bibliothek Warburg* XVIII (Leipzig 1930) 110n and his illustrations. Urania's is the last portrait of
this group to be described, but see note 31 below.

30 The eleventh portrait of the Triumph is of Princess Zelmane, but no description is
given. Being dead, and spoken about only in terms of reflections and images, she
perhaps represents a kind of 'pure spirit.'

31 Urania is perhaps herself the juxtaposition that Turner suggests for the opening
scenes of the *New Arcadia*: she moves from being a Neoplatonic vision of love to
embodying 'the ethic of love – *caritas* – acted out in a fallen world' ('Disfigured
Face' 116).

32 Josephine A. Roberts' analysis of Phalantus' Tourney suggests that the overall action of the episode has been determined by the matter-spirit topos as well. Pyrocles' victory while clothed in 'rustie pooreness' demonstrates the triumph of inner beauty, virtue, over Phalantus' belief in the supremacy of external features, 'the beauty which gave it the praise' (Architectonic Knowledge in the New Arcadia (1590): Sidney's Use of the Heroic Journey, Elizabethan Studies 69 [Salzburg 1978] 198).

33 Sidney introduces the terms on I, 33 in the New Arcadian material concerning Argalus and Parthenia; the quotation is given on p 25 below. Georgia Ronan Crampton, The Condition of Creatures: Suffering and Action in Chaucer and Spenser (New Haven 1974), offers a fine opening chapter tracing the history and development of this topos.

34 John F. Danby, Poets on Fortune's Hill: Studies in Sidney, Shakespeare, Beaumont and Fletcher (London 1952) 51, 63

35 Davis, 'Thematic Unity in the New Arcadia,' SP 57 (1960) 138

36 This opposes Danby's argument concerning patience, pp 66-70.

37 Topics for epideictic oratory are found in Aristotle, Rhet. II.9, Ad. Her. III.vi.10 and Quintilian III.vii.10-25; see Lausberg's tables of Lobgegenstände (para. 245) and argumenta or loci a persona (para. 376), and Edmond Faral, Les arts poétiques du XIIe et du XIIIe siècles (Paris 1924) 75-81. O.B. Hardison, jr, The Enduring Monument: A Study of the Idea of Praise in Renaissance Literary Theory and Practice (Chapel Hill 1962), discusses the connection between encomium and biography (p 30), and, interesting for the princes' education in Book II, the connection between exemplary narrative and epideictic (pp 54-6).

38 One benefit of having a list of standard virtues (whether compiled from rhetoric books or from an author's own practice) is that omissions become as significant as what is included in any given description. The topoi can be applied 'normatively' in this way to Phalantus (I, 97) with interesting results.

39 The description actually continues by speaking of his liberality rather than magnificence and his one 'spot' of over-vehement constancy, which cannot be counted a spot.

40 See Eugene M. Waith, The Herculean Hero in Marlowe, Chapman, Shakespeare and Dryden (New York: Columbia University Press 1962) and Myron Turner, 'The Heroic Ideal in Sidney's Revised Arcadia,' SEL 10 (1970) 63-82. Argalus is associated with Hercules again at I, 420.

41 Sidney's insistence on balancing opposites shows in another clause of this description: 'in whom strong making tooke not away delicacie, nor beautie fiercenesse.' See note 45 for more on the combination of male and female perfection.

42 Richard Rainolde, The Foundacion of Rhetorike (1563), introd. Francis R. Johnson (New York 1945), fol. xlr, offers the following topics for praise based on Aphthonius:

(1) *Genus eius:* of what nation, country, ancestors, parents
(2) education: institution, arts, laws
(3) chief ground: acts done, which proceed from
   – excellencies of mind (fortitude of mind, wisdom, magnanimity)
   – excellencies of the body (beautiful face, amiable countenance, swiftness, might and strength)
   – excellencies of fortune (dignity, power, authority, riches, substance, friends)

43 *Iliad* IX.443. See Curtius' discussion of the topos *sapientia et fortitudo* 172ff. Lawry, on the contrary, makes much of the difference between the princes, as does Roberts, *Architectonic Knowledge* 63-78. See Jon S. Lawry, *Sidney's Two Arcadias: Pattern and Proceeding* (Ithaca 1972).

44 See the *New Arcadia's* description of their battle against each other in the Helot rebellion. Sidney usually makes some distinction between combatants, but here 'bothe had bothe' is the keynote (I, 42-3).

45 Danby's treatment of the two princes is standard: Musidorus represents the purely masculine, but Pyrocles, 'a Marses heart in a Cupides bodye' (I, 48), combines male and female qualities and is therefore 'pre-excellent' (Danby, *Poets on Fortune's Hill* 57). The conjunction of Mars and Cupid may well be conventional. Tasso describes his Rinaldo thus: 'se' l miri fulminar ne l'arme avvolto, / Marto lo stimi; Amor, se scopre il volto' (If you saw him raging in battle dress you would think him Mars; Cupid if he reveals his face), *La Gerusalemme liberata*, ed. Fredi Chiapelli (Florence 1957) I.58.

46 C.S. Lewis, *English Literature in the Sixteenth Century* (Oxford 1954) 338

47 See Baldassare Castiglione, *The Book of the Courtier*, trans. Sir Thomas Hoby, Everyman's Library (London 1928) 190 and Book III in general for many of these traditional views of women.

48 There is an earlier implicit contrast between sweetness and wisdom in Book II (*OA* 97-8) when they fall in love. In the *New Arcadia* a further alteration takes place in the relationship of the two sisters. Sidney makes them confidantes (I, 176ff., 307), which they are explictly not in the original version (*OA* 368). See Roberts, *Architectonic Knowledge* 79-84.

49 *Poems*, xxvii-xxviii. See also Robert W. Parker, 'Terentian Structure and Sidney's Original *Arcadia*,' *ELR* 2 (1972) 64-70

50 Giambattista Guarini, *The Compendium of Tragicomic Poetry* (1599), in *Literary Criticism: Plato to Dryden*, ed. Allan H. Gilbert (Detroit 1962; 1st pub. 1940) 528-9

51 This 'dedication' is repeated in the *New Arcadia* (I, 168-9), but seems radically unsuited to the revision's tone and narrative technique. See Chap. 4.

52 In the *New Arcadia* Musidorus' increased importance is shown by the central role he plays in Book I: the narrative follows him at and away from the shipwreck

scene, and goes with him on his search for Pyrocles. More attention is also given to Pamela's wooing, and she emerges as the dominant figure in the Captivity sequence.

53 The next paragraph begins by making the comparison explicit: 'The sight whereof so diverse from her sister ...' See the analysis of Pamela here in Turner, 'Disfigured Face' 133-4.

54 Castiglione's examples of female virtue include women who 'with learning in disputation have confuted so many Idolators' (p 203).

55 Almost the same words are repeated on I, 384.

56 Danby, *Poets on Fortune's Hill* 58-9

57 In fact, the art-nature conflict is rarely presented in its pure form. The question it usually poses is 'whether nature simply, or nature helped by cunning, be more excellent' (I, 75).

58 The passage continues with an account of the servants containing a minor crux that has interesting stylistic overtones: 'The servants not so many in number, as cleanlie in apparell, and serviceable in behaviour, testifying even in their countenaunces, that their maister tooke as well care to be served, as of them that did serve.' The 1613 Folio, E, which Ringler commends for intelligent editorial emendation (*Poems* 537), reads 'aswell care of them that did serve, as to be served.' As the more expected reading, it is perhaps the less probable. (It is also inferior in rhythm.) Apart from scribal probabilities, though, if one looks at the criss-crossing pattern of beauty and utility or function that runs through the passage, this final segment can be seen as another variant of care for function rather than care for a thing itself. Then the statement resembles 'as the one cheefly heeded, so the other not neglected,' but without the ranking into primary and secondary. One is tempted to think that Sidney meant 'as well one as another' quite precisely, making which element comes first irrelevant. I am not familiar with other examples in English, but it is Seneca's standard use of the *tam ... quam* construction in his *Epistles*.

59 The words 'handsome' and 'homely' are interesting in this connection. According to the *OED*, the prevalent modern sense of both these words dates from about 1590; Sidney apparently had these connotations in mind, but he was also dealing with the then-prevailing meanings of 'handsome' as easy to handle or use and seemly or decent, and of 'homely' as simple and unpolished (in addition to the modern sense of physically unattractive).

60 The two are not totally reversible, however, since extreme beauty would not become functional. The reconciliation of these apparent opposites is a lesson the princes learn on their first shipboard voyage: 'to see how beautie, and use can so well agree together, that of all the trinckets, where with they [the ships] are attired, there is not one but serves some necessary purpose' (I, 191).

61 Leo Spitzer, *Linguistics and Literary History: Essays in Stylistics* (Princeton 1948) 18

62 *Ibid.* 19

63 Lausberg, *Handbuch der Literarischen Rhetorik*, para. 800

64 *Ad Her.*, IV.xxviii.39

65 Quintilian, IX.iii.85; Hoskins, 14. For the author of *Ad Her.*, chiasmus seems to be an added beauty to the figure, not part of its essence.

66 John Hoskins, *Directions for Speech and Style*, ed. Hoyt H. Hudson (Princeton 1935) 14-15, 67-8. The examples are from I, 278, 7, 199.

67 Hoskins, *Directions for Speech and Style* 15. Brother Simon Scribner, *Figures of Word-Repetition in the First Book of Sir Philip Sidney's Arcadia* (Washington, DC 1948) 64n, counts forty-six examples of what he calls inverse repetition (equating *antimetabole* and chiasmus) in Book I alone. On my count, there are about forty examples of the rhetoric of reciprocity in the *New Arcadia*.

68 The main functions treated in Lausberg's discussion of *correctio* (paras. 284-6) are to heighten the effectiveness of an original statement or to apologize for overbold speech. See the excellent discussion by Elizabeth McCutcheon, 'Denying the Contrary: More's Use of Litotes in the *Utopia*,' in *Utopia*, trans. and ed. R.M. Adams, Norton Critical Edition (New York 1975) 224-30 (orig. publ. *Moreana*, 31-2 [1972], 116-21), for an example of how such minor rhetorical devices can yield stylistic insights.

69 Heinrich Wölfflin, *Principles of Art History: The Problem of the Development of Style in Later Art*, trans. M.D. Hottinger, 7th ed. (New York nd) 166

70 Katherine Everett Gilbert and Helmut Kuhn, *A History of Esthetics*, 2nd ed. (Bloomington 1953) 187

71 Marsilio Ficino, *De amore*. Struever, *The Language of History*, refers to some exceedingly interesting material from Augusto Rostagni in this connection: 'The original Gorgian figures, such as antithesis, derived, according to Rostagni, from the Pythagorean doctrine that only a recognition of multiplicity contributes to a sense of unity, that disharmony invokes harmony' (p 133). The citation is to 'Un nuovo capitolo nella storia della retorica e della sofistica,' in *Scritti minori* I, *Aesthetica* (Turin 1955) 16-17. See also Untersteiner, *The Sophists*, 119-20.

72 A note on the relation of Sidney's manipulation of antithesis to the Renaissance tradition of the transcendence of opposites. The connection is real, but not profound, by which I mean that Sidney's usage reflects his participation in his age, but not his sharing of the tradition's underlying concerns. The tradition is philosophical, based on the 'theory that "transcendence" is a souce of "balance" because it reveals the coincidence of opposites in the supreme One' (Edgar Wind, *Pagan Mysteries in the Renaissance*, 2nd ed. [Harmondsworth, Eng. 1967] 97). The metaphysical difficulty it resolves, the Platonic duality between the realms of existence and of meaning, was the central problem of Cusanus (see Ernst Cassirer, *The Individual and the Cosmos in Renaissance Philosophy*, trans. M. Domandi [New York 1963] 16-23)

and remains central to Bruno's *Degli eroici furori*, but seems unrelated to Sidney's *Arcadia*. For example, the answer offered by Bruno – that the lover need renounce neither the corporeal nor the spiritual element in his soul, but should harmonize the two in order to contemplate Diana, 'the finite mode of the infinite being' (P.E. Memmo, jr, trans. *Giordano Bruno's The Heroic Frenzies* [Chapel Hill 1966] 45) – is relevant to Sidney only in its first and less significant half, and even this is qualified by Bruno's extremely abstract formulation of the 'lover.' The *coincidentia oppositorum* is, as Wind suspects, 'a subject too esoteric for the wide success it apparently enjoyed' in the Renaissance (*Pagan Mysteries* 97). Use of the form need imply no commitment to the mystical Platonism at its source; for Sidney and for most of his age it satisfied their pleasure in paradox and their basic aesthetic preferences for a beauty that was not simple but was an 'inherently "contrarious" principle' (*Pagan Mysteries* 88, citing Pico). One common mythological embodiment of the theory, that Harmony is the daughter of Venus and Mars (*Pagan Mysteries* 86-7), seems seminal enough in just its ordinary exoteric readings (if, indeed, Sidney needed any specific impetus or emblem for something so deeply rooted in his temperament and intellectual training).

73 Lewis, *Sixteenth Century* 342

74 Note, incidentally, that beauty and utility are equally 'services.' The terminology 'Being, Life, Sense, Reason' is from *The Trewenesse of the Christian Religion*, Chap. 1, thought to have been translated in part from the French of Duplessis-Mornay by Sidney, though what we have is only Golding's. See Katherine Duncan-Jones, ed., *Miscellaneous Prose*, 155-7. Golding's text can be found in Feuillerat, *Works* III, 205ff.

75 Aristotle, *Politics*, Benjamin Jowett, trans., I.ii (1253[a]). The Chain of Being in *Trewenesse*, as in Elyot, leads of course not to the state but to God.

76 The emphasis upon democracy (and this entire passage) is added to the *New Arcadia*, as is the account of the evils of oligarchy which Euarchus confronts upon assuming the throne of Macedon (I, 185-7). One may recognize in this an 'encyclopedic' motive governing Sidney's selection and organization of material. See discussion Chap. 7, p 148.

77 The beast fable of *OA*'s Third Eclogues offers yet another political perspective, suggesting the need to counteract the monarch's power with a strong aristocracy. The view is placed in the eclogues probably because it is an alternative perspective that questions the political assumptions of the principal action just as the pastoral felicity questions its heroic and amorous assumptions.

78 Sidney's extension of this idea provides a charming gloss on romance practices in naming offspring: Pamela carves in the barks of trees 'pretty knots which tied together the names of Musidorus and Pamela, sometimes intermixedly changing them to Pamedorus and Musimela' (*OA* 198).

79 Danby, *Poets on Fortune's Hill* 50

CHAPTER THREE: RHETORICAL EXPLORATIONS – TWO TOPOI

1 Xenophon, *Memorabilia of Socrates*, trans. J.S. Watson, Temple Classics (London 1904) III.i.21-33

2 Jane Aptekar, *Icons of Justice: Iconography and Thematic Imagery in Book V of The Faerie Queene* (New York 1969) 188-200, documents iconographically this conflation between Omphale and Prodicus' Vice.

3 The slippery quality of the antithesis shows immediately. Xenophon (Socrates? Prodicus?) clearly thinks of it as Virtue vs *Vice*, but (except perhaps for the accusation of 'using men as women' at i.30) the lures are purely sensuous and not compounded, for example, by violence and fraud. The figure may thus have some claim to the more ambiguous name of 'Happiness,' or in later formulations, 'Pleasure.'

4 I have summarized the fable in such detail because it offers some interesting parallels with the general concerns of the *Arcadia*. Nor is the connection surprising; Cicero had commended the fable to all young gentlemen making the major educational decision of what career to follow (*De officiis*, ed. Walter Miller, Loeb Classical Library, I, xxxii).

5 Panofsky, *Hercules am Scheidewege, Studien der Bibliothek Warburg* XVIII (Leipzig 1930) 102, speaks of 'die *Anpassungsbereitschaft der Form*, die sich dem jeweils "Modernen" zu fügen gewillt ist, und die *Beharrungstendenz des Gehaltes*, der stets durch eine frömmere oder jedenfalls weniger heroische als moralistiche Auffassung bestimmt bleibt ...' (emphasis in text). My interpretation of this passage is that form might lend itself to modern content, but moral implication remained constant. I have made the elements three instead of two because I think this is closer to Sidney's aesthetics: at I, 381, Sidney speaks of the workmanship of the form, the sumptuousness of the matter, and the invention of the application as aesthetic standards.

6 Moral implication and form became so indissoluble that the purely abstract Pythagorean 'Y' could convey the essential meaning (Panofsky, *Hercules* 64ff.). Panofsky notes (p 49) the tendency of all non-mythical abstractions to lack inner stability, undergoing on the one hand various kinds of allegorizing, and on the other, a constant striving for living embodiment which leads to their assimilation to figures of history and myth.

In connection with the various contents the form could be made to serve, Hallett Smith in *Elizabethan Poetry: A Study in Conventions, Meaning and Expression* (Cambridge, MA 1952) 297, notes that in Thomas Bradshaw's *The Shepherds Starre* (1591) Hercules is the Protestant champion and his two paths are the old and the reformed religion.

7 Edgar Wind, *Pagan Mysteries in the Renaissance*, 2nd ed. (Harmondsworth, Eng. 1967) 205. The disjunction may be influenced by the Stoic belief that Virtue is possessed entirely or not at all, that there are no degrees of evil.

8 Cf. Stephen K. Orgel 'Sidney's Experiment in Pastoral: *The Lady of May*,' JWCI 26 (1963) 198-203. A.C. Hamilton's reading of the masque is suggestive but unconvincing (*Sir Philip Sidney: A Study of His Life and Works* [Cambridge, Eng. 1977] 23-6).

9 Eugene F. Rice, jr, *The Renaissance Idea of Wisdom*, Harvard Historical Monographs, XXXVII (Cambridge, MA 1958) 155-6, citing Le Caron, *Les Dialogues* (Paris 1556) 53^r.

10 See Cristoforo Landino, *Disputationes Camaldulenses*, Book I.

11 Rice, *The Renaissance Idea of Wisdom* 46. Tudor humanism was of course strongly civic in orientation. See G.K. Hunter, *John Lyly: The Humanist as Courtier* (Cambridge, MA 1962) Chap. 1.

12 See G. Karl Galinsky, *The Herakles Theme: The Adaptations of the Hero in Literature from Homer to the Twentieth Century* (Oxford 1972): Homer and Hesiod in Chap. 1, Pindar in Chap. 2, Greek Drama Chap. 3. Good also on the *Aeneid* in Chap. 6 and Seneca in Chap. 8.

13 Pp 115-16. The example represents for Sidney an illustration of ideal humour because it fuses the elements of delight and laughter, though 'in themselves they have, as it were, a kind of contrariety' (p 115).

14 Coluccio Salutati, *De laboribus Herculis*, ed. B.L. Ullman (Zurich 1951) 317, citing Fulgentius, *Mythologiae* II, 2 (Helm) (my translation)

15 See Hesiod, *Works and Days* 286-92 for the whole passage. This is Watson's translation given in *Memorabilia* II.i.21. Peter V. Marinelli in a splendid article on the Italian romances makes the Logistilla episode central to the *Furioso*, because it sets up the contemplative and active lives, the divine and human loves of Astolfo and Ruggero respectively. The third part of the scheme – *amor ferinus* or sensual pleasure – is filled by Orlando. See 'Redemptive Laughter: Comedy in the Italian Romances,' in *Versions of Medieval Comedy*, ed. Paul G. Ruggiers (Norman, OK 1977) 239-45

16 Ludovico Ariosto, *L'Orlando furioso*, ed. Giacinto Casella (Florence 1931) VII.54. The translation is by Allan Gilbert, *Orlando Furioso*, 2 vols (New York 1954). The jewellery motif comes from Ovid, *Heroides* IX.57-60.

17 The confusion between Omphale and Iole (daughter of Eurytus, defeated King of Oechelia) is rampant in the Renaissance, based probably on Deianeira's accusation in the *Heroides* that both had conquered Hercules, and centred on the motif of the weak woman wearing the lion skin. See FQ V.v.24 and *Gerusalemme liberata* XVI.3; Salutati, *De laboribus Herculis* 315 makes the conflation deliberate. Sidney confuses the two in the *Old Arcadia* (*OA* 225) but distinguishes correctly in the *Defence* and the *New Arcadia* (I, 18, 76, 452).

18 The translation is by Edward Fairfax. Smith discusses this passage and the Choice of Hercules in *Elizabethan Poetry* 299.

19 In addition to the biblical allusion, these lines set right an earlier passage in the garden (xvi.21) that must have stayed in Milton's mind: 'L'uno di servitù, l'altra d'impera / si gloria, ella in sé stessa, ed egli in lei.' One takes pride in servitude, the other in mastery, she in herself and he in her.

20 Aptekar also is interested in reconciling the choice legend (virtuous Hercules) with the legend of Omphale. But she sees it being done 'sequentially' – first he succumbs and then he changes his mind. Disjunction and choice are therefore dominant. Isabel G. MacCaffrey suggests that Britomart herself, 'Radigund's *alter ego*,' offers a possible rapprochement: 'For Spenser, the alternative to the Judgment of Paris is not to repudiate Venus, but to choose a *Venus armata.*' *Spenser's Allegory: The Anatomy of Imagination* (Princeton 1976) 237 and n. MacCaffrey's assertion of synthesis is attractive, but note that Spenser does not give up the form and idea of rejection expressed in the defeat of Radigund.

21 My text is *Spenser's Faerie Queene*, ed. J.C. Smith, 2 vols (Oxford 1909).

22 Panofsky, *Hercules* 82-3 (emphasis in text). The reference to Goethe is the passage in *Götter, Helden und Wieland* where, reproving Wieland's and Prodicus' presentation of Virtue and Pleasure as incompatible extremes, Goethe has Hercules deny that the crossroads episode actually happened: 'Wären mir die Weiber begegnet, siehst du, eine unter den Arm, eine unter den, und beide hätten mit fortgemuszt' ('Had the women met me, you see, one under this arm, one under that, and both would have had to go with me' [my translation]), *ibid.* 136n.

23 See the chapter of the same name in Wind, *Pagan Mysteries*, which suggests many other examples of the tradition. He speaks of paintings and medals depicting the opposites Mars and Venus in which 'Venus is not only joined to Mars, but ... his nature is an essential part of her own and *vice versa*. True fierceness is thus conceived as potentially amiable, and true amiability as potentially fierce' (p 94).

24 Richard C. McCoy, *Sir Philip Sidney: Rebellion in Arcadia* (New Brunswick, NJ 1979) 45ff., makes much of the point that these debates are not resolved but are repeated without being settled.

25 This is carried out also in the coronet of gold and feathers that is 'not unlike to an helmet' (I, 75). That Zelmane's doublet is of 'skie colour sattin' may be significant, for 'blue, as the color of the sky, was symbolic of the aspiring mind according to Lomazzo: "Persius sat. i. speaking of Blew garments, sheweth that they belong only to such persons, as aspire unto higher matters: and Cicero used sometimes to wear this color, giving men thereby to understand, that he bare an aspiring minde"' (A *Tracte Containing the Artes of Curious Paintinge*, trans. Richard Haydock [1598] 122, cited by Smith, *Elizabethan Poetry* 10).

26 The *Old Arcadia* device of a dove preying on an eagle did not have this 'positive' function (*OA* 27).

27 As readers we may well be shocked to discover that Rinaldo's love is real, but Tasso's is a legitimate interpretation of the Dido and Aeneas material he is 'rectifying' here.

28 See discussion in Chap. 7.

29 P 98. The reference is to the *Phaedrus* 250, *De finibus* II, xvi, and *De officiis* I, v.

30 Aristotle, *Nicomachean Ethics*, trans. W.D. Ross, VII, ii-iii, esp. 1146^b30-1147^a10. The reference to Socrates is to *Protagoras*, 352 BC. See James J. Walsh, *Aristotle's Conception of Moral Weakness* (New York: Columbia University Press 1963) 102-4, 149-50.

31 Lawry, *Sidney's Two Arcadias* 74

32 The relation of the *Old Arcadia* to the *New Arcadia* is significant here. The passage is *more* emblematic in the *Old Arcadia* because it is the major form of love depicted there. But the *New Arcadia* has by this time presented Strephon and Claius, Argalus and Parthenia, and has somewhat elevated the tone of the princes' disguises and the scene in which the princesses are attacked by fierce animals. In the *New Arcadia*, therefore, this soliloquy offers a perspective rather than a paradigm, though Sidney still insists that it expresses an element in the love of 'all this noble companie.' See Elizabeth Dipple, 'Metamorphosis in Sidney's Arcadias,' *PQ* 50 (1971) 47-62, for the importance of context in reinterpreting identical material in the *Old* and *New Arcadia*.

33 Recapitulated in even stronger terms in old book *III*, *OA* 183

34 C.S. Lewis, *English Literature in the Sixteenth Century* (Oxford 1954) 338. Andrew D. Weiner has an excellent discussion of Gynecia as a Calvinist conception: *Sir Philip Sidney and the Poetics of Protestantism: A Study of Contexts* (Minneapolis 1978) 87-94, 100.

35 *Nic. Eth.* 1103^b 25

36 Italics mine. The corresponding passage in the *New Arcadia* is at I, 118. In the *Old Arcadia* this is our first notification of Basilius' feelings; in the *New Arcadia* Pyrocles has already told Musidorus about them, naturally with less sententiousness. 'Cleophila,' incidentally, is the *Old Arcadia's* name for Zelmane, Pyrocles in Amazonian disguise.

37 Philanax is generalizing apropos of Dametas. A similar remark is omitted later because of the change in narrative point of view (cf. *OA* 44 with I, 117-18).

38 *Astrophel and Stella* 10

39 See Stephen J. Greenblatt, 'Sidney's Arcadia and the Mixed Mode,' *SP* 70 (1973) 269-78.

40 If kept, this would be Pyrocles' second attempt to commit suicide by braining himself; in the revision he tries it after Philoclea's supposed death (I, 483). The *OA* scene is discussed in Chap. 7.

41 Eg, *Works* I, 436, 466

42 *The Republic of Plato*, trans. and ed. Francis M. Cornford (Oxford 1941) 271-3, 547A-550C. See also Walsh, *Aristotle's Conception of Moral Weakness* 33-52. Sidney's concern is with anger, too: Pyrocles is an example of 'overmastered courage and spite,' and at I, 436 he boils over with spite and disdain.

43 Classical writers were aware of the problem. Euripides' Medea and Phaedra were probably conceived as a challenge to Socrates' views (see Walsh, 16-22). Interestingly for Gynecia, the speaker of Ovid's famous 'video meliora proboque / deteriora sequor' is Medea (*Met.* VII, 20-1).

44 Weiner, *Poetics of Protestantism*, discusses Philoclea in connection with the problem of knowledge and virtue, pp 96, 161.

45 *OA* 108 has the interesting reading of 'to fall' for the *New Arcadia*'s 'to be altered.'

46 *Nic. Eth.* 1103ª 20

47 Seneca, *Ad Lucilium epistulae morales*, trans. R.M. Gummere, Loeb Classical Library Vol. II, Ep. 90, para. 46

48 Altered in the *New Arcadia* to 'minds, which nether absolutly clime the rocke of Vertue, nor freely sinke into the sea of Vanitie' (I, 260)

49 See *Chanson de Roland*, ll 1999-2004 (Roland's reply when Oliver wounds him), for an indication of how the depth of their bond could have found expression.

50 Especially since Sidney increases the pathos with the death of Philoxenus' father (Amphialus' foster-father) from 'sorrow of his sonne and (I think principally) unkindnes of Amphialus' (I, 71), and with the joyful greeting he receives from Philoxenus' dog.

51 Amphialus knows that love cannot be forced, and later admits knowing that his action against Basilius is treason, yet he does not permit himself to think this way while the Captivity continues.

CHAPTER FOUR: TONAL STRUCTURE

1 See Eugene M. Waith, *The Pattern of Tragi-Comedy in Beaumont and Fletcher* (New Haven 1952) 5-10 for the way characters are ranged to illustrate the idea of chastity in *The Faithful Shepherdess*. Muriel C. Bradbrook has studied thematic structure more generally in *Themes and Conventions of Elizabethan Tragedy* (Cambridge, Eng. 1935).

2 William Empson, *Some Versions of Pastoral* (London 1935) 55

3 *Ibid.* 54, where the discussion is explicitly about romances like *The Faerie Queene* and the *Arcadia*

4 Amphialus' horse is described as well, in terms of the sure service of age and well-proportioned greatness. The combat may well be paradigmatic or semi-allegorical.

5 Some writers take a harsher view. McCoy finds the contest 'frivolous, even deca-
dent,' with Sidney 'subtly satirizing their mannered chivalric gestures' (Richard C.
McCoy, *Sir Philip Sidney: Rebellion in Arcadia* [New Brunswick, NJ: 1979] 177).
His strongest argument is that these combats take place after the grimness of the
first day of battle, when war is made 'real.' Roberts considers the whole series of
combats part of a critical exposure of chivalry as a 'self-centered struggle for personal glory'; the point is epitomized by this contest, but is for her central to
Sidney's conception of Amphialus (Josephine A. Roberts, *Architectonic Knowledge
in the New Arcadia (1590): Sidney's Use of the Heroic Journey*, Elizabethan
Studies 69 (Salzburg 1978) 260.

6 The situation of the kidnapping and siege could have been treated as such a crisis.
'Imminent social disaster' does form the basis of Basilius' call for Argalus' service,
but locally Sidney emphasizes instead the issue of Argalus' honour.

7 I find this a more powerful moment than either Parthenia's hysteria when trying to
stop their combat or than her own melodramatic death, though Sidney's comment
on the latter – 'the rarenes of the accident, matching together (the rarely matched
together) pittie with admiration' (I, 449) – suggests that he considered it tragedy. An
important element missing from Sidney's 'version' of the Andromache scene, incidentally, is Astyanax, Hector's infant son. Roberts, *Architectonic Knowledge*, also
compares Parthenia with Andromache here (p 267).

8 The later combat between Musidorus and Amphialus offers yet another variation.
It is a display of sheer courage, ferocity, and technique; rules are obeyed, but most
of the courtesy and humanity have been eliminated.

9 Empson, *Pastoral* 31. See also Richard Levin, *The Multiple Plot in English Renaissance Drama* (Chicago 1971) 146-7, on clown subplots.

10 The third 'female' is Pyrocles, disguised as the Amazon Zelmane. This both allows
freer handling of the sexual idea and sets up the most obvious comic situation.

11 The second oracle (I, 510) says that Basilius' daughters will return 'safely and
speedily.'

12 Separation and reunion is as it were the thematic action of the first section; other
instances occur between Argalus and Parthenia and between Kalander and his son
Clitophon. Separation alone is the keynote of the opening invocation, though the
first sentence of the book presages fruitful union (see Jon S. Lawry, *Sidney's Two
Arcadias: Pattern and Proceeding* [Ithaca, NY 1972] 167).

13 The section runs from one debate between the princes to the other; since they
were originally part of the same sequence in the *Old Arcadia*, the division is logical.
I use chapter numbers for convenience; they were provided not by Sidney but by
the 1590 editors. There are only one or two places where their judgment seems
questionable.

14 Argalus proves a 'rare ensample' of 'trueth of love ... a vertuous constancie, and even a delight to be constant, faith geven ...' (I, 35).

15 This offers a much different picture of Helen and her court from that given in Book II, which critics often quote as presenting the ideal towards which the *Arcadia* strives (I, 283-4). I rather suspect that since the description in Book II is our second acquaintance with Corinth, it is qualified by our earlier knowledge.

16 Basilius' passion also interferes with his natural relation to his daughter: in Book II he uses Philoclea as a pander or go-between in his affair with Zelmane.

17 Ismenus tells of having seen Amphialus, who when he discovered that his page was following him, 'rase up in such rage, that in truth I feared he would kill me ...' (I, 73).

18 The idea is picked up again in Book III when Musidorus and Amphialus assume that they are fighting over the same woman. The tone is much more grim there, however, since the mistake is largely responsible for the incredible viciousness of their battle (I, 453-62, esp. 456).

19 Also omitted are Musidorus' even greater amorous liberties after he kills the bear: 'he turned to his lady Pamela (at that time in a swoon with extremity of fear), and softly taking her in his arms, he took the advantage to kiss and re-kiss her a hundred times ...' (OA 52).

20 Zelmane's 'impatient delight' is the restrained revision of Cleophila's 'painful delight she had to see without hope of enjoying' (OA 48).

21 See Lausberg, *Handbuch der Literarischen Rhetorik* para. 805 and *Ad Herennium* III.iii.6, with its references to Thucydides 3.82 on the moral effects of the Peloponnesian War and Sallust, *Cat*. 52.11. Sidney himself uses the figure to describe how Andromana translates all her stepson's actions into the 'language of suspition' (I, 247; the passage is quoted here on p 105 and on OA 324, ll 16-18).

22 The 'relativist' tendencies of an analysis such as Stephen Greenblatt's of the 'mixed mode' (SP 1973) seem to falsify the solidity of Sidney's values; his stance is closer to the moral awareness that Paul J. Alpers has analysed for Spenser (*The Poetry of The Faerie Queene*, Princeton 1967) and that we normally attribute to Shakespeare.

23 Arthur C. Kirsch, *Jacobean Dramatic Perspectives* (Charlottesville, VA 1972) 10. Professor Kirsch makes a further observation that seems relevant to the *Arcadia*: 'Where tragicomedy ... presents an action in which oppositions are being continuously transformed, [in] satiric comedy ... [the] vision of the oppositions which govern man's behavior is characteristically static' (p 15).

24 Cf. the pattern of tragicomedy Waith sets up for Beaumont and Fletcher.

25 *AS* 25, *Poems* 177. Cf. also *AS* 4, 10, 14, 34 and 35, 52, 68.

26 *AS* 18, *Poems* 173-4. Cf. also *AS* 5, 19, 21, 51, 71. I don't mean to push the parallels too far. The tensions generated in *AS* are much greater than one feels in the *Arcadia*, perhaps because the 'humour' of the sonnets is most often irony.

27 Rudenstine's distinction in *Sidney's Poetic Development* (Cambridge, MA 1967) between the royal poems and those by the shepherds and Philisides, which offer more colloquial rhythms and diction, is necessary for talking about the *Arcadia's* verse.

28 Robert L. Montgomery, jr, *Symmetry and Sense: The Poetry of Sir Philip Sidney* (Austin 1961) 119, 58-9

29 The Narrator has a whole range of distancing tricks: he employs the modesty topos (*OA* 11, 49), disclaims having 'feeling insight enough' into passion (*OA* 42), chats playfully with his readers (always addressed as 'Ladies') at several points, talks of the conduct of women 'in these worthy days' (*OA* 50), and so on. The influence for some of this may well not be Ariosto's narrator but Chaucer's in the *Troilus* (see *Defence* 112). On the Narrator see Margaret E. Dana, 'The Providential Plot of the *Old Arcadia*,' *SEL* 17 (1977) 40-4 and Rudenstine, *Sidney's Poetic Development* 28-35. Weiner documents what might be called a 'Protestant' Narrator who manipulates the reader's responses (see, eg, Andrew D. Weiner, *Sir Philip Sidney and the Poetics of Protestantism: A Study of Contexts* (Minneapolis 1978) 75.

30 There is only one exception to this in the 500 pages that Sidney revised, the Narrator's apostrophe to Philoclea: 'And alas (sweete Philoclea) how hath my penne till now forgot thy passions, since to thy memorie principally all this long matter is intended?' (I, 168-9). The wording, but not the sense, is altered slightly from *OA* 108. The lapse, if it is such, is genuinely puzzling, since whatever truth it contains is not reflected in the work.

31 Sidney saw this in his *Arcadia* despite the strong insistence on 'poetic justice' in the *Defence* (eg, p 88).

32 *The Epic of Gilgamesh*, Eng. version by N.K. Sandars, Penguin Classics (Baltimore 1960) 87

33 Cedric H. Whitman, *Homer and the Heroic Tradition* (Cambridge, MA 1958) 198-9. Patroclus is both Achilles' 'double' and an aspect of Achilles (his 'humanity').

34 See Sigmund Freud, *The Interpretation of Dreams*, 3rd English ed., in *The Basic Writings of Sigmund Freud*, trans. and ed. A.A. Brill, Modern Library (New York 1938). Another technique germane to narrative literature would be condensation, which allows one symbol or figure simultaneously to represent several disparate events capable of meaningful association by the dreamer.

35 *Ibid.* 349. See the discussion of the dream process in *The Faerie Queene* in Graham Hough, *A Preface to The Faerie Queene* (New York 1963) 97, 131-5.

36 Carl G. Jung, *Archetypes of the Collective Unconscious*, in *The Basic Writings of Carl G. Jung*, ed. Violet Staub de Laslo, Modern Library (New York 1959) 304-17. The key factor here is that these two archetypes are embodiments or projections of some aspect of the human psyche. They are relevant to the dreamer himself but appear as alien figures.

37 Kenneth Burke, *A Grammar of Motives and a Rhetoric of Motives* (Cleveland and New York 1962) 406

38 There is thus also a contrast in their ages, but Sidney does not pick it up elsewhere. Cf. the four-way comparison of Philoclea, Pamela, Helen, and Parthenia in I, 32 and 100. Sidney seems to have paired the women in his mind, for Pamela and Helen share certain characteristics and Philoclea and Parthenia others.

39 Dorothy L. Sayers' introduction to her translation of *The Song of Roland*, Penguin Classics (London 1957), sheds interesting light on the education motif. Apparently it is of feudal rather than classical derivation:

> It was the ancient custom to send a boy of good family to be brought up ('nurtured,' or 'fostered') in the household of one's over-lord, where he received such education as was to be had, learned good manners, and was trained in arms, sports, and horsemanship. Two boys thus bred up side by side from early youth, and competing together in their work and play, would become special friends, or 'companions'; and this intimacy and friendly rivalry would be continued in after life. The affection between companions, and that between the lord and the lads nurtured in his house was a very strong one, frequently overshadowing those of blood-relationship. (p 37)

40 This and the emphasis on Amphialus' masculinity seem to promote comparison with Musidorus, but other incidents fit better with Pyrocles. See Roberts, *Architectonic Knowledge* 268-73, for comparisons between Amphialus and the princes.

41 In apparent contrast to this pattern is the passage at I, 375 where Amphialus considers the charge that love is nurtured in idleness and refutes it: he is both desperately in love *and* engaged in 'urgent affaires.' Rudenstine calls attention to this passage as a 'glimpsed vision of harmony' (*Sidney's Poetic Development* 26), but the narrative context must surely qualify it. This is heroic action for the wrong purpose, and his *love* is what has allowed him to become his mother's tool. If Amphialus' combination of love and the active life is relevant to the synthesis Sidney desired, it is to guarantee that the princes' triumph will not be thought an easy one.

42 The incident is quite Virgilian in feeling: it later provides Philanax the motive for killing Amphialus' page Ismenus despite inner promptings towards mercy (cf. *Aeneid*, XII 940-51).

43 The lightning rod metaphor is Northrop Frye's, as are most of the elements in this list. See *Anatomy of Criticism: Four Essays* (Princeton 1957) 209-11.

44 The particular statement belongs to E.M.W. Tillyard, *The English Epic and Its Background* (London 1954) 314, but this must be the assumption of all users of the 1593 text.

CHAPTER FIVE: NARRATIVE STRUCTURE – RETROSPECTIVE HISTORY

1 The subject has been taken up by John Danby, Walter Davis, Jon Lawry, Arthur
Amos, and Josephine Roberts. See also the earlier discussions of Edwin Greenlaw,
'Sidney's Arcadia as an Example of Elizabethan Allegory,' in Kittredge Anniversary
Papers (Boston 1913) 327-37 and Kenneth Myrick, Sir Philip Sidney as a Literary
Craftsman (Cambridge, MA 1935). For an account of weaknesses in Davis' and
Greenlaw's analyses, see my article, 'Sidney's Arcadia, Book II: Retrospective Narrative,' SP 64 (1967) 159-62. The article is a version of this chapter.
2 The distinction between the princesses is carried out in the stories they tell: Philoclea narrates Erona's unfortunate love; Pamela dwells more on the political repercussions of Plangus' error.
3 Greenlaw distinguishes them as political wrongs to be righted and sins against love;
Davis distinguishes between stories having public ahd psychological emphases.
4 Surprisingly, there is no mention made of learning through negative example,
though this is ordinarily included in such educational programs. Vice as a necessary
foil to virtue is part of the theory of the Defence and of the actual practice of the
Arcadia.
5 Musidorus' ecstatic view of love here is also relevant to the dramatic situation in
the frame of his narrative.
6 As retrospective narrative, these stories have all taken place before Book I.
7 Sidney's sense that the 'hero' must develop in a world which is so shifting and problematic seems to me to be related to his preference for a figure I have described in
the introduction as an 'Orator-King' (p 12ff.), an Isocratean rhetoricist conception.
8 Pamphilus seems to be a parody of the lover on the third step of Diotima's ladder
in the Symposium. His devotion is to beauty wherever he finds it; it is constancy
to a principle residing in many objects rather than to a particular person.
9 Cf. Defence, 89: the feigned example depends for its power to move on the ability
to 'be tuned to the highest key of passion.'
10 Significantly, the only reference to love in Musidorus' tales occurs in the vision of
harmonious order at the outset of their voyage, where it is described in terms of the
chivalric ideal of heroic deeds inspired by one's mistress; marriage occurs more frequently, and as one might expect, each instance is arranged for the state's convenience.
11 Since the speaker is Musidorus, the idea of demonstrating nobility by wearing a
base disguise has obvious reference to his dramatic situation in the frame as well.
12 Cf. these Giants with Anaxius, whom Sidney associates with the giants of Greek
myth (I, 263). In so far as both concern the idea of power potentially at the service
of the good, the allegorical root of Sidney's conception may be the control of the
nobler passions, such as anger, by reason.

13 The sections are roughly equal in length and Sidney seems to have marked the divisions himself, first with the arrival in Asia Minor and then with the summarizing commentary comparing his heroes with Aeneas and Ulysses (quoted above, p 205).

14 The moral disorder of Pyrocles' narrative may also be reflected in its rearrangement of the tonal scheme as it handles problems of love: it begins with comedy and parody (Dido and Pamphilus), moves to the negative with Andromana's lust for both Pyrocles and Musidorus, and then to the positive with the account of Helen's court. Love in the 'positive' section is further qualified by being predominantly sad, since the noble loves are all unrequited (Palladius for Zelmane, Zelmane for Pyrocles, Leucippe for Pamphilus).

15 Despite my having stressed the need not to simplify the episodes for the purposes of neat schematization, I must confess my present neglect of about 15 pages in the second section of Pyrocles' narrative for reasons of convenience in handling.

16 See Lawry's discussion of the positive value the Zelmane story has for the meaning of the princes' Asia Minor adventures (*Sidney's Two Arcadias* 238). See also Roberts, *Architectonic Knowledge* 75, 102-4.

17 D.M. Anderson, 'The Dido Incident in Sidney's *Arcadia*,' *N&Q*, NS III, Vol. 201 (1956) 418

18 This is Anderson's opinion as well (*ibid*. 418). The idea is not unknown in romance – in Chrétien's *Yvain*, the giant Harpin threatens to turn the knight's daughter over to his scullery boys, though not while her father is watching (ll 4112-42 Foerster ed.).

19 Pyrocles suggests that his error in not suspecting Chremes' sudden politeness can be traced to what we would ordinarily call his virtue: 'a sufficient token to me, if Nature had made me apte to suspect; since a churles curtesie rathely comes but either for gaine, or falshood' (I, 275).

20 Davis, 'Thematic Unity' 131 and 133n.

21 The words quoted belong to Pyrocles, not Leucippe. These, incidentally, are the Baccha and Leucippe who appeared together in Artesia's Triumph in Book I. Leucippe adds her own note suggesting the complexities of judgment to the narrative by resolving to spend her life 'in bewayling the wrong, and yet praying for the wrong-dooer' (I, 290).

22 Erona's dilemma is itself significant because it represents a situation where no action is clearly right. The passage is greatly expanded from the bare statement of the *Old Arcadia* (*OA* 69).

23 Cf. the traditional antithesis between force and fraud.

24 Plangus' 'dilemma' is set up with verbal resemblances to Erona's, 'she being drawne to two contraries by one cause' (I, 235). Cf. the figure *paradiastole*.

25 In addition to the studies cited in note 1, see Winifred Schleiner, 'Differences of
Theme and Structure of the Erona Episode in the Old and New Arcadia,' SP 70
(1973) 377-91. McCoy, Rebellion in Arcadia, discusses Plangus extensively as well,
pp 144-56, though it seems to me that Sidney's point is distorted by the conflation
made between Pyrocles and Plangus.

26 See Samuel Lee Wolff, The Greek Romances in Elizabethan Prose Fiction (New
York: Columbia University Press 1912) 143-4.

27 Cf. Works I, 205: 'But ... high honor is not onely gotten and borne by paine, and
daunger, but must be nurst by the like, or els vanisheth as soone as it appeares to
the world ...'

28 Even what we might consider a change of character, Sidney takes as a progressive
unfolding of something essentially complete and always potentially ready to be
expressed. This is his description of the paranoiac King of Phrygia:

> Yet while youth lasted in him, the exercises of that age, and his humour (not
> yet fullie discovered) made him something the more frequentable, and less daun-
> gerous. But after that yeares beganne to come on with some, though more sel-
> dome shewes of a bloudie nature, and that the prophecie of Musidorus destinie
> came to his eares ... Then gave he himselfe indeede to the full currant of his
> disposition ... (I, 196)

The classical antecedents of Sidney's conception of character are discussed under
the term 'substantialism' by R.G. Collingwood, The Idea of History (Oxford 1936),
especially in his remarks on Tacitus, p 44. See also William Nelson, The Poetry of
Edmund Spenser: A Study (New York: Columbia University Press 1963) 122-3.

CHAPTER SIX: NARRATIVE EXPLORATION – SCOPE

1 See the chapter 'Et in Arcadia Ego: Poussin and the Elegiac Tradition,' included in
Erwin Panofsky, Meaning in the Visual Arts (Garden City, NY 1955), for the history of Arcadian interpretation. See also Bruno Snell, The Discovery of the Mind:
The Greek Origins of European Thought, trans. T.G. Rosenmayer (New York
1953) Chap. 13; Thomas G. Rosenmayer, The Green Cabinet: Theocritus and the
European Pastoral Lyric (Berkeley 1969) Chap. 11; and Elizabeth Dipple, 'Harmony
and Pastoral in the Old Arcadia,' ELH 35 (1968) 309-28.

2 David Kalstone, Sidney's Poetry: Contexts and Interpretation (Cambridge, 1965),
Chap. 1; published separately as 'The Transformation of Arcadia: Sannazaro and Sir
Philip Sidney,' CL 15 (1963) 234-49

3 Recently there has been a swing to making the Arcadia 'politically relevant' to its
times, but this, as in McCoy's Rebellion in Arcadia, largely means anchoring it in

its historical moment by making connections with the Huguenot cause or the Alençon affair. My own concern here is not so topical; I have in mind Sidney's interest in 'politics' – in political theory, political possibilities, generalizable historic experience, the relation between ruler and state, rather than even in such particul. ideas as the subaltern magistrate or the legitimizing of tyrannicide.

4 The dichotomy is in neither case a disjunction. It is 'knowing' incorporated in 'doing,' and for Rixus' plea about the hunter's life, contemplation incorporated in action: 'for ours, besides that quiet part, doth both strengthen the body, and raise up the mind with this gallant sort of activity' (Miscellaneous Prose 29).

5 The earlier discussion appears on pp 75-7.

6 Nic. Eth. I .ii (1094^b). This passage is to be put in the balance against the Ethics' final statement that the intellectual virtues are higher than the moral – in Renaissance terms, that the contemplative life is higher than the active.

7 Erich Auerbach, Mimesis: The Representation of Reality in Western Literature, trans. Willard Trask (Garden City, NY 1957) 116-17

8 Richard W. Barber, The Knight and Chivalry (London 1970) 103, for both the quotation and the preceding material. See also p 36.

9 See John E. Stevens, Medieval Romance: Themes and Approaches (London 1973) 238 and his discussion in general.

10 Morte Arthure, ed. John Finlayson, York Medieval Texts (London 1967) 11. See th introduction on the development of Arthurian legend, esp. pp 5-10, 'Chanson de geste and romance.'

11 See Eugene Vinaver, ed. The Works of Sir Thomas Malory, 1st ed. (Oxford 1947) III, 1363-4, and also Charles Moorman, The Book of Kyng Arthur: The Unity of Malory's Morte Darthur (Lexington, KY 1965) 24-7.

12 Auerbach, Mimesis 117

13 Ibid. 123

14 This alteration in political interest and fierceness has of course already occurred in the material Ariosto inherits. See C.P. Brand, Ariosto: A Preface to the 'Orlando Furioso' (Edinburgh 1974) Chap. 3, 'The Literary Tradition.'

15 Rinaldo is in some senses a more 'human' figure than the other heroes, with relatively greater complexity in his social ties. His status as ruler and general as well knight is given unique emphasis in the poem (XXXI.56-8).

16 The 1532 additions include also the decidedly political Marganor episode (Canto XXXVII) and the Castle of Tristram (XXXII) with its courtesy and hospitality themes. See Brand, Ariosto 171-82. The purely political context of the poem is al thin, whether one defines this in terms of concern for good government, interest problems of succession or of genuine rebellion, or presentation of the populace as force to be served or even manipulated rather than merely punished.

17 Brand, Ariosto 89-92

18 *Defence* 98 talks of 'heroical' poetry, listing such champions as Achilles, Cyrus, Aeneas, Turnus, Tydeus, and Rinaldo. I do not mean to imply that Ariosto did not consider his poem to be an 'epic.'

19 Finlayson, ed. *Morte Arthure* 10

20 The Helot rebellion can be found on I, 36-47. I discuss it in more detail later in this chapter, pp 129-30.

21 McCoy's most interesting explorations are of the political ramifications of the Amphialus rebellion, both in relation to Machiavelli and the Huguenots and in discussing the shift between large-scale battle and single combats (*Rebellion in Arcadia* 174-8).

22 William Empson, *Some Versions of Pastoral* (London 1935) 23. Page references appear in the text. See also in this connection Renato Poggioli, 'Naboth's Vineyard: The Pastoral View of the Social Order,' *JHI* 24 (1963) 3-24, collected in his *The Oaten Flute: Essays on Pastoral Poetry and the Pastoral Ideal* (Cambridge, MA 1975).

23 '"This member of the class is the whole class, or its defining property: this man has a magical importance to all men." If you choose an important member the result is heroic; if you choose an unimportant one it is pastoral' (Empson, *Pastoral* 79). See also pp 12, 21, 198-9.

24 Rosenmeyer's highly restrictive definition of pastoral as 'what Theocritus did' negatively establishes how wide and varied one's account of pastoral must be (see, eg, his chapter in *The Green Cabinet* called 'Anatomy'), but it also isolates some sense of 'pure' pastoral, of what it is always possible that pastoral might retreat back to. Rosenmeyer's position is succinctly stated on p 214.

25 *Sannazaro's Arcadia and Piscatorial Eclogues*, trans. Ralph Nash (Detroit 1966) 25. Nash continues by describing the impetus of Sannazaro's *Arcadia* as a movement 'away from the imperfect flux and toward contemplation of the eternal and ideal.'

26 See Poggioli, *The Oaten Flute* 27, 200-2.

27 Their role in the interludes remains unclear because Sidney never revised this part of the work.

28 Kalstone, *Sidney's Poetry* 64. The previous quotation is from pp 65-6. See also the discussions of the eclogues in Jon Lawry, *Sidney's Two Arcadias: Pattern and Proceeding* (Ithaca, NY 1972), Andrew Weiner, *Sir Philip Sidney and the Poetics of Protestantism: A Study of Contexts* (Minneapolis 1978) and Elizabeth Dipple, 'The "Fore Conceit" of Sidney's Eclogues,' *Literary Monographs* I (1967).

29 Walter R. Davis, *Sidney's Arcadia* (New Haven 1965) 38. Arcadia itself, the royal lodges, and the cave are the three geographical areas meant here; Asia Minor is yet another concentric circle in Davis' scheme.

30 The translation is from Michael C. Putnam, *The Poetry of the Aeneid: Four Studies in Imaginative Unity and Design* (Cambridge, MA 1965) 135.

31 See Putnam, *ibid.* 129-36 and Chap. 3 generally; also G. Karl Galinsky, *The Herakles Theme: The Adaptations of the Hero in Literature from Homer to the Twentieth Century* (Oxford 1972) Chap. 6.

32 As I shall argue later, I consider this scene essential to a fuller appreciation of the *New Arcadia*. It seems probable that Sidney meant to include the imprisonment scene (though altered) as well. See pp 136, 139.

33 In this single aspect, it resembles Musidorus' narrative, which may be significant for Sidney's evaluation of Xenophon, since Musidorus' concept of virtue is incorporated into a more complex one.

34 Xenophon does not, however, share the buoyant ethical position Shaw brought to a similar conception of the hero in *Caesar and Cleopatra*.

35 E.M.W. Tillyard, *The English Epic and Its Background* (London 1954) 58. The identification of Euarchus with Aristotle's μεγαλόψυχος was made by Kenneth Thorpe Rowe, 'Romantic Love and Parental Authority in Sidney's *Arcadia*,' *University of Michigan Contributions in Modern Philology* 4 (1947) 38ff.

36 This aspect of polity is, however, present in the early description of the Persian society in which Cyrus was reared (*Cyropaedia*, trans. Henry G. Dakyns, Everyman ed. [London 1914] 6-11). But Cyrus is a different type of king once he gains power.

37 Arthur Heiserman, *The Novel before the Novel: Essays and Discussions about the Beginnings of Prose Fiction in the West* (Chicago 1977) 186-202, in emphasizing the primacy of Heliodorus' general religious orientation in the *Aethiopica*, seems to play down the political and social scope of the work.

38 It is very important also that Pyrocles and Musidorus *pursue* virtuous action and do not merely (like Theagenes and Chariclea) have things happen to them that they must endure well. Cf. Sidney's point in the *Arcadia* concerning the insufficient heroism of Ulysses and Aeneas (I, 206). It is interesting to note that Heliodorus' sixteenth-century French translator, Jacques Amyot, voices a similar objection to what I have called the work's double focus:

> (quand tout est dit) ce n'est qu'une fable, à laquelle encore default (à mon jugement) l'une des deux perfections requises pour faire une chose belle, c'est la grandeur, à cause que les contes, mesmement quant à la personne de Theagenes, auquel il ne fait executer nulz memorables exploitz d'armes, ne me semblent point assez / riches ... (Le Proïsme du Translateur, *L'Histoire Aethiopique de Heliodorus* [Paris 1547], sigs. A iii^r-iii^v).
>
> (when all is said and done) it is only a fable, which still lacks (in my opinion) one of the two kinds of perfection required for creating a beautiful object, that is, grandeur, because the tales – even concerning the person of Theagenes, whom he does not have carry out any memorable feats of arms – do not seem to me rich enough ... (my translation)

(Note Amyot's transmutation of Aristotle's neutral 'magnitude' into a moral category.)

39 B.P. Reardon, 'The Greek Novel,' *Phoenix* 23 (1969) 293. The material of this article is condensed from Reardon's *Courants littéraires grecs des IIᵉ et IIIᵉ siècles après J.-C.*, Annales Littéraires de l'Université de Nantes, No. 3 (Paris 1971) 309-403.

40 Reardon, 'The Greek Novel' 292. Heiserman in his 'Discussions' under the figure of 'Kappa' speculates interestingly on ways of relating these romances to the history and sociology of the period.

41 Ben Edwin Perry, *The Ancient Romances: A Literary-Historical Account of their Origins* (Berkeley 1967) 48. He also describes Greek romance as fundamentally Hellenistic drama in substance and [rhetorical] historiography in form (pp 78, 140). The influence of Heliodorus was therefore simultaneously the influence of Sophistic historiography.

42 Northrop Frye, in *The Return of Eden: Five Essays on Milton's Epics* (Toronto 1965), says that the implication of Sidney's remark is that the *Cyropaedia* 'represents the prose counterpart of the encyclopaedic epic' (p 11). Frye's whole discussion here of major prose genres is significant for the appraisal of the *Arcadia*'s genre.

43 See also Underdowne's own introduction to his translation of Heliodorus (*An Aethiopian Historie* [1587 ed.], ed. Charles Whibley, Tudor Translations, V [London 1895]). This kind of interpretation was possible also because they saw the work as an imitation of virtues and vices rather than with Aristotle as an imitation of an action. See Marion Trousdale, 'A Possible Renaissance View of Form,' *ELH* 40 (1973) 192: a story might have meaning 'not by virtue of its ordering but by virtue of its gloss. And schoolchildren were taught to draw from any tale at all points all of the moral truths they were able to find.' Amyot's comment, cited in note 38 above, suggests that readers had other Aristotelian concepts available to them for correcting this imbalance.

44 See Eduard Norden, *Die Antike Kunstprosa vom VI. Jahrhundert vor Christus bis in die Zeit der Renaissance*, 2 vols (Leipzig 1898).

45 Torquato Tasso, *Discorsi del poema heroico* (1594), in Allan H. Gilbert, ed., *Literary Criticism: Plato to Dryden* (Detroit 1962; 1st pub. 1940) 483-4. This is a slight alteration of the 1587 text, which substitutes 'fatti di cortesia, di generosita' for 'magnanimous resolution to die.' The earlier text is quoted in Bernard Weinberg, *A History of Literary Criticism in the Italian Renaissance* (Chicago 1961) II, 648n.

46 Fritz Caspari, *Humanism and the Social Order* (Chicago 1954)

47 *Ibid.* 6

48 G.K. Hunter, *John Lyly: The Humanist as Courtier* (Cambridge, MA 1962) 29

49 *Ibid.* 15. A good contrast to Sidney's English approach is offered by Landino's interpretation of the *Aeneid* as the 'ascent of the hero from the fleshly concerns of Troy

to the purity of the contemplative life symbolized by the conquest of Latium,'
quoted in Nelson, *Poetry of Edmund Spenser* 123, citing *Disputationes Camaldulenses*, Books III and IV.

50 English 'princes' were less plentiful than rulers of small Italian courts, and English
expectations must have been more of service and less of this kind of influence. But
Sidney's own experience might well lead him to some such idea, since he was himself the recipient of similar advice and 'education' by Languet.

51 Spenser's suggested hierarchy in I.x puts contemplation higher than action, but the
context is specifically religious rather than philosophical.

52 Sidney's relation to sophistic rhetoric here reflects the mediation of Cicero and Stoic
rationality. The emphasis of the episode is so decidedly on Pyrocles' rhetorical
skill – he is demonstrating both the validity of his education and his qualifications as
a potential king – that interpretation of the parallel episode in *The Faerie Queene* in
terms of the Gallic Hercules seems very attractive (see T.K. Dunseath, *Spenser's
Allegory of Justice in Book Five of The Faerie Queene* [Princeton 1968] 99-101).

53 Dunseath, *Spenser's Allegory of Justice* 94-112

54 The same is true of the final remedy. The reduction to class prejudice is disquieting
both morally and for its sense of 'polity': Artegall, being loath 'his noble hands t'
embrew / In the base blood of such a rascall crew' (V.ii.52), sends in Talus, who
disperses and kills them all with his flail.

55 This might be the result of Spenser's plan to have these twelve books centre on private rather than public virtues, though Book V is ambiguous in this respect.

56 Rudenstine, *Sidney's Poetic Development*, is particularly good on these tensions,
though he talks about leisure and relaxation rather than love. He would not, I
think, agree with my sentence, recognizing the 'firmness of acceptance' instead as
only one half of the tension.

57 Dedicatory letter, *Works* I, 3

58 'S.P. Sidney had ane intention to have transferr'd all his Arcadia to the stories of
King Arthure' (Jonson, *Conversations with Drummond*, cited in Tillyard, *English
Epic* 294).

59 The Helot rebellion has generally been thought to reflect Sidney's ideas on Ireland,
where his father, Sir Henry, served as Elizabeth's Viceroy.

60 This applies to Basilius in the *Old Arcadia* (*OA* 358); the gist of the 1593 version is
probably the same: Euarchus and Basilius together are 'in effect the whole strength
of Greece' (*OA* 355 variants).

61 The *New Arcadia* also adds an interesting passage to the first description we have
of Basilius, distinguishing virtues which inspire admiration from those which stir
affection and then proceeding to state that Gynecia is of more princely virtue than
her husband (I, 19).

CHAPTER SEVEN: NARRATIVE STRUCTURE – RELATIONSHIP BETWEEN EPISODES AND FABLE

1 In addition to Ringler, *Poems* xxxviii, see Robert W. Parker, 'Terentian Structure and Sidney's Original *Arcadia*,' *ELR* 2 (1972) 61-78 and Clark L. Chalifour, 'Sir Philip Sidney's *Old Arcadia* as Terentian Comedy,' *SEL* 16 (1976) 51-63.

2 Except for Elizabeth Dipple, 'The Captivity Episode and the *New Arcadia*,' *JEGP* 70 (1971) 418-31. She also sees Book III as a narrative impasse, but seems to feel that Sidney intended it that way, that is, that he had more or less abandoned the *Old Arcadia*'s plot by 'burying' the controlling significance of the oracle in newer material.

3 See, for example, the index to Bernard Weinberg's *A History of Literary Criticism in the Italian Renaissance* (Chicago 1961), s.v. 'episode.'

4 Gerald F. Else, *Aristotle's Poetics: The Argument* (Cambridge, MA 1957) 325-6nn, on *Poetics* IX (51^{b}34-5). Author's italics

5 *Ibid.* 505n. Author's italics

6 This position is supported by David Riggs, '"Plot" and "Episode" in Early Neoclassical Criticism,' in *Renaissance Drama* NS VI (1973), ed. Alan C. Dessen (Evanston, Ill. 1975) 161-70. See also Madeleine Doran, *Endeavors of Art: A Study of Form in Elizabethan Drama* (Madison, WI 1954) 273-7.

7 Antonio Minturno, *L'Arte poetica*, in Allan H. Gilbert, ed., *Literary Criticism: Plato to Dryden* (Detroit 1962) 279. The resemblance to the *Iliad* is deliberate, for this follows a similar plot summary of Homer's epic. Riggs, '"Plot" and "Episode",' usefully cites Minturno on Aristophanes as well.

8 See Doran, *Endeavors of Art* 274.

9 Technically, this turns Kalander's narration of the material surrounding the oracle, which the 1590 editors call 'the ground of all this storie' (I, 17), into an episode; but exposition in drama also has this ambiguous status with relation to plot.

10 Artesia and apparently Anaxius have also been killed. The only important characters remaining from the episodes (except for Helen, who is nursing Amphialus back to health as she once did Parthenia) are Plangus and Erona, Artaxia and Plexirtus. It is likely from the revised passage concerning Euarchus in the 1593 text (OA 355-6) that this incident had to be left unresolved at the end of the book.

11 See OA 369 for Sidney's original conception of Philoclea. The scene occurs while the two princesses are awaiting the trial in tears, 'especially the tender Philoclea who, as she was in years younger and had never lifted up her mind to any option of sovereignty, so was she apter to yield to her misfortune, having no stronger debates in her mind than a man may say a most witty childhood is wont to nourish ...' The 1593 edition keeps the passage (*Works*, II, 162).

12 Peter Lindenbaum, 'Sidney's *Arcadia*: The Endings of the Three Versions,' *HLQ* 35 (1971) 216, considers it a major contradiction to have Pamela flee Arcadia with

Musidorus 'after she had so adamantly asserted to Cecropia ... that to marry without her father's consent would be an offense to God' (I, 405).

13 C.S. Lewis, *English Literature in the Sixteenth Century* (Oxford 1954) 333. The issue seems freshly relevant because Maurice Evans has chosen the 1593 edition for his Penguin text (1978).

14 Ringler, *Poems* 375-8, discusses these emended passages and on p 378 argues for Sidney's responsibility. See also William L. Godshalk, 'Sidney's Revision of the *Arcadia*, Books III-V,' *PQ* 43 (1964) 171-83; Robertson, *OA* lx-lxii; Lindenbaum, 'Endings' 205-18; A.C. Hamilton, *Sir Philip Sidney: A Study of His Life and Works* (Cambridge, Eng. 1977) 169-70; Dorothy Connell, *Sir Philip Sidney: The Maker's Mind* (Oxford 1975) 144n.

15 Thus, Davis' reinterpretation of the comic intrigues in the old Books III and IV to accord with the moral tone of the new Book III is indefensible: 'Upon the return from Cecropia's castle to the retreat, each of the heroes embarks on a rigorous program of Stoic endurance ... By great labor and self-restraint, Musidorus manages to maneuver his persecutors into traps so that he can escape to Thessalia with Pamela ... Pyrocles' task is the more heroic as the difficulties he faces are greater; his first job is to pacify the lustful Gynecia, a task which calls for tact and great continence ...' (*Sidney's Arcadia* 77-8).

16 In addition to the arguments cited in note 14, I have noted three examples of Sidney's characteristic use of *antimetabole* in the longer passage, which may be taken as corroborating stylistic evidence for its being authorial.

17 The argument for Christian patience is Danby's, for Neoplatonic transformation Davis'.

18 This seems to be a playfully ironic comment by the Narrator, for it must apply not to the debate itself but to the immediately previous emotional statement, which may have its own logic but can hardly be termed 'wisely uttered.'

19 The problem of character is always difficult. What, for example, is Gynecia's *real* character: is her action in the plot the determining factor rather than her past and subsequent life? Elizabeth Dipple in 'Metamorphosis in Sidney's *Arcadias*,' *PQ* 50 (1971) 53-4, seems to suggest this, but I disagree. Again, as for Pyrocles and Musidorus in the *Old Arcadia*, the plot records a specific lapse, though hers is worse and more widespread in the psyche. Sidney is willing to hold her generally responsible (see the final paragraph of the work), but he does not, I think, mean to judge her solely on this one action. Gynecia incidentally can be spoken of in this way, while Basilius does not have 'character' in this sense at all.

20 Greville, *Life of Sidney* 16

21 The discussion occurs on *OA* 372ff. Though it is possible to cite Christian sources for these ideas as well, my point is that they are not exclusively Christian in content. The ideas shared by the *Phaedo* and the *Arcadia* concern the opposition of

body and soul, the connection between passion and the senses, speculation about life prior to birth (Sidney's interpretation of this in terms of the fetus in its mother's womb and his insistence that what we know about the experience comes through knowledge, not memory, seem to be aimed at refuting Socrates' doctrine of recollection). Davis (*Sidney's Arcadia* 63n) and Robertson following Davis (*OA* 479ff.) cite Duplessis-Mornay, Chap. 14, which is also based on the *Phaedo*, a natural locus for discussion of the immortality of the soul.

22 The intellectual context of this issue and other specific arguments are examined in 'Vision, Revision, and the 1593 Text of the *Arcadia*,' *ELR* 2 (1972) 142-5. The article is an earlier version of the first 15 pages of this chapter.

23 An answer to the accusation that the princes display incredible smugness at the pre-trial scene because they show no remorse for the disastrous results of their activity in Arcadia can be found in my review of McCoy and Weiner in *Seventeenth Century News* 39 (1981) 5-6. One might expect, however, that had Sidney revised this much of his original, the *NA* princes would here demonstrate fuller self-knowledge and awareness of their moral dilemma.

24 See Dipple, 'Metamorphosis' 47-8.

25 I maintain that this is generally true, though some readers – eg, Lawry, Weiner, and Franco Marenco in both 'Double Plot in Sidney's *Old Arcadia*,' *MLR* 64 (1969) 248-63 and *Arcadia Puritana* (Bari 1968) – apparently do not feel this good will. Dipple's assessment in her articles is more complex, but frequently unsympathetic.

26 Sidney intensifies this conception of Musidorus when he picks up the thread later on: 'and the every way enraged Musidorus rase from her – enraged betwixt a repentant shame of his promise-breaking attempt and the tyrannical fire of lust (which, having already caught hold of so sweet and fit a fuel, was past the calling back of reason's counsel) ...' (*OA* 306). The original promise had been made with these significant words: '"What I am," said he, "the gods, I hope, will shortly make your own eyes judges ..."' (*OA* 197).

27 Lanham, in Davis and Lanham, *Sidney's Arcadia* 349. Though this is true of the passion felt by the princes, it is not an adequate evaluation of their total experience. Rudenstine offers much the best account (*Sidney's Poetic Development* 24-35). In summary he says that if Sidney 'generally asks us to see Pyrocles and Musidorus as noble, idealistic and pardonably human in their minor faults, he also frequently reminds us of the debilitating and destructive effects of unrestrained desire' (pp 34-5).

28 These include Erona's unfortunate passion for Antiphilus (containing the immoderate desire of another suitor that nearly causes the destruction of her country and also Antiphilus' betrayal because of his new love for Artaxia); the inconstant and unchaste love of Andromana of Palestine, which fixes on an Arabian prince, then on Pyrocles and Musidorus simultaneously, and finally on an applemonger; and a separate tale of the Queen of Egypt's lust for her stepson Amasis.

29 Dicus' account is connected with Erona's story also in the revision (where his Cupid is described by Miso). Erona's story is of course a tale of 'Cupid's revenge' and talks about his pictures and images.

30 This statement is perhaps misleading: the distancing mechanism in the Narrator's comments often is not moral judgment but wit, irony, or playful deflation. Weiner has a rather different assessment of the Narrator's function in the OA (see Sir Philip Sidney and the Poetics of Protestantism: A Study of Contexts [Minneapolis 1978] 169-70, 174-5).

31 By this I mean that we probably exaggerate when we describe the action as a thwarted 'rape': Musidorus' 'desires' could be only one element had the scene continued, and the traditional behaviour of the over-eager lover suggests that in such a situation the mistress is totally in control. (Cf. Astrophel himself, though the OA's tone is much darker.) Is it conceivable that Sidney's Pamela could be less effective in this than her namesake in Richardson's novel?

32 But see Dipple, 'Metamorphosis' 57-8, for the difference in Sidney's handling of Pyrocles' disguise in the two versions.

33 The emphasis given to love in this passage is notable because the princes are not motivated in their Asia Minor adventures by love; it must refer then to Arcadia as the final stage of their education.

34 See Jon S. Lawry, Sidney's Two Arcadias: Pattern and Proceeding (Ithaca, NY 1972) 237-8; Josephine A. Roberts, Architectonic Knowledge in the New Arcadia (1590): Sidney's Use of the Heroic Journey, Elizabethan Studies 69 (Salzburg 1978) 102-4, 188-9; Dipple as cited in note 32.

35 Rudenstine, Sidney's Poetic Development 19-21

36 Perhaps we are to take Lalus' appearance in the incident of Phalantus' tourney as an emblem of this lack of comprehension between the two ideals. Thyrsis and Lalus may be the same character with a different name in each version.

37 The NA also omits the poem's distinction between the shepherds' ages and the motif of parental authority in arranging marriages. I have discussed the poem's more negative evaluation of love on pp 182-3 n22. Connell, The Maker's Mind 116-27, examines the Strephon-Claius-Urania material as an index of Sidney's revised conception of love in the NA.

38 'Diana apparelled in the garments of Venus,' though a common idea in the Renaissance (like the Virgilian original, however, it is usually stated the other way round), seems to supply an emblem of the vanishing distinction, notwithstanding the absence of the reversible rhetoric that one might expect in ideal descriptions. The emphasis of the emblem is perfectly Sidneian: The figure is the active Diana, not the amorous Venus, at heart.

   This passage is frequently quoted in the criticism as flat statement, but it in fact offers problems of interpretation. It reads like a simple account of what Pyrocles believed to be possible at an earlier stage in his education. But he and the reader are both familiar with the other description of Helen's court given in Book I, in which she disregards her people's needs, keeps spies, and engages in love games and subterfuges (I, 66-72). Moreover, from the explicit point of view of his greater knowledge and experience, Pyrocles seems to affirm the simple earlier judgment (I, 284), though the reader finds it hard to concur.

39 *Sidney's Arcadia* 54

40 Pastoral plots can be used for many purposes: see my 'King Lear as Pastoral Tragedy' in R. Colie and F.T. Flahiff, eds *Some Facets of King Lear* (Toronto 1974), or consider the relevance to *Walden* in the next note.

41 This is where Davis comes out as well when he sees the pastoral pattern as having to go through the pastoral circle in order to emerge on the other side, back in 'civilization.' The difference in emphasis is all-important, as examination of Thoreau's *Walden*, a good example of Davis' pastoral pattern, suggests. The emphasis in *Walden*, as in the *Diana* and Sannazaro's *Arcadia*, is not on the outside world for which this experience of contemplative withdrawal and self-realization prepares one, but on the experience itself. In Sidney, emphasis falls on the active world. The education and most of the achievements that count (in the princes' own minds as well as in the world's) are gained in active experience and do not have to be relearned or cast off before rebirth, as Thoreau implies. *Walden*, though an extreme case, is a fair reduction of the *tendency* of Davis' pastoral pattern, and it cautions us that we must make a sharp distinction between the pattern itself and Sidney's use of it. Poggioli implicitly takes issue with the educational bias of Davis' pastoral pattern by insisting that pastoral is concerned not with renewal but with *retreat* (Renato Poggioli, *The Oaten Flute: Essays on Pastoral Poetry and the Pastoral Ideal* [Cambridge, MA 1975] 1).

42 See how this works, for example, in James E. Phillips, 'Renaissance Concepts of Justice and the Structure of *The Faerie Queene*, Book V,' *HLQ* 33 (1970) 103-20. Roberts, *Architectonic Knowledge*, Chap. 4, deals with the retrospective narrative as 'encyclopedically' concerned with modes of narrative fiction, using Virginia Woolf as a starting point: 'In the *Arcadia*, as in some luminous globe, all the seeds of English fiction lie latent' ('The Countess of Pembroke's *Arcadia*,' in *The Common Reader, Second Series* [New York 1948] 40).

43 See above, pp 14-16.

44 Weinberg, *Literary Criticism in the Italian Renaissance*, I, 44-5, discusses poetry as a 'universal science'; it claims hegemony in the arts because it includes materials of all other sciences.

45 The passage goes on to suggest models for princes, virtuous men, and whole commonwealths.

46 As a gloss on the 'generalities' and 'specialities' of virtue, cf. Cicero, *De inventione* II.liii.159: 'Virtue may be defined as a habit of mind in harmony with reason and the order of nature ... It has four parts: wisdom, justice, courage, temperance.'

47 See Cicero, *De inv*. II.iv.12; *Ad Her*. III.ii.3 considers honour a subdivision of advantage. See also Lorna Challis, 'The Use of Oratory in Sidney's *Arcadia*,' *SP* 62 (1965) 561-76.

48 The omission is prepared for by *Ad Her*. III.viii.15: 'And if epideictic is only seldom employed by itself independently, still in judicial and deliberative causes extensive sections are often devoted to praise and censure.' See the earlier discussion of epideictic in character descriptions, p 25ff.

49 See Ringler's notes, *Poems* 412-15.

50 Sidney may have timocracy in mind with the rebellion of Amphialus and Cecropia, since so much emphasis is given to ambition, pride, and honour. This would reflect Plato's scheme, not Aristotle's.

51 Kenneth O. Myrick, *Sir Philip Sidney as a Literary Craftsman* (Cambridge, MA 1935) 269-70

52 Davis, 'Thematic Unity' 135 (his italics)

53 McCoy's psychoanalytic emphasis in *Rebellion in Arcadia* leads him instead to see the episodes (especially that of Plangus) as versions of Pyrocles' own experience.

54 See *OA* 159, 368. Though the *New Arcadia* seems on paper to have a considerable number of sibling relationships, many of them are perfunctory, with no corresponding effect on behaviour and action (eg, Phalantus and Helen, Kalander and Parthenia's mother).

55 'Two things that contribute greatly to friendship are a common upbringing and similarity of age ... and people brought up together tend to be comrades; whence the friendship of brothers is akin to that of comrades' (*Nic. Eth.* VIII.xii.1161[b] ad fin.); see also 1162[a]1-14. Friendship is an important chivalric motif as well.

56 As fanciful as the statue may seem, the allegorical import is clear: Love has the hero cradled in her arms, but it is to nourish and not merely divert him from his proper course, as an Armida or an Alcina would. It also displays a decidedly *active* bias: surely this is beauty nurturing heroism rather than serving as a rung on a Platonic ladder; Venus Urania would not be conceived of as a *mother*. The other two references to the parental theme are Kalander's 'fatherly love' for Musidorus (I, 16) and his genuine parenthood of Clitophon.

57 *OA* 11 offers a similar statement as a rumour, but since the oracle explicitly fixes a one-year period, there is no need for such drastic measures. The revision mitigates a problem concerning Pyrocles' behaviour in the *Old Arcadia*, when he dissuades Basilius from returning to his court after the Duke mistakenly believes the oracle to have been fulfilled (*OA* 178; cf. *OA* 133 with I, 328). There seems to be no reason for Pyrocles' objection in the *Old Arcadia* since return to Mantinea should enable him to pay court to Philoclea in his own person without any restrictions. Because Pyrocles' dissuasion has such serious and deleterious effects on Arcadia, as well as being against the principles of public good in which he has been educated,

the reader has a right to demand that the issue be more pressing before Pyrocles will act this way. Revising the oracle to connect Basilius' death with his daughters' marriages probably forestalls the need for the scene between Pyrocles and Basilius, but the argument cannot be conclusive.

58 Cf. *Nic. Eth.* VIII.ix.1160ª5: 'the injustice increases by being exhibited towards those who are friends in a fuller sense; eg, it is a more terrible thing to defraud a comrade than a fellow citizen, more terrible not to help a brother than a stranger, and more terrible to wound a father than any one else.'

59 *Defence* 98, on Aeneas' leaving Dido

60 Yet Philanax might be wrong. He has not analysed the situation accurately: the prisoners' safety has had nothing to do with Basilius' power and raising the siege does not cause their death, nor do we know what would have happened had Basilius not raised it.

61 Sidney probably meant to signal the weakness in Kalander's argument by having him plan to persuade Basilius at some other time to let Amphialus marry his daughter (I, 467).

62 The same holds true for our reaction to his making Philoclea his procuress in the affair with Zelmane.

63 See R.S. Crane, 'The Concept of Plot and the Plot of *Tom Jones*,' in *Critics and Criticism* (abridged), ed. R.S. Crane (Chicago 1957) 63-4n.

64 In addition to most of the books and editions cited earlier, see Kenneth Thorpe Rowe, 'Romantic Lore and Parental Authority in Sidney's *Arcadia*,' *University of Michigan Contributions in Modern Philology* 4 (1947); D.M. Anderson, 'The Trial of the Princes in the *Arcadia*, Book V,' *RES* 8 (1957) 409-12; Elizabeth Dipple, 'Harmony and Pastoral' and '"Unjust Justice" in the *Old Arcadia*,' *SEL* 10 (1970) 83-101; Clifford Davidson, 'Nature and Judgment in the *Old Arcadia*,' *Papers on Language and Literature* 6 (1970) 348-65, and Margaret E. Dana, 'The Providential Plot of the *Old Arcadia*,' *SEL* 17 (1977) 39-57.

65 See *OA* 384 for the Narrator's judgment, which links Gynecia's action firmly to the suicide-providence debate.

66 *Rhet.* I.13.1374b, trans. Grant. Quoted in C.K. Allen, *Law in the Making*, 7th ed. (Oxford 1964) 391

67 See, for example, the discussion of Phillips, 'Renaissance Concepts of Justice.'

68 This sentence condenses the discussion on pp 12-18 of F.W. Maitland, *Equity: A Course of Lectures*, 2nd ed. (1936), eds A.H. Chaytor and W.J. Whittaker, rev. by John Brunyate (Cambridge, Eng. 1949).

69 Although equity is strictly applicable only to civil law, its topics as listed by Aristotle are obviously also of interest to criminal trials (where they form the substance of the argument for the defence). F.W. Maitland implies that the connection might have been more relevant to the sixteenth century: 'Since the destruction of the Star Chamber we have had no criminal equity' (*Equity* 19).

70 Plato in *The Statesman* compares law to 'an obstinate and ignorant tyrant' (294a, Jowett's trans., quoted by Allen, *Law in the Making* 388).

71 *OA* 404. The passage continues:

> For although out of them [reason and philosophy], these [laws] came, and to them must indeed refer their offspring, yet because philosophical discourses stand in the general consideration of things, they leave to every man a scope of his own interpretation; where the laws, applying themselves to the necessary use, fold us within assured bounds, which once broken, man's nature infinitely rangeth.

This will hardly bear the astonishing interpretation Davis places on it, that the work exonerates the princes of all the faults and crimes they are accused of at the trial, 'so that at the end Euarchus can condemn them only for ravishment, and that, he insists ... by law and not by philosophy or reason' (*Sidney's Arcadia* 166).

72 *Nic. Eth.* v.x.1137^{b}15-27. Earlier in the same passage, Aristotle has said that equity is 'not the legally just but a correction of legal justice' (^{b}10).

73 Most objections to Euarchus' judgment of the princes stem from some sense of equity (whether recognized by the critic or not), since they mostly assume that the princes are only 'technically' but not 'really' guilty. Margaret Dana, for example, thinks the conflict between Euarchus and the princes is merely a 'tragic and ironic misunderstanding' ('Providential Plot' 54). She seems to take *consent* as crucial (p 55n), but it is clear that Euarchus does not, because he knows Pamela left willingly (*OA* 406: 'though both consent'). Cf. the irrelevance of consent between Julietta and Claudio in *Measure for Measure*. Elizabeth Dipple feels 'intellectual scorn' for Euarchus and the proceedings ('"Unjust Justice"' 93; cf. p 99 on the reader's indignation), but I think this runs counter to Sidney's intention and to his interest in what the Narrator calls 'the nature of arguing' (*OA* 399). Rhetorical interest lies in finding arguments; weighing truths is a separate operation. The legal situation, where one can only insist that the prosecution and defence do not deliberately lie, magnifies the general rhetorical dictum that what each side presents is an *account* of experience, not experience itself. The perspective is thoroughly rhetoricist. Sidney takes the submerging of truth for granted; his secondary interest, once the arguments have been found, is how much truth Euarchus can nevertheless discover.

74 These are aspects of equity present in Aristotle's definition. Euarchus, however, explicitly rejects yet another argument from equity when he denies the validity of past deeds in favour of a more stringent (more Protestant) notion of moral judgment (*OA* 405). The relevance of past deeds brings up the problem of Gynecia again, as discussed p 208 n19. (See A.P. Rossiter on assessing Hamlet's character, *Angel with Horns: Fifteen Lectures on Shakespeare*, ed. Graham Storey [London 1961].)

75 See my discussion of the Asia Minor adventures in Chap. 5. Even Laconia, that triumphant example of Pyrocles' political sagacity, apparently refuses to have its problems solved: the 1593 revisions say that 'immediately upon [Pyrocles'] departure [war] had broken out more violently than ever before' (OA 357 var.).

76 On p 139. Joan Rees, rev. of Arcadia Puritana, Yearbook of English Studies 1 (1971) 235, seems to concur.

77 Nic. Eth. v.i.1129^{b}30. The passage in which Aristotle makes this point runs from 1129^{b}15-1130^{a}14; it forms the conclusion to his first chapter.

78 The argument here seems a deliberate 'reworking' of the problem of equity, in which 'private conveniency' traditionally means the old, the poor, and the weak. Untersteiner (The Sophists 183n8), however, mentions a Gorgian theory of equity which, 'as opposed to positive Right, tends towards a natural Right, "in which the importance of the communal standard expressly prevails over that of individual nature",' citing Victor Ehrenberg, Anfänge des griechischen Naturrechts, Archiv für Geschichte der Philosophie, 1 Abt., 35 (1923) Heft 3-4, pp 119-43, esp. p 133. Struever discusses this as a significant humanist historical attitude on p 123, The Language of History.

79 Ringler's attempt to construct a new trial scene from the revised oracle (Poems 378-9) seems motivated by a desire to make Euarchus represent 'Absolute Justice' in an unproblematic way, thus losing some of the special resonance of the trial within the NA.

CHAPTER EIGHT: CONCLUSION

1 Nic. Eth. v.i.1129^{b}25 ad fin. I have rearranged the final clauses of this passage for my own emphasis. In the text they run: 'what, as a relation to others is justice is, as a certain kind of disposition without qualification, virtue' (Ross translation, emended by readings from the Loeb edition, trans. H. Rackham).

2 Again, comparison with Dante is striking: the goal of man's activity, considered in some way stripped of specifically Christian trappings, is Justice, also seen as the achievement of complete virtue and the fulfillment of the active life. The Arcadia goes as far along Dante's journey as Virgil does.

3 John F. Danby, Poets on Fortune's Hill: Studies in Sidney, Shakespeare, Beaumont and Fletcher (London 1952) 80

APPENDIX A

1 Elizabeth H. Haight, Essays on the Greek Romance (New York 1943) 77. See also Arthur Heiserman, The Novel before the Novel: Essays and Discussions about the Beginnings of Prose Fiction in the West (Chicago 1977) 188-94.

2 Gerald F. Else, *Aristotle's Poetics: The Argument* (Cambridge, MA 1957) 513
3 Based on the Russian formalist distinction between 'fable' (my 'story') and 'sujet' (my 'plot'), cited in René Wellek and Austin Warren, *Theory of Literature* (New York 1956) 208

INDEX

Important characters, episodes, and ideas are indexed as well as names, but certain of these appear too frequently to be usefully noted. Thus the reader will find Friendship but not Love, Amphialus and Basilius but not Pyrocles and Pamela, *Arcadia*'s plurality of structures but not *Arcadia*'s revisions.

218 Index

Argalus: matter-spirit 19-20; doing-
suffering 25, 34, 185 n33; character 26,
185 nn39-40, 196 n14; combat with
Amphialus 65-7, 77, 114, 135, 152, 195
n6; as subordinate hero 81-2, 166. See
also Argalus and Parthenia.
Argalus and Parthenia 19-20, 25, 33-4,
40-1, 65-7, 70, 74-5, 118, 129, 134-5,
144-6, 155, 193 n32, 195 n12. See also
Argalus, Parthenia.
Ariosto, Ludovico (Orlando Furioso) 65,
75, 80, 197 n29; Ruggero-Alcina 46-51,
191 nn15-16, 212 n56; scope 112-13,
134, 202 nn14-17, 203 n18
Aristotle
Nicomachean Ethics 52, 53, 60, 107,
110, 118, 150, 153-4, 156, 160-1,
166, 194 n46, 202 n6, 212 n55, 213
n58, 214 n72, 215 nn77, 1
Poetics 133, 157, 204-5 n38, 205 n43
Politics 39, 109, 150, 212 n50
Rhetoric 8, 9, 14-15, 60, 150, 159, 179
nn24, 25, 26, 180 n37, 185 n37, 213
nn66, 69, 214 n74
Artesia 55, 74-5, 207 n10; Triumph 21-4,
29, 182-3 n22, 184 nn29-31
Asia Minor adventures 24, 51, 59-60,
87-108, 110, 113-14, 118, 125, 129, 135,
141, 143-4, 150-1, 161, 165-7, 199-201
nn1-28, 210 n33, 215 n75
Attack by wild animals 51, 70, 73, 76,
135, 143, 193 n32, 196 n19
Auerbach, Erich 111, 112
Augustine, St 10, 53-4, 179 n31

Bacon, Sir Francis 16, 181 n5
Barber, Richard W. 202 n8
Basilius: retirement 44-5, 70, 110, 116,
128-30, 206 n60; knowledge and virtue
54, 60; in love 72-4, 141, 143, 193 n36,

196 n16, 213 n62; as ruler and father
153, 155-7, 212 n57, 213 nn60-1; char-
acter 206 n61, 208 n19
Bochenski, I.M. 181 n12
Bradbrook, Muriel C. 194 n1
Brand, C.P. 113, 202 nn14, 16
Bruno, Giordano 184 n27, 188-9 n72
Burke, Kenneth 82

Caplan, Harry 15, 181 n8
Captivity episode 24-5, 55-6, 114, 118,
131, 133, 135-7, 139-40, 144, 156-7,
161, 165-6, 186-7 n52, 207 n2
Caspari, Fritz 122-3
Cassirer, Ernst 188-9 n72
Castiglione, Baldassare 123, 186 n47, 187
n54
Cecropia: Captivity 24, 32, 68, 131;
Amphialus 26-7, 61-2, 114, 155; self-
knowledge 61-2; in psychological
scheme 151-2
Chalifour, Clark L. 207 n1
Challis, Lorna 178 n14, 212 n47
Chanson de Roland 194 n49, 198 n39
Chaucer, Geoffrey 197 n29
Chivalry 6, 110, 111-14, 115-16, 143,
145-6, 147, 199 n10, 212 n55
Chrétien de Troyes 46, 111-12, 200 n18
Cicero 8, 52, 179 n24, 181 n8, 181-2 n15,
192 n25, 193 n29, 206 n52; De inven-
tione 211 n46, 212 n47; De officiis
190 n4, 193 n29; De oratore 9-10,
179 nn24, 26-7; Topica 14-15, 181 nn7,
11
Colish, Marcia 179 n31
Collingwood, R.G. 201 n28
Comedy 54, 142; Terentian comedy 30,
132, 186 n49, 207 n1
Connell, Dorothy 178 n11, 179 n30, 208
n14, 210 n37